MAHATMA GANDHI

MAHATMA GANDHI: HIS OWN STORY

C. F. ANDREWS

GYAN

Published by

GYAN

Gyan Publishing House
5, Ansari Road
Daryaganj, New Delhi-110002
Phone: 011-47034999, 9811692060
E-mail: books@gyanbooks.com

Distribution Network
gyanbooks.com
India, USA, Canada, UK, Australia

ISBN: 978-93-6920-242-3 (PB)

First Published, 1930

2nd Impression 2025

Printed at: Gyan Press, Delhi.

MAHATMA GANDHI
Author: C. F. ANDREWS

MAHATMA GANDHI—HIS OWN STORY

(*By courtesy of the Artist.*)

MAHATMA GANDHI

A drawing by Sjt. Kanu Desai

MAHATMA GANDHI
HIS OWN STORY

Edited by

C. F. ANDREWS

With an Introduction by

JOHN HAYNES HOLMES

NEW YORK
THE MACMILLAN COMPANY
1930

DEDICATED

WITH MUCH AFFECTION

TO

DR. AND MRS. BAHADUR SINGH

AND THE SETTLERS FROM INDIA

IN THE WEST INDIES

PREFACE

THE MATERIAL OF THIS AUTOBIOGRAPHY, which Mahatma Gandhi has called "The Story of My Experiments with Truth," was first dictated by him in his own mother-tongue to one of his fellow political prisoners during a long imprisonment in the years 1922-24. It was afterwards continued in a serial form, as a feature of his Gujarati paper, called "Navajivan," and translated into English by his intimate friends, Mahadev Desai and Piyarelal Nair, receiving at the same time his own careful revision. Miss Slade, who is known in Mr. Gandhi's Ashram as Mirabehn, also assisted in shaping its final English form. The whole series of short chapters has now been published by the Navajivan Press at Ahmedabad in two large volumes, containing over twelve hundred octavo pages. These chapters have also been printed serially in America in Dr. John Haynes Holmes' paper, "Unity."

Another book of equal importance has been used, wherein Mahatma Gandhi describes personally his own experiences in South Africa. The volume is called "Satyagraha (Soul-force) in South Africa," and the translation has been made by Valji Govindji Desai. This book has never been printed in America. Its Indian publisher is Mr. S. Ganesan, Triplicane, Madras, India. In using freely all these documents and making abbreviations, I would wish very warmly to express my admiration for the manner in which the spirit of the author has been kept by the translators.

When we turn to the three volumes and try to gain the clue to Mahatma Gandhi's estimate of human conduct, it will be found to centre in three cardinal virtues, recurrent in all his writings. These are Truth, Loving-kindness, and Inner Purity.[1] The first pair of these form together the Eternal Quest of the soul and denote its infinite yearning to pass through this mortal existence without transgressing more than can be possibly avoided the ultimate spiritual realities. The full music of life demands the harmony of Truth and Love. But so difficult is the music to master, and so complete is the renunciation required, that success can only be attained through a body and soul kept clean from all sensual passion. Therefore the constant refrain of Inner Purity runs through all his writings, wherein at one time Love is the dominant note, and at another time Truth. He believes intensely that only the pure in heart can see God; and he gives a very concrete and plain-spoken definition of what that Purity means. In his own person, it has implied the abandonment of the married life for one of entire abstinence from all sexual relations. How far he would demand this from others in their search for God will be revealed in his own words.

In one part of his Autobiography, Mahatma Gandhi declares that he has continually sought the guidance of the Spirit in all that he has written. He has felt assured, he tells us, that this guidance has been granted in due measure. It is this sincere attempt, so searchingly keen, to lay bare before God and man the hidden secrets of his inner life, and to bring out into the light anything evil along with what is good, that seems to me to make these writings so vitally authentic.

Two points need to be made clear to the reader before the present abridged volume is taken in hand.

(1). The most prolonged and intricate of all his passive

[1] *Satya, Ahimsa, Brahmacharya.*

resistance struggles, undertaken in the Transvaal, has been reluctantly omitted from this book. The complete narrative could not easily be condensed, and therefore after much hesitation I have left it out with a view to later publication. The sequence of the life-story is not, however, seriously broken because I have given at some length the picture of the Natal passive resistance which was the crown of his moral achievement in South Africa.

(2): Diet restriction, combined with fasting, was one of the avenues along which Mr. Gandhi tried to approach reality in human affairs. A great deal has been written by him about this. Since, however, his description of these things would have taken up too much space, I have been unable to reproduce it. Yet here again it has been a regret to me to make this omission, because his experiments tend to correct the idea that his outlook on life is altogether unscientific. They show what a daring explorer he has been, and how his mind in its own peculiar way is of that scientific order, which proceeds from hypothesis to rigid examination of facts in order to sift out Truth.

The need for the present edition of the Autobiography has long been recognised both in Europe and America. Dr. Holmes had at first intended to fulfil this labor of love. His insight into Mr. Gandhi's character made him peculiarly fitted for such a task. But he was summoned away from America to Palestine, at a critical moment, and it happened that at the same time my own duties called me to the West. It was therefore decided that I should be responsible. Dr. Holmes, on his part, undertook to write the Introduction; and his appreciation will be read with the deepest interest by all who recognise that he was the very first to make the name of Gandhi known and loved in America. What Romain Rolland has done in Europe, he himself has accomplished in the New World.

In preparing this edition, the main difficulty throughout, as I have already suggested, has been the large amount of material as contrasted with the stringent limitation of space. Many times over, what was first selected has been put on one side in order to insert some other portion which could not possibly be omitted. Even after what seemed a final selection had been made, the work had to be begun all over again. Yet a certain experience was gained as I went on, and at last I have a reasonable hope that the narrative will carry the reader along with it. What I have aimed at throughout is to make the book easily intelligible in the West without sacrificing any of its peculiarly Eastern setting. It is my sincere hope that those who read it will study along with it the former volume entitled "Mahatma Gandhi's Ideas."

I would specially thank the Indian publishers, M. M. Bhatta and S. Ganesan, and also the translators, Mahadev Desai, Piyarelal Nair and Valji Desai, for the use they have allowed me to make of their work. Above all I am indebted to Mahatma Gandhi himself whose full permission was granted to me to abbreviate his own writings. Along with him I would wish to devote any profits which may come from this book (as well as from the former volume) to the Pearson Memorial Hospital at Santiniketan. This hospital has been built in memory of our mutual friend, Willie Pearson, who died by a railway accident in Italy at the end of September, 1923. Ten years earlier, in 1913, he had gone out with me to Natal to help Mr. Gandhi in his passive resistance struggle, and the bond of love thus formed has remained unbroken by death.

My affectionate gratitude is due to the Indian residents in British Guiana, Trinidad and Dutch Guiana, for the inspiration which they gave me while carrying through this work during the months that I recently spent among them as their guest. It was out of the scanty leisure snatched from a protracted enquiry in those lands that the book had to be prepared. Yet no environment could have given me more encouragement than daily intercourse with warm-hearted Indian companions in those distant countries. Therefore, I have ventured to dedicate this volume to them. It is an equal joy to me to record with deep affection the kindness of many friends in this New World. Along with those I have already mentioned in my former volume I would add the names of Mr. George Foster Peabody, Miss Anna Bogue and Mrs. James, Dr. Rufus Jones, Miss Cooley and Miss House, Dr. Sunderland, Lawrence Tombs, Frank Moore, Hari Govil, Murray Brooks, Nonie Gregg, E. C. Carter, S. D. Joshi and D. J. Fleming. I would wish also to thank in this same connection the Rt. Rev. the Bishop of Guiana and Mrs. Beatrice Gregg of Trinidad for their exceeding kindness.

My warmest thanks are due to the staff of the Phelps-Stokes Foundation and its Chairman; the staff and students of Hampton Institute, Virginia; and Penn School, St. Helena's Island, where I have been able to finish this volume. The work of editing it was a far longer and more difficult task than I had anticipated and without constant acts of unselfish kindness on the part of these and other friends too numerous to mention it would have been impossible for me to complete it in the midst of a very arduous programme of duties.

May I venture to add how very deeply grateful I have

been to the people of the United States and Canada among whom I had come with some trepidation for the first time. I had heard of their great material wealth and had expected to be repelled by its hardening influences upon the soul. Wherever I have seen this deterioration I have spoken plainly in warning about it. But I have found a wealth of affection that has surprised me by its generosity and simplicity, and I go away with a very grateful heart.

Since this book was compiled and edited the Indian situation has become very grave indeed. A deadlock appears to have been reached. Mahatma Gandhi has again been imprisoned. Yet it is well-nigh universally admitted that his influence remains one of the paramount factors in Indian affairs. Therefore a study of his character, which has documentary authority behind it, is a necessity, if the best minds in India and Great Britain are not to drift still further apart. While in my former book his thoughts and ideas were presented, in this volume the aim has been to set forward briefly in a readable form for Western readers his own life-story.

In a similar manner and with the same object in view I have already published Tagore's "Letters to a Friend"; and it is my sincere hope, if health permits, to complete the picture of Tagore in another volume just as this present book completes the picture of Gandhi. For it is my firm conviction that through the eyes of these two men the West may learn at last to appreciate the East.

C. F. ANDREWS.

CONTENTS

CONTENTS

ILLUSTRATIONS

INTRODUCTION

THE AUTOBIOGRAPHY OF MAHATMA GANDHI, of India, is a document of the first order of importance as the intimate revelation of the life and thought of a man who must be ranked as one of the supremely great personalities not only of his own but of all time. At this critical moment in the history of India, this autobiography takes on an added significance as the "*apologia pro vita sua*" of the leader who holds in his hands, by virtue of his unchallenged spiritual ascendancy among his people, the destiny of his country in its relation to the great Empire from whose rule she seeks release. Here is related the story of the drama of inward conviction and outward circumstance which has brought Gandhi to the center of the stage in an hour big with fate for all mankind.

In the light of present events in India, and of Mahatma Gandhi's place in these events, one turns to the pages of this autobiography with a feeling akin to awe. They have a simplicity that is almost naïve, a frankness that is frequently startling, an integrity that is always sublime. They also had in their original form, as published serially in "Young India" (Ahmedabad) in India, and in "Unity" (Chicago) in this country, a fullness of detail that was embarrassing from the standpoint of general interest among readers far removed from the peculiar circumstances of Indian history and life. For publication outside of India, it was evident that the book must be drastically revised. It is fortunate that this delicate and difficult task fell into the hands of the one man most competent to perform it. Mr. C. F. Andrews, the editor of this volume, is an Englishman who has lived more than twenty-six years in India. He is Gandhi's most trusted and beloved friend outside the ranks of his own countrymen. He knows through long and intimate personal experience the varied elements of Gandhi's character, and he shares through kinship of spirit the beauty of his ideals. What is essential to the understanding of the man, he has preserved in this version of the Autobiography; only what is incidental and accidental has he removed. In its present form this "Story" should become a classic of autobiographical literature in the English tongue.

In a recent article in the "Century Magazine," I declared that if Mahatma Gandhi is to be understood by the Western mind, he must first of all be seen as the immediate successor to Leo Tolstoy in that unbroken line of saints and seers, running like the stitches of a golden thread through the tangled pattern of human affairs, who have insisted that man, like God, is spirit, and can achieve his ends and thus fulfil his life only by using the spiritual powers of his nature. Gandhi, in other words, like Tolstoy, Garrison, Fox, St. Francis, Jesus, Isaiah, is a "non-resistant."

This is an awkward and inaccurate word, since it expresses only that negative quality of refusing to meet evil with evil, violence with violence, injury with retaliation in kind, which the average man finds it so difficult to differentiate from inertia and cowardice. "Non-resistance," as a descriptive term, neglects altogether that superbly positive, even aggressive quality, which Gandhi has defined so nobly in his famous phrase, "Soul-force," and which Jesus has exalted in his immortal injunction—"Love your enemies, bless them that curse you, do good to them that hate you." The non-resistant should be known as one who would lift man altogether above the plane of brute physical existence, where he had his origin, to that loftier plane of reason and the spirit, where he has his proper destiny. He would have humanity begin now to live that life of intelligence, constructive good-will, creative love and self-sacrificing service, which distinguishes the human from the animal. Such life is the one thing which can bring God's kingdom upon earth, to displace these innumerable kingdoms of the rod and sword which have cursed man in every age, and now threaten to destroy him altogether. The phrase, "non-resistance," expresses not at all these ultimate and positive implications of the repudiation of physical force. But it is the one generally accepted phrase we have to describe the group of men whom I have named, and the phrase, therefore, that we must use to give Gandhi his proper classification.

But Gandhi is not merely one among many non-resistants. On the contrary, he is unique among them all for a use of his essential genius on a scale and with a power never achieved or even attempted before. The non-resistant way of life has always had its pure and heroic individual exemplars. It has been adopted and practised by small groups, like the Dukhobors, as a basis of community existence apart from the encompassing society of men. It has been lifted high by certain organized religious bodies, like the Moravians and the Quakers, as a guiding light amid the confusion of a world where "ignorant armies clash by night." But never till Gandhi came along was it deliberately adopted and used by a whole people as a program of statesmanship to the great end of political and social liberation.

Gandhi's great campaign in South Africa (1894-1914)

must stand forever, I believe, not only as the first but also as the classic example of the use of non-resistance by organised masses of men for the redress of grievances. Here was a situation which was as old, and as new, as human history itself—the repression of a despised minority of men by an arrogant, cruel and all-powerful majority. Certain thousands of Gandhi's fellow-countrymen, brought to South Africa to do the menial labor of the land, were outlawed from justice, tortured by discriminative legislation, despised and spat upon by a so-called superior race, and thus visited with misery and threatened with death. In such a situation the downtrodden in other ages have either abjectly endured and died, or else have risen in mad revolt, and perished or escaped amid the horrors of struggle and slaughter. Gandhi, determined that his fellow-countrymen should not bow "like dumb, driven cattle" beneath the yoke of oppression, was equally determined that they should not plunge themselves and their oppressors into the agonies of violence and death. Out of the mystery of his own devoted and highly disciplined spirit, he found a better way. With a skill, patience, and heroism well-nigh unexampled, he took these thousands of ignorant, untrained indentured laborers, sore oppressed in an alien land, and, by sheer power of personal example, welded them into a single body, and instigated a non-resistant revolt which brought them, after years of struggle, the freedom they sought. Gandhi's first step was to teach his followers to have no part in the life of a society which denied them the elementary rights of men (Non-co-operation). His next step was to discipline his followers to do no violence upon their oppressors—to suffer injury themselves, but to return no injury to others (Non-violence). And his last step was to lead his followers to the heroic achievement of serving their oppressors—helping them, coming to their relief and rescue, whenever they fell into need (Soul-force). Thus, when a Zulu rebellion broke out, Gandhi and his followers suspended their opposition campaign, and gave aid and comfort to their enemies. When the plague seized Johannesburg, they nursed the sick and buried the dead among their persecutors. When war engulfed the country, they marched to the battlefields of Englishmen, to serve and save the wounded. For the first time in history, a great fight for freedom was conducted on the principle of "be not overcome of evil, but overcome evil with good." And the moral law, regnant in the universe and in the hearts of men, justified itself, as it always will in the long run, by bringing to Gandhi and his followers the reward of victory. Henceforward, when men doubt the efficacy of non-resistance, they have their answer in South Africa.

What the Mahatma attempted and achieved in South Africa, great as it was as compared with all previous undertakings of the kind, shrinks into insignificance in the light of his vast non-violent non-co-operation campaign in opposition to British imperialism in India in 1919-1922. Here Gandhi became the leader of a great people, numbering more than three hundred millions of men and women, in an uprising for national autonomy. He took his place at this hour with Bruce, Washington, Garibaldi, Sun Yat-sen, as one of the supreme patriots of human liberty. But he stands apart from and above these men, also, as one who refused to draw the sword as the necessary weapon of liberation. Alone among national leaders striving for the freedom of their people, he sought a spiritual weapon; and in this search, he worked out a peaceful program of revolt which stands as a supreme achievement of world statesmanship. In this program of "non-co-operation," as it was called, Gandhi showed himself one of the wisest as well as bravest of men. In his success in disciplining a vast population to its performance, he looms as the most potent personal force the world has known. In one year he demonstrated the efficacy of a non-violent campaign to win liberty against odds that no sword could ever overcome. If, at the critical moment, he failed to reach his goal, it was because, in the intensity of the conflict and in the momentousness of the issue, Gandhi forgot, or ignored, what he had himself taught in South Africa: that the non-resistant method must have time to achieve its end. The sword may win or lose everything in one heroic moment. The soul must have years, perhaps decades, to make its slow but perfect way. This principle that non-resistance can win only when trusted and tried "in the long run," established for all time by the twenty years of patient conflict in South Africa, Gandhi himself violated in 1921, just as Jesus violated it in his time, by promising that victory would be immediate. This inevitably rushed both expectation and effort on the part of the Indian people, and resulted in the collapse of the great movement from its own inward momentum. Gandhi, in other words, put suddenly on the masses a greater spiritual strain than they were prepared all at once, even under his leadership, to bear. But in India, as in South Africa, the principle was proved. Gandhi, no more than Jesus, is discredited by a failure that shall yet be retrieved by the law which he himself discovered and proclaimed.

It is Gandhi's greatest glory, and the surest evidence of

his spiritual stature, that he himself saw the reason of his failure, and was the first to undertake the stupendous labor of its correction. Understanding came to him in the silent hours of his imprisonment at Yeravada, after his arrest on March 10, 1922, and in the long, quiet hours of his convalescence after his release. He had achieved a miracle with the people of India. He had done what had never been done, and what had been said could not be done—namely, united the whole nation in one great and sustained mass movement against imperialism in its tyrannous form; a movement so nearly successful that it shook the British Empire to its foundations. "Gandhi's was the most colossal experiment in world history," said Sir George Lloyd, the English Governor of Bombay, "and it came within an inch of succeeding." But the strain was too great; and under it the people broke. Now the work must be begun all over again. What had been done in South Africa on a small scale, he must now do in India on a large scale. He must train the Indian people for their great task of independence. He must make them inwardly worthy of what they desired, and thus spiritually capable of winning and holding it. He must cleanse India of its social abominations; end forever the political, racial and religious hatreds which divide the nation and make it impotent; discipline the masses everywhere to self-dependence, outwardly in their political and economic, inwardly in their intellectual and spiritual, life. He must teach them, in other words, the law of love, and, by making them obedient to this law, fit them to be at last the masters of their destiny.

It was when Gandhi, after his long convalescence, undertook this gigantic labor of the spiritual regeneration of a whole people, that he entered upon the greatest period of his career. He abandoned, now, the political field to other and lesser men. His was no longer the task of organizing political parties, presiding at political congresses, leading nationalistic political campaigns. This work might well go on—indeed, must go on! But always there was the deeper and higher task of reaching the souls of the people, and this henceforward was his task. Promptly he defined certain tests, or standards, of spiritual discipline which must be met as a condition of the attainment of Swaraj. Moslems and Hindus must end their age-old hate, and live together as brethren in a common cause. The Untouchables must be delivered from the outer darkness of prejudice into which they had been cast, and thus restored in love and sympathy to the common life of India. Women must be raised up to a plane of political, economic and social equality with men. The liquor traffic must everywhere be prohibited. The home-weaving and home-spinning of cloth worn by patriotic persons must become everywhere the national custom, and thus the token at once of inward purity and outward freedom. Above all, must every man eschew violence, banish hate and fear from out his heart, and seek deliverance from the national enemy (Britain) by transforming this enemy, through the alchemy of love, into a friend. Long since had Gandhi begun this work in his own personal life. He had organized it on a modest scale at his religious school (Ashram) and fraternal community at Ahmedabad. Now he sent forth the challenge throughout the length and breadth of all the land, and set himself patiently but resolutely to the task of its fulfilment.

Suddenly and sublimely Gandhi became what in essence he had been from the beginning—a religious leader. In South Africa, he had appeared as the skilful and successful organizer of a local social revolt. In India, in 1919-1922, he had loomed high as the patriotic leader of a far-flung nationalistic struggle for independence. In both these instances, however, Gandhi was greater than the rôles which he was playing. His non-resistant program, hitherto unheard of on such a scale and to such ends, was the outward and visible sign of mightier forces inwardly at work. From the beginning, in other words, in his most practical endeavors for reform, Gandhi had been concerned not merely with political and social aims, but with moral and spiritual ideals. More truly than he himself realized for a time, he was moving, under the impulse of his essential nature, on the religious plane. And now, in an instant, as it were, he became deliberately in action what he had always instinctively been in motive and idea —a seer and prophet of the soul! No longer was he to be numbered merely with political reformers and nationalistic leaders. Henceforth he was to be reckoned with the supreme religious geniuses of history—those half-dozen timeless spirits who have changed the order of the world.

One wonders, as this period of Gandhi's life is recalled in the light of present events, what Britain was doing at such a moment. What a chance was this for reconciliation and readjustment between two great peoples! The Mahatma had never before been so powerful. In his days of political leadership, Gandhi had been beyond all compare the most potent single influence ever known. One may search the pages of history in vain to find any man in any age—religious teacher, military conqueror, political statesman—who has held at one time so vast a power over so many millions of human beings during his own lifetime. Throughout all India, Gandhi had been supreme. The great bowed before his sanctity; the learned reverenced his wisdom; the myriad common people hailed his sacrifice and love. In a far-flung population speaking different languages, acknowledging different traditions, worshipping different gods, and the vast majority of them illiterate, Gandhi's name had been everywhere known, and his word everywhere obeyed. This personal influence of one man over more than three hundred millions of his fellow-men is a fact unparalleled in the recorded annals of the race. And now this influence was suddenly deepened! Not so immediate in its appeal, not so dramatic in its expression, not so definite and tangible in its character, as formerly, it yet ranged as far over the surface of society, and at the same time penetrated to central sources of thought and life. No longer sweeping like a flood that engulfed, it flowed rather as a hidden river which feeds and thus renews the landscape. Gandhi now held not merely the political allegiance but also the spiritual awe of his countrymen. By his own choice he was removed from the field of controversial political reform. He was suddenly now become a spiritual leader, concerned with the souls of his people and their dedication to great causes of brotherhood and peace. Was there no statesman in England wise enough to see this fact? Is there a doom upon our days that the Empire could not take advantage of this opportunity to join hands with Gandhi for the salvation of India, the Empire, and the world?

What prevented this happy consummation was unquestionably the stupidity of English Tories in interpreting Gandhi's voluntary retirement as a sign of his loss of influence, and thus of the end of his activities as a popular leader. The Mahatma, they argued, is a broken reed, a shattered idol. The courage of the British administration in arresting and imprisoning him has achieved the decisive result of scattering his followers and shattering his power. His refusal, after his release and recovery, to resume the political headship of his people, is a confession of failure and defeat. His influence is gone. He no longer leads because there is none to follow. What was for a few months, according to British official sources, the greatest single menace ever faced by the Empire, has now dwindled to the insignificant proportions of a naked little man surrounded by a few fanatical reformers in an obscure corner of the land. With the passing of this man, they continued, the danger is over, and Britain can proceed to work out in her own way, and to her own advantage, the destinies of the Indian people. So Britain went ahead—stupidly, blindly, selfishly—and repeated that earlier record of arrogance and oppression which had wrought such peril at the close of the Great War. Four things happened in these years which drove the people of India into an even more furious frenzy of despair and wrath than that which led to Gandhi's non-co-operation campaign of 1919-1922.

First, the affairs of India, to quote an English Liberal, were entrusted to "hands that should never have been allowed to touch them, and India was provided with the distressing spectacle of a Gandhi confronted by a Birkenhead. In that contrast, perhaps, the destiny of British power in Asia may be symbolized. Such collocations may seem trivial in themselves. They are not seldom the turning-point of national and imperial destiny."

Secondly, in anticipation of a necessary revision of the

Indian constitution, the Simon Commission was appointed, with no representation of India in its membership. In all the more than three hundred millions of Indians, that is, there was found not one man—Gandhi, or anybody else—who was deemed worthy to sit with Englishmen in the determination of Indian affairs! Instantly, India exploded in one vast eruption of indignation and revolt. Political and religious differences disappeared as men of all parties and all creeds united in one high resolve to boycott the Commission and repudiate its work. Wherever Sir John Simon and his associates went in India, they were met by vast uprisings of the people, armed with insulting banners, which paralyzed all efforts of the Commission to achieve results.

Thirdly, and in some ways worst of all, the Simon Commission was supported not only by Tories and Liberals in England, but also by Laborites. With a degree of stupidity which at this date seems fairly incredible, Mr. MacDonald not only voted for the Commission in the House of Commons, but actually allowed representatives of the Labor Party to serve as members of the Commission. When this happened, the last remnants of confidence in England disappeared from the hearts of Indians. From Gandhi down, all now believed that there was henceforth no Englishman in church or state, in private or public life, who could be trusted. The Labor Party had been the last hope, and in this crisis of Indian affairs the Party had gone over to the enemy. From this moment on all contacts with England were definitely and forever at an end.

Lastly, as a crowning irony of circumstance, came the publication of Katherine Mayo's "Mother India." This curious and wicked book may seem to be a trivial phenomenon in the perspective of the tremendous events of this present hour. But in relation to the situation which pertained when it was published, the volume was a disaster of the first magnitude. Into a problem of utmost difficulty and delicacy, needing for its solution every influence of moderation and goodwill, there was suddenly precipitated this work which held up India to the ridicule and contempt of men. Nobody in India will ever believe that this vicious slander, which spared not even such men as Gandhi and Tagore from libellous attack, was not inspired by British influences. Whether or not this be true, "Mother India" was one of the central influences of the time which made co-operation between Englishmen and Indians impossible.

Thus was disillusionment renewed and severance completed. Again, as in 1919, Britain had lost its opportunity and driven all India to revolt. Gandhi in his retirement, preaching the regeneration of his people and their inner spiritual preparation for the fulfilment of their nationalistic dreams, watched the drift of the times, and noted its steady progress towards disaster. On the one hand was an England which was obdurate, stubborn, stupid, steadfastly resolved to rely in the last resort upon that sheer brute force of arms and men which had sustained the Empire hitherto. On the other hand was an India aflame with wrath, and, worst of all, beginning to turn away, in sheer loss of patience and self-control, from that ideal of non-resistance which had been the moving passion of the Mahatma's life. The new generation of Indians seemed no longer to be with him in his program of non-violent non-co-operation, but, like young blood everywhere, was dallying with the quick and easy way of striking at the foe and delivering themselves by force from the bondage in which they suffered. Was it possible for him, in such a situation of seething unrest and disturbance, to continue that basic work of social and spiritual change to which he had deliberately set his hand? Could he retain any influence, or serve any useful or effective end, if he stayed aloof from his people in such an hour of national humiliation and distress? Was he not an Indian, and did he not feel at this time, as in 1919, the duty to act in concert with all Indians in defense of their dignity and rights as men? Above all, must he not strive again, as in 1919, to turn the tide of violence which seemed sweeping upon the land, and guide it into safe channels of protest and revolt? He was old and feeble, but his power was still as great as ever. Did there not remain for him one last effort to save the situation from the final cataclysm of ruin, and by some supreme demonstration of non-resistant love, achieve an emancipation of India which would not be inconsistent with a reconciliation with England?

It was some such line of thought as this which persuaded Gandhi to emerge from his retirement, and assume again the active leadership of India in her revolt against the British crown. At the All-India Congress of 1928, the great Mahatma entered upon the third, and in all probability the last period of his heroic service of the cause of India. Exercising his old mastery of his people, even of the younger men and women who still reverenced him as their country's saint and savior, Gandhi served upon Britain an ultimatum that Swaraj must be granted to India within the period of the next year—i.e., before January 1, 1930. On the other hand, the Mahatma gave solemn pledge to his people that, if Britain did not act within the period named, he would again organize and personally lead a nation-wide non-resistant movement for independence.

It is this pledge which Gandhi is fulfilling at this hour. In this return to public life, and this new organization of a great non-co-operative campaign against the Empire, certain critics see a repudiation of the Mahatma's conviction that the Indian people must learn to master themselves before they undertake the mastery of their government—that preparation must precede attainment. But have not events since January demonstrated that preparation is attained? Have not Gandhi's spiritual labors already produced their fruit? How otherwise explain that sublime spectacle of discipline, patience, forbearance, fortitude, non-resistant sacrificial suffering on the part of millions of humble beings, which is to-day writing in India a new chapter of human history? Furthermore, the Indian leader seems suddenly to have come to a new revelation of his "Soul-truth." He sees at last that struggle is itself attainment—that the very suffering incident to the battle for independence is the sure and perfect preparation for such independence! The present campaign, said Gandhi, in a recent issue of his paper, *Young India*, is designed "not to establish independence, but to arm the people with the power to do so." We must deliberately seek wounds, and even death itself, he now declares, that by the discipline of sacrifice we may conquer our enemies and at the same time fit ourselves for emancipation from their rule. This is the new Gandhi—a Gandhi more profound, more rigorous, more terrible than before. He has at last become, like Jesus, one of "the terrible meek"—the meek who "inherit the earth."

What may well be the last days of his life Gandhi is dedicating to the herculean task of winning for India the recovery of her ancient dignity and power—the liberation of the most august and venerable of civilizations to new and greater life. At the same time, and by the same process, is he seeking to save India and Britain, in their final struggle, from the unnecessary horrors of violence, bloodshed, and destruction. It is this which justifies Gandhi's claim that he is acting on Britain's behalf to-day quite as much as on behalf of his own land. And on the world's behalf as well! For Gandhi's influence is spreading from India to all the East, and from the East to the distracted West. The Mahatma is to-day a universal figure. No man, to be sure, more Oriental than he! A hundred ideas, native to his very life, must forever be alien to the imagination of other men. But his spirit, like a star, shines down through darkness. Wherever men struggle and falter, they hail his light. His name has become a symbol of dedication, his life a program of salvation. What men everywhere are at first dimly, and then ever more clearly, coming to see, is that we have on the earth to-day, in the person of Mahatma Gandhi, the latest in the august succession of the supreme spiritual geniuses of all time—Lao-tsze, Confucius, Buddha, Zoroaster, Isaiah, Jesus. The comparison with Jesus in inevitable, and not merely from the standpoint of the non-resistant ideal which binds the two in perpetual fellowship. Long before the War the Mahatma was compared with the Christ for the sheer beauty and sanctity of his inner life. Now this comparison is immeasurably clarified and strengthened by the spectacle of what Gandhi is seeking to do for India and for the world. If we would know what Jesus was as a saint, and also what he did, or tried to do, as a savior, we have only to look across the seas to this greatest man in the world to-day.

To discover the secret of Gandhi, we must "behold the man." In no leader of the race has the power of the spirit ever come to such utter singleness of expression as in this Indian. Nothing else avails to explain the matchless character of his influence. His person is stripped as naked of grace as his body of clothes. His physical presence is completely insignificant. His intellectual capacity, as compared with Tolstoy's, is meagre. Unlike Jesus, he commands no magic of words. Unlike Mohammed, he has no consuming passion of temperament and will. Among religious leaders, he comes nearer to St. Francis, perhaps, than to any other; but even here he lacks that lovely esthetic sensibility, that native instinct of poetry and song, which blossoms with such immortal fragrance in the Assisian's "Little Flowers." A frail, puny, utterly unimportant-looking man is the Mahatma. But in this trivial lantern of the flesh, there burns a light that "never was on land or sea." His deep and lustrous eyes, his lovely smile, his utter clarity of mind, his gentleness and peace and unfailing compassion—these reveal at once the inner glory. The poverty of Gandhi's personality in every other respect serves but to isolate and thus make plain his essential quality of life. Other men can be explained by gifts of birth, or education, or personality, or intellect, or speech. Gandhi knows none of these things. Clothed upon with the frailest garment of fleshly incarnation ever known, the Mahatma walks among us as pure spirit.

It is this fact which makes so formidable Mahatma Gandhi's return to active political leadership. The inherent spiritual power of the man, coupled with his control of the people in matters of fundamental human relationships, makes him a factor of overwhelming importance in the life of India and of the world. If they had been wise, the English administrators would have welcomed his new assumption of active leadership, and used it as a constructive influence for peace. Nor is it now too late! It is never too late to do the one thing needful. For it is Gandhi, and Gandhi alone, "now as always," to quote C. F. Andrews, "the central driving force in Indian political life," who has it within his power to save the existing situation. Failing his intervention by the glad accord of all good men, India will not subside again in meek submission, but flame into a revolt which may consume the world. Gandhi has for India, the Empire and mankind, "the way of life." Will men refuse this now again, as they refused it once before?

JOHN HAYNES HOLMES.

New York City,
June 15, 1930.

A SHORT LIST OF COMMON INDIAN WORDS

Titles of Reverence and Respect

Word	*Meaning*
Mahatma . .	A title of Gandhi meaning "Great Soul"
Gurudeva . .	A title of Tagore meaning "Revered Teacher"
Deshbandhu . .	A title of the late C. R. Das meaning "Friend of the Country"
Lokamanya . .	A title of the late B. G. Tilak meaning "Beloved by the People"
Srijut (Sjt) . .	A common title equivalent to Esquire

Religious Institutions

Sabarmati Ashram	The religious institution of Mahatma Gandhi near Ahmedabad
Santiniketan . .	The religious institution of Rabindranath Tagore near Calcutta
Gurukula . .	The religious institution of Mahatma Munshi Ram near Hardwar

Terms Used in Passive Resistance

Ahimsa . . .	Non-violence
Satya	Truth
Satyagraha . .	Truth-force or Soul-force
Satyagrahi . .	One who practises Soul-force
Brahmacharya .	The practice of Chastity

Mahatma Gandhi's Hand-spinning Movement

Charka . . .	The spinning-wheel
Khaddar . . . / Khadi . . .	Home-spun cloth

Muhammadan Religious Terms

Islam . . .	The religion of the Prophet Muhammad
Muslim . . .	Belonging to Islam

Word	*Meaning*
Musalman . .	Follower of Islam
Khilafat . . .	The office of Caliph
Maulana . . .	Religious Teacher

SACRED SANSKRIT BOOKS

Vedas . . .	The Earliest religious hymns of India
Upanishad . .	The earliest religious philosophy
Puranas . . .	The Sacred Hindu Legends

HINDU RELIGION

Dharma . . .	Religion or religious duty
Varnashrama Dharma	Religion of Caste
Sanatana Dharma	Orthodox Hindu religion
Sanatani . . .	An orthodox Hindu

THE FOUR CASTES

Brahman . . .	The first Caste (knowledge)
Kshattriya . .	The second Caste (rule)
Vaishya . . .	The third Caste (trade, agriculture)
Shudra . . .	The fourth Caste (labour)

THE FOUR RELIGIOUS STAGES

Brahmacharya .	The first stage of the religious life (chastity)
Grihastha . .	The second stage of the religious life (householder)
Vanaprastha . .	The third stage of the religious life (gradual retirement)
Sanyas . . .	The fourth stage of the religious life (complete retirement)

THE TWO GREAT EPICS

Mahabharata . .	The National Epic wherein Krishna is the

Word	*Meaning*
	Divine Hero. The Bhagavad Gita is part of this Epic
Ramayana . .	The Sacred Epic of North India wherein Rama is the Divine Hero

Political Terms

Swadeshi . . .	Belonging to, or made in, one's own country
Swaraj . . .	Self-government

Indian Coinage

Anna . . .	Very slightly more than two cents	16 annas=1 rupee
Rupee . . .	About thirty-two cents	
Lakh . . .	About thirty-seven thousand five hundred dollars	
Crore . . .	About three million seven hundred and fifty thousand dollars	

MAHATMA GANDHI—HIS OWN STORY

CHAPTER I

BIRTH AND HOME

THE GANDHIS belong to the Bania caste [1] and seem to have been originally retail traders. But for three generations they had been Prime Ministers in several Kathiawar [2] States. Uttamchand Gandhi, called Ota Gandhi, my grandfather, must have been a man of principles. State intrigues compelled him to leave Porbandar, where he was Diwan, and to seek refuge in Junagadh. There he saluted the Nawab with the left hand. Some one noticing the apparent discourtesy asked for an explanation which was thus given: "The right hand is already pledged to Porbandar."

Ota Gandhi married a second time, having lost his first wife. He had four sons by his first wife and two by his second wife. In my childhood I do not think I ever felt or knew that these sons of Ota Gandhi were not all of the same mother. The fifth of these six brothers was Karamchand Gandhi, who was called Kaba Gandhi; the sixth was Tulsidas Gandhi. Both these brothers were Prime Ministers in Porbandar one after the other. Kaba Gandhi was my father. He was for some time the Prime Minister in Rajkot and then in Vankaner. He was a pensioner of the Rajkot State when he died.

Kaba Gandhi married four times in succession, having lost his wife each time by death. He had two daughters

[1] The Modh Bania is a sub-division of the Vaishya Caste. Its original occupation was that of trade or agriculture. See "Mahatma Gandhi's Ideas," page 28.

[2] Kathiawar is a small peninsula on the extreme west of India. It is divided into a large number of Indian States which have their centre at Rajkot. The chief minister in each state is called Diwan.

by his first and second marriages. His last wife, Putlibai, bore him a daughter and three sons, of whom I was the youngest.

My father was a lover of his clan, truthful, brave and generous, but short-tempered. To a certain extent he may have been even given to carnal pleasures. For he married for the fourth time when he was over forty. But he was incorruptible and had earned a name for strict impartiality in his own family as well as outside. His loyalty to the state was well known. An Assistant Political Agent spoke insultingly of his prince, and he stood up to the insult. The agent was angry and asked Kaba Gandhi to apologise. This he refused to do and was therefore kept under detention for a few hours. But when the agent saw that Kaba Gandhi was adamant he ordered him to be released.

My father never had any ambition to accumulate riches and left us very little property. He had no education, save that of practical life. Of history and geography he was ignorant. But his rich experience in practical affairs helped him towards the solution of the most intricate questions and enabled him to manage hundreds of men. He had very little religious training, but he possessed that culture which comes from the frequent visiting of temples and listening to discourses on Hindu religion. In his last days, he began reading the Gita at the instance of a learned Brahman friend of the family, and he used to repeat aloud some verses every day at the time of worship.

The outstanding impression that my mother has left on my memory is one of saintliness. She was deeply religious and would never think of taking her meals without her daily prayers. Her visit to the temple was one of her daily duties. As far as my memory can go back, I do not remember her having ever missed her religious fasts. She would take the hardest vows and keep them without flinching. Illness was no excuse for relaxing them. I can recall her once falling ill when she was observing a special vow of fasting; but the illness was not allowed to interrupt the religious discipline. To keep two or three consecutive fasts was nothing to her. Living on one meal a day during her fasts was a habit with her. Not content with that, she fasted completely on each alternate day during one such period. At another time, she vowed not to take food without seeing the sun. We children on those days would stand, staring at the sky, waiting to announce to our mother the sun's appearance. At the height of the rainy season the sun not seldom remains invisible throughout the day; and I can recall days when, at the sun's sudden appearance after the rain, we would rush in and announce it to her. She would come out to see with her own eyes; but by that time perhaps the fugitive sun would be gone, thus depriving her of her meal. "That does not matter," she would say cheerfully. "God did not want me to eat to-day." Then she would return to her round of duties.

My mother had strong common sense. She was well informed about all matters of State, and ladies of the Court thought highly of her intelligence. Often I would accompany her, exercising the privilege of childhood; and I still remember many lively discussions she had with the widowed mother of the Thakor Sahib.

It was from these parents that I was born at Porbandar on October 2, 1869. There I passed my childhood and went for the first time to school. It was with some difficulty that I got through the multiplication tables. The fact that I recollect nothing more of those days than of having learnt, in company with other boys, to abuse our teacher, would strongly suggest that my intellect must have been sluggish at that time and my memory raw.

I must have been about seven years old when my father left Porbandar for Rajkot to become a member of the Court. There I was put to a primary school, and I can well remember those days, including the names and other particulars of the teachers who taught me. As at Porbandar, so at Rajkot, there is hardly anything special to note about my studies, and I could only have been a mediocre student. From this school I went to the suburban school and thence to the high school, having already reached my twelfth year. I do not remember having ever told a lie, during this short period of my life, either to my teachers or to my schoolmates. I used to be very shy and avoided all company. Books and lessons were my sole companions. It was my daily habit to be in school at the stroke of the hour and to run back home as soon as the school was over. Literally I ran back, because I could not bear to talk to anybody and was even afraid lest anyone should poke fun at me.

There is an incident which occurred at the examination during my first year at the high school, which is worth recording. Mr. Giles, the Educational Inspector, had come on a visit of inspection. He had set us five words to write as a spelling exercise. One of the words was "kettle." I had misspelt it. The teacher tried to prompt me with the point of his boot, but I would not be prompted. It was beyond me to see that he wanted me to copy the spelling from my neighbour's slate; for I had thought that the teacher was there to supervise us against copying. The result was that all the boys, except myself, were found to have spelt each word correctly. Only I had been stupid. The teacher tried later to bring this stupidity home to me, but without effect; for copying was something I could never learn to do. Yet the incident did not in the least diminish my respect for my teacher. I was by nature blind to the faults of elders. Later, I came to know of many other failings of this teacher; but my regard for him remained the same. For I had learnt to carry out the orders of elders, not to scan their actions.

Two other incidents belonging to the same period have always clung to my memory. As a rule I had a distaste for any reading that went beyond my school books. The daily lesson had to be done, because I disliked being taken to task by my teacher as much as I disliked deceiving him. Therefore I would do the lessons, but often without my mind in them. Thus when even the lessons could not be done properly, there was of course no question of any extra reading. But somehow my eyes fell on a book purchased by my father. It was a play about Shravana's devotion to his parents and I read it with intense interest. There came to our house about the same time some itinerant showmen. One of the pictures that was shown by them was Shravana carrying, by means of slings fitted for his shoulders, his blind parents on a pilgrimage. The book and the picture left an indelible impression on my mind. "Here is an example for you to copy," I said to myself. The agonised lament of the parents over Shravana's death is still fresh in my memory. The melting tune moved me deeply and I played it on a concertina which my father had purchased for me.

There was a similar incident connected with another play. Just about this time, I had secured my father's permission to see a play performed by a certain dramatic company, called "Harishchandra." It captured my heart and I could never be tired of seeing it. But how often should I be permitted to go? It haunted me, and I must have acted "Harishchandra" to myself times without number. "Why should not all persons be truthful like Harishchandra?" was the question I asked myself day and night. To follow truth and to go through all the ordeals that Harishchandra went through was the one thought that this play inspired in me. Quite literally I believed in the story of Harishchandra. The memory of it all often made me weep. My common sense tells me to-day that Harishchandra could not have been a historical character. But for me, both Harishchandra and Shravana are living realities; and I am sure I should be deeply touched as before if I were to read those plays again to-day.

Before I finish this narrative I know that I shall have to swallow many bitter draughts; but I can not do otherwise, if I claim to be a worshipper of Truth. It is my painful duty to have to record first of all my marriage at the age of thirteen. As I see the youngsters of the same age about me, who are under my care, and think of my own marriage, I am inclined to pity myself and to congratulate them on having escaped my lot. I can see no moral argument in support of such a preposterously early marriage as mine. Let the reader make no mistake. I was married, not betrothed. For in Kathiawar there are two distinct rites, betrothal and marriage. Betrothal is a preliminary promise on the part of the parents of the boy and girl to unite them in marriage, and it is not inviolable. The death of the boy entails no widowhood on the girl. It is simply an agreement between the parents; the children have no concern with it. Often they are not even informed of it. Thus it appears that I was betrothed thrice, though I do not know when. I was told that two girls who were chosen for me had died in turn; and therefore I infer that I was betrothed three times. However, I have a faint recollection that the third betrothal took place in my seventh year. Nevertheless I do not recollect having been informed about it. In what I now put down, I am writing not about my betrothal but about my marriage, of which I have the clearest recollection.

It will be remembered that we were three brothers. The first was already married. The elders decided to complete the marriage of my second brother, and a cousin and myself all at the same time. In this there was no thought of our welfare, much less our wishes. It was purely a question of their own convenience and economy. Marriage among Hindus is no simple matter. The parents of the bride and the bridegroom often bring themselves to ruin over it. They waste their substance and their time. Months are taken up over making clothes and ornaments and preparing budgets for dinners. Each tries to outdo the other in the number and variety of courses to be prepared. Women, whether they have a voice or no, sing themselves hoarse and even get ill, and disturb the peace of their neighbours. These in their turn quietly put up with all the turmoil and bustle, dirt and filth, which represents the remains of the wedding feast, because they know that a time will come when they also will be behaving in a similar manner. It would be better, thought my elders, to have all this bother over once and for all. For in this way there would be less expense and greater display. For money could freely be spent, if the expense had not to be repeated three times over. My father and my uncle were both old men, and we were the last children they had. It is likely that they wanted to have this last best time of their lives before they died. In view of all these considerations, a triple wedding was decided upon; and as I have said before, months were taken up in preparations for it.

It was only through these preparations that we got warning of the coming event. I do not think it meant to me anything more than the prospect of good clothes to wear, drum beating, marriage processions, rich dinners, and a strange girl to play with. The carnal desire came later. I propose to draw the curtain over my shame, except for a few things worth recording. To these I shall come later.

My brother and I were taken back from Rajkot to Porbandar. My father was a Diwan, but a servant of the State and all the more so because he was in favour with the Thakor Sahib. The latter would not let him go until the last moment. When he did so, he ordered my father special stage coaches, reducing the journey by two days. But the fates had willed otherwise. Porbandar is one hundred and twenty miles from Rajkot, which means a cart journey of five days. My father was to complete the distance in three, but the coach toppled over during the third stage, and he sustained severe injuries. He arrived bandaged all over. Both his and our interest in the coming event was half destroyed, but the ceremony had to be gone through. For how could the marriage dates be changed? Yet I forgot to grieve over my father's injuries in the childish amusement at the wedding.

To both my parents I was a devoted son, but none the less was I devoted to the passions of the flesh. I had to learn that all happiness should be sacrificed in devoted service to my parents. And yet, as though by way of punishment for my desire for pleasure, an incident happened, which will be told later on, that has ever since rankled in my mind. Nishkulanand sings: "Renunciation of objects, without the renunciation of desires, is short-lived, however hard one may try." Whenever I sing this song, or hear it sung, this bitter untoward incident rushes to my memory and fills me with shame.

My father had put on a brave face in spite of his injuries, and took full part in the wedding. As I think of it, I can even to-day call before my mind's eye the places where he sat as he went through the different details of the ceremony. Little did I dream then, that I should have to criticise my father in later life for having married me as a child; for everything on that day seemed to me right and proper and pleasant. There was also my own eagerness to get married; and as everything that my father did then struck me as beyond reproach, the recollection of these things is still fresh in my memory. I can picture to myself how we sat on our wedding seat; how we performed the "seven steps";[3] how the newly wedded husband and wife put the sweetmeat into each other's mouth; how we began to live together. Two innocent children were all unwittingly hurling themselves into

[3] The "seven steps," called "Saptapada," are taken together by a Hindu bride and bridegroom while they make promises of mutual fidelity and devotion, after which the marriage becomes irrevocable. The sweetmeat, called "Kansar," is a preparation of wheat, which the pair eat together after the completion of the ceremony.

the ocean of life. My brother's wife had thoroughly coached me about my behaviour on the first night. I do not know who had coached my wife. I have never asked her about it, nor am I inclined to do so now. The reader may be sure that we were too nervous to face each other. We were certainly too shy. How was I to talk to her and what was I to say? The coaching could not carry me far. But no coaching is really necessary in such matters. The impressions of the former birth are potent enough to make all coaching superfluous. We gradually began to know each other, and to speak freely together. We were the same age. But I took no time in assuming the authority of a husband.

It has already been explained that I was a pupil at the high school at the time when I was married. We three brothers were learning at the same school. My eldest brother was in a much higher class, and the brother who was married at the same time as I was only one class ahead of me. Marriage resulted in both of us wasting a year. Indeed, the result was worse for my second brother; for he gave up his studies altogether. Heaven knows how many youths suffer the same plight as he. Only in our present Hindu Society do school and marriage go thus hand in hand together.

My own studies were continued. I was not regarded as a dunce at the high school but always enjoyed the affection of my teachers. Certificates of progress and character used to be sent to our parents every year and mine were always good. As far as I can recollect I had not any high regard for my own intellectual ability, but I very jealously regarded my character. The least little blemish drew tears from my eyes. When I merited (or seemed to the teacher to merit) a rebuke, it was quite unbearable for me. Once I received corporal punishment. The punishment itself did not affect me so much as the fact that it was considered my desert. When it happened I wept piteously. That was when I was in the first or second standard. There was another similar incident during the time when I was in the seventh standard. Dorabji Edulji Gimi was the headmaster. He was popular among the boys, as he was a disciplinarian, a man of method and a good teacher. He had made gymnastics and cricket compulsory for boys in the upper standards. I disliked school sports and had never taken part in any exercise such as football or cricket before they were made compulsory. My shyness was one of the reasons for this aloofness, which I now see was wrong. But at that time I had the false notion that gymnastics and school games had nothing to do with education. To-day I know that physical training should have as much place in the curriculum as mental training. I may mention, however, that I was none the worse for abstaining from exercise, because I had read in books about the benefits of long walks in the open air; and having liked the advice I had formed a habit of taking walks. This habit has remained with me ever since, and these walks have given me a fairly hardy constitution.

The reason of my dislike for gymnastics was my keen desire to serve as a nurse to my father. As soon as the school was over, I would hurry home and begin serving him. Compulsory exercise came directly in the way of this service and therefore I requested Mr. Gimi to exempt me from gymnastics so that I might be free to serve my father. But he would not listen to me. Now it so happened that one Saturday, when we had our school in the morning, I had to go from home to the school for gymnastics at four o'clock in the afternoon. I had no watch, and the cloudy weather deceived me. Before I reached the school the boys had all left. The next day Mr. Gimi examining the roll found me marked absent. Being asked the reason for absence, I told him what had occurred, but he refused to believe me and ordered me to pay a small fine.

I was convicted of lying! That deeply pained me. How was I to prove my innocence? There was no way. I cried in deep anguish. I saw that a man of truth must also be a man of care. This was the first and last instance of my carelessness in school. I have a faint recollection of finally succeeding in getting the fine remitted.

The exemption from exercise was of course obtained, as my father wrote himself to the headmaster saying that he wanted me at home after school. But though I was none the worse for having neglected exercise, I am still paying the penalty of another neglect. The notion came to me somehow that good handwriting was not a necessary part of education, and I retained it until I went to England. When later, in South Africa, I saw the beautiful handwriting of lawyers and young men who were born and educated in that country I was ashamed of myself and repented of my neglect. I saw that bad handwriting should be regarded as a sign of imperfect education. I tried later to improve mine, but it was too late. The negligence of my youth could never be repaired. It is now my opinion that children should first be taught the art of drawing before learning how to write. Let the child learn his letters by observation just as he draws different objects, such as flowers and birds. Let him learn handwriting only after he has learnt to draw objects. He will then write a beautifully formed hand.

Two more reminiscences of my school days are worth recording. I had lost one year because of my marriage, and the teacher wanted me to make good the loss by skipping a class, which was a privilege usually allowed to industrious boys. I therefore had only six months in the third standard and was promoted to the fourth after the examinations. English became the medium of instruction in most subjects from the fourth standard onward, and at first I found myself completely at sea. Geometry was a new subject in which I was not particularly strong, and the English medium of instruction made it still more difficult for me. The teacher taught the subject well, but I could not follow him. Often I would lose heart and think of going back to the third standard, feeling that the packing of two years' studies into a single year was too ambitious. Yet this would not only discredit me, but also the teacher; because counting on my industry he had recommended my promotion. So the fear of the double discredit kept me to my post. When, however, with much effort I reached the thirteenth proposition of Euclid, the utter simplicity of it all was suddenly revealed to me. A subject which only required the simple use of one's reasoning powers could not be difficult. Ever since that time geometry has been both easy and interesting for me.

Sanskrit however proved a harder task. In geometry, there was nothing to memorise; whereas in Sanskrit everything had to be learnt by heart. This subject also was commenced from the fourth standard. As soon as I entered the sixth I became disheartened. The teacher was a hard taskmaster anxious, as I thought, to force the boys. There was a sort of rivalry going on between the Sanskrit and the Persian teachers. The Persian teacher was lenient. The boys used to talk among themselves that Persian was very easy and that the teacher was very good and considerate to the students. This "easiness" of Persian tempted me and one day I sat in the Persian class. The Sanskrit teacher was grieved. He called me to his side and said: "How can you forget that you are the son of a Vaishnava father? [4] Won't you learn the language of your own religion? If you have any difficulty, why not come to me? I want to teach you students Sanskrit to the best of my ability. As you proceed further, you will find in it things of absorbing interest. You should not lose heart. Come and sit again in the Sanskrit class."

This kindness put me to shame. I could not disregard my teacher's affection. To-day, I cannot but think with gratitude of Krishnashankar Pandya. For if I had not acquired the little Sanskrit that I learnt then, I should have found it difficult to take any interest in our sacred books. In fact, I deeply regret that I was not able to acquire a more thorough knowledge of the language because I have since realised that every Hindu boy and girl should possess sound Sanskrit learning.

It is now my opinion that in all Indian curricula of higher education there should be a place for Hindi, Sanskrit, Persian, Arabic and English, besides of course the vernacular. This list need not frighten any one. If our education were more systematic, and the boys free from

[4] The followers of Vishnu, as the One Supreme God, are called by the name "Vaishnava." The Vaishnavas have a repugnance against taking the life of any animal and are usually strict vegetarians. The appeal of love and compassion is very strong among them.

the burden of having to learn their subjects through a foreign medium, I am sure learning all these languages would not be an irksome task, but a perfect pleasure. A scientific knowledge of one language makes a knowledge of other languages comparatively easy.

CHAPTER II

SCHOOL DAYS

AMONGST MY FEW FRIENDS at the high school I had, at different times, two who might be called intimate. One of these friendships did not last long, though I never forsook my friend. He gave me up, because I made friends with the other. This latter friendship I regard as a tragedy in my life. It lasted a long time and I began it in the spirit of a reformer. This companion was originally my elder brother's friend. They were classmates together. I knew his weaknesses, but I regarded him as a faithful friend. My mother, my eldest brother, and my wife warned me that I was in bad company. I was too proud a husband to heed my wife's warning. But I did not dare at first to go against the opinion of my mother and my eldest brother. Nevertheless I pleaded with them, saying, "I know he has the weaknesses you attribute to him, but you do not know his virtues. He cannot lead me astray, because my association with him is meant to lead him right. For I am sure if he mends his ways, he will be a splendid man. I beg you not to be anxious on my account."

I do not think this satisfied them, but they accepted my explanation and let me go my way. Since then, I have seen that I had calculated wrongly. One who tries to reform another cannot afford to have close intimacy with him during the process. True friendship is an identity of souls rarely to be found in this world. Only between like natures can friendship be altogether worthy and enduring. Friends react on one another. Hence, in friendship, there is very little scope for the reformation of a friend. I am of opinion that all exclusive intimacies are to be avoided; for man far more readily takes in vice than virtue. And he who would be friends with God must remain alone, or make the whole world his friend. I may be wrong, but my effort to cultivate an intimate friendship proved a failure.

A wave of "reform" in other directions was sweeping over Rajkot at the time when I first came across this friend. He told me that many of our teachers were secretly taking meat and wine. He also named many well known people of Rajkot as belonging to the same company. There were also some high school boys among them. When I heard this, I was painfully surprised and asked my friend the reason. He explained it to me in this way. "We are a weak people," he said, "because we do not eat meat. The English are able to rule over us, because they are meat-eaters. You know how hardy I am, and a great runner, too. It is because I am a meat-eater. Meat-eaters do not have boils or tumours; and even if they sometimes happen to have any, they heal quickly. Our teachers and other distinguished people who eat meat are no fools. They know its virtues. You should do likewise. There is nothing like trying. Try and see what strength it gives."

All these pleas on behalf of meat-eating were not advanced at a single sitting. They were the substance of a long and elaborate argument which my friend was trying to impress upon me from time to time. My elder brother had already fallen. He therefore supported him. I certainly looked feeble-bodied by the side of my brother and this friend. Both of them were hardier, stronger, and more daring than I was. This friend's exploits cast a spell over me. He could run long distances with extraordinary speed and excelled in high and long jumping. He could put up with any amount of corporal punishment. He would often display his exploits to me; and as one is always dazzled when he sees in others the qualities that he lacks himself, I was also dazzled by my friend's exploits. This was accompanied by a strong desire to be like him. I could hardly jump or run. Why should not I also be as strong as he?

Again I was a coward. I used to be haunted by the fear of thieves, ghosts, and serpents. I did not dare to stir out of doors at night. Darkness was a terror to me. It was almost impossible for me to sleep in the dark, since I would imagine ghosts coming from one direction, thieves from another, and serpents from a third. I could not therefore bear to sleep without a light in the room. How could I disclose my fears to my wife sleeping by my side, now at the threshold of youth? I knew that she had more courage than I, and this made me ashamed of myself. She knew no fear of serpents and ghosts. She could go out anywhere in the dark. My friend knew all these weaknesses of mine. He would tell me that he could hold in his hand live serpents, could defy thieves and did not believe in ghosts. And all this was, of course, the result of eating meat.

A doggerel of Narmad's was in vogue amongst us schoolboys as follows:

> Behold the mighty Englishman;
> He rules the Indian small,
> Because being a meat-eater
> He is five cubits tall.

All this had its due effect upon me, and I was at last defeated. It began to grow on me that meat-eating was good; that it would make me strong and daring; that if the whole country took to it the English could be overcome.

A day was thereupon fixed for beginning the experiment. It had to be conducted in secret. The Gandhis were Vaishnavas. My parents were particularly staunch in their faith. The family had even its own temples. Jainism[1] was strong in Gujarat, and its influence was felt everywhere and on all occasions. The opposition to and abhorrence of meat-eating that existed in Gujarat among the Jains and Vaishnavas was to be seen nowhere else either in India or outside India in such strength. These were the religious traditions in which I was born, and I was extremely devoted to my parents. The moment that they would come to know of my having eaten meat they would be shocked to death. Moreover, my love of truth made me especially reluctant. It is not possible for me to say that I did not know that I should have to deceive my parents if I began eating meat. But my mind was bent on "reform." It was not a question of pleasing the palate. There was no thought in my mind that meat had a particularly good relish. It was simply that I wished to be strong and daring and desired my countrymen also to be the same, so that we might be able to defeat the English and make India free. The word "Swaraj" (self-government) I had not yet heard. But I knew what freedom meant. The

[1] The Jain religion was established in India during the same epoch as the Buddhist religion. One of its chief tenets is the strict abstention from taking the life of any living creature. It was owing partly to the influence of the Jain faith that the doctrine of Ahimsa obtained such a hold of the religious consciousness of India. In western India Vaishnavas sometimes retain, along with their own faith, the Jain philosophy of life. This was the practice in the Gandhi family.

frenzy of "reform" blinded me. And having ensured secrecy, I persuaded myself that mere hiding the deed from my parents was no departure from truth.

So the day came. It is difficult fully to describe my condition. There was, on the one hand, the zeal for "reform" together with the novelty of making a momentous departure in life. There was on the other hand the shame of hiding like a thief in order to do this very thing. Which of the two swayed me most it would be impossible to say. We went in search of a lonely spot by the river, and there I saw meat for the first time in my life. We had also bread baked in English fashion. Neither gave me any relish. The goat's meat was as tough as leather and I simply could not eat it. Indeed, I became so sick that I had to leave off in disgust.

Afterwards I passed a very bad night. A horrible nightmare haunted me. Every time I dropped off to sleep, it would seem as though a live goat were bleating inside me; and I would jump up full of remorse. But then I would remind myself that what I had done was a duty, and so I would become more cheerful. My friend was not one to give in easily. He now began to cook various delicacies along with the meat and dress them neatly. And for our place of dining, no longer the secluded spot on the river was chosen, but a State house, with its dining hall and tables and chairs, about which my friend had made arrangements in collusion with the chief cook there. This bait had its effect. I got over my dislike for English bread; forswore my compassion for the goats, and became a relisher of meat dishes, if not of meat itself. This went on for about a year. But not more than half a dozen of such dinners were enjoyed in all; because the State house was not available every day, and there was the difficulty about preparing frequently expensive savoury meat dishes. I had no money to pay for this "reform." My friend had therefore always to find the wherewithal and I had no knowledge from whence he found it. But find it he did, because he was bent on turning me into a meat-eater. But even his means must have been limited, and hence these dinners had necessarily to be few and far between.

Whenever I had occasion to indulge in these surreptitious meals, dinner at home was out of the question. My mother would naturally ask me to come and take my food and want to know the reason why I did not wish to eat. "I have no appetite to-day," I would say, "there is something wrong with my digestion." It was not without compunction that I devised these pretexts. I knew I was lying, and lying to my mother. Also I was aware that if my mother and father came to hear of my having become a meat-eater, they would be shocked beyond words. This knowledge was gnawing at my heart. Therefore I said to myself: "Though it is essential to eat meat, and also to take up food 'reform,' yet deceiving and lying to one's father and mother are worse than abstinence from meat. In my parents' lifetime, therefore, such things must be out of the question. When my parents have passed away and I have found my freedom, then I will eat meat openly. But until that moment arrives I will abstain from it."

This decision I communicated to my friend, and I have never since gone back upon it. My parents never knew what an offence two of their sons had committed. Thus meat was abjured by me at last out of the purity of my desire not to lie to my parents; but I did not abjure the company of my friend. My zeal for setting him right had proved disastrous for me, and all the time I was completely unconscious of the fact.

The same company would have led me into faithlessness to my wife. But I was saved by a narrow margin. My friend once took me to a brothel. He sent me in with the necessary instructions. It was all prearranged. The bill had already been paid. I went into the jaws of sin, but God in his infinite mercy protected me against myself. I was almost struck blind and dumb in this den of vice and came away without committing the deed for which my friend had taken me. I felt as though my manhood had been injured, and wished to sink into the ground for shame. But I have ever since given thanks to God for having saved me. I can recall four more similar incidents in my life; and in most of them my good fortune rather than any effort on my part saved me. From a strictly ethical point of view, all these occasions must be regarded as moral lapses; for the carnal passion was there, and this was as bad as the act. But from the ordinary point of view, a man who is preserved from physically committing sin is regarded as saved. And I was kept from sin only in that sense. There are some actions from which an escape is a godsend both for the man who escapes and for those about him. Man, as soon as he gets back his consciousness of right, is thankful to the divine mercy for the escape. As we know that a human being often succumbs to temptation, however much he may resist it, we also know that divine providence often intercedes and saves him in spite of himself. How all this happens; how far man's will is free; to what extent he is a creature of circumstances; how far fate enters on the scene—all this is a mystery and will remain a mystery.

But to go on with the story. Even this was far from opening my eyes to the viciousness of my friend's company. Therefore I had many more bitter draughts in store until my eyes were actually opened by an ocular demonstration of some of his lapses quite unexpected by me. These will come later. One thing, however, I must mention now, as it pertains to the same period. One of the reasons of my differences with my wife was undoubtedly the company of this friend. I was both a devoted and jealous husband, and this friend fanned the flame of my suspicions about my wife. I never could doubt his veracity. And I have never forgiven myself the violence of which I have been guilty in often having pained my wife by acting on his information. Only a Hindu wife tolerates these hardships, and that is why I have always regarded woman as an incarnation of tolerance. A servant wrongly suspected may throw up his job; a son in the same case may leave his father's roof; a friend may put an end to the friendship. A wife, even if she suspects her husband, will keep quiet. But if the husband suspects her, she is ruined. Where can she go? A Hindu wife may not seek divorce in a law court. Law has no redress for her. And I can never forget or forgive myself for having driven my wife to that desperation.

The canker of suspicion was rooted out only when I understood Ahimsa[2] in all its bearings. I saw then the glory of Brahmacharya[3] and realised that the wife is not

[2] Ahimsa means literally innocence, non-violence. In its positive aspect, it has the equivalence of love.

[3] Brahmacharya means, literally, conduct that leads one to God. Its technical meaning is self-restraint, particularly continence.

the husband's bondslave but his companion and his helpmate, and an equal partner in all his joys and sorrows—as free as the husband to choose her own path. Whenever I think of those dark days of doubt and suspicion, I am filled with loathing at my folly and my lustful cruelty, and I deplore my blind devotion to my friend.

I have still to relate some of my failings during this period and also previous to it, which date from before my marriage or soon after. A relative and I became fond of smoking. Not that we saw any good in smoking, or were enamoured of the smell of a cigarette. We simply imagined a sort of pleasure in emitting clouds of smoke from our mouths. My uncle had the habit; and when we saw him smoking, we thought we should copy his example. But we had no money. So we began pilfering stumps of cigarettes which had been thrown away by my uncle.

The stumps, however, were not always available, and could not give much smoke either. So we began to steal coppers from the servant's pocket money in order to purchase Indian cigarettes. But the question was where to keep them. We could not, of course, smoke in the presence of our elders. Somehow we managed for a few weeks with these stolen coppers to get Indian cigarettes. In the meantime, we heard that the stalks of a certain plant were porous and could be smoked. So we got them and began this kind of smoking. But we were far from being satisfied with such things as these. Our want of independence began to hurt us. It was unbearable that we should be unable to do anything without the permission of our elders. At last, in sheer disgust, we decided to commit suicide!

But how were we to do it? From what place were we to get the poison? We heard that Datura seeds were an effective poison. Off we went to the jungle in search of these seeds, and obtained them. Evening was thought to be the auspicious hour. We went to Kedarji Mandir,[4] put melted butter in the temple-lamp, paid a visit to the shrine and then looked for a lonely corner. But our courage failed us. Supposing we were not instantly killed? And what was the good of killing ourselves after all? Why not rather put up with the lack of independence? Nevertheless, we swallowed two or three seeds. We did not dare to take more. Both of us now fought shy of death. We decided to go to Ramji Mandir to compose ourselves and to dismiss the thought of suicide. Thus I realised that it was not as easy to commit suicide as to contemplate it. Since that evening, whenever I have heard of someone threatening to commit suicide, it has had little effect on me.

The thought of suicide ultimately resulted in both of us abandoning the habit of smoking stumps of cigarettes and of stealing the servant's coppers for the purpose of smoking. From that time onward, ever since I have reached manhood, I have never desired to smoke. The habit of smoking has come to appear to me barbarous, dirty and harmful. I have never understood why there is such a rage for smoking throughout the world. It is almost unbearable to me to travel in a compartment full of tobacco smoke and I become choked for want of fresh air.

But much more serious than this theft was the one I was guilty of a little later. This other theft was com-

[4] Temple.

mitted when I was fifteen. In this case, I stole a bit of gold out of my meat-eating brother's armlet. This brother had run into a debt of about twenty-five rupees. He had on his arm an armlet of solid gold. It was not difficult to clip a bit out of it.

Well, it was done, and the debt cleared. But this became more than I could bear. I resolved never to steal again. I also made up my mind to confess it to my father. But I did not dare to speak. Not that I was afraid of my father beating me; for I do not recall his ever having beaten any of us. No, I was afraid of the pain I should cause him. But I felt that the risk must be taken; that there could not be a cleansing without a clean confession. At last I decided to write out the confession and then submit it to my father and ask his forgiveness. So I wrote it on a slip of paper and handed it to him myself. In this note, not only was my guilt confessed but I also asked adequate punishment for it. The note was ended with a request to him not to punish himself for my offence, and also a pledge that I would never steal again.

I was trembling all over as I handed the confession to my father. He was then suffering from fistula and was confined to bed. His bed was a bare plank of wood. I handed him the note and sat opposite. As he read it through, tears like pearl drops trickled down his cheeks, wetting the paper. For a moment he closed his eyes in thought and then tore up the note. He had sat up to read it. He again lay down. I also shed tears when I saw my father's agony. If I were a painter I could draw a picture of the whole scene to-day. It is still so vivid in my mind. Those pearl drops of love cleansed my heart, and washed my sin away. Only he who has experienced such love can know what it is. As the hymn says:

> Only he
> Who is smitten with the arrows of love,
> Knows its power.

This was, for me, an object lesson in Ahimsa. Then I could read in it nothing more than a father's affection. But to-day I know that it was pure Ahimsa. When such Ahimsa becomes all-embracing, it transforms everything it touches. There is no limit to its powers. This sort of sublime forgiveness was not natural to my father. I had thought that he would be angry, say hard things, and strike his forehead. But he was wonderfully quiet; and I believe this was due to my clean confession. A clean confession, combined with a promise never to commit the sin again, when offered before one who has the right to receive it, is the purest type of repentance. I know that my confession made my father feel absolutely safe about me, and increased his affection for me beyond measure.

The time about which I am now writing was my sixteenth year. My father was bedridden, suffering from fistula. My mother along with an old servant of the house and myself were his principal attendants. The duties of a nurse devolved upon me. These mainly consisted in dressing the wound, giving my father his medicine, and compounding drugs whenever they had to be made up at home. Every night I massaged his legs and retired only when he asked me to do so or after he had fallen asleep. Such service was dear to me. I do not remember ever having neglected it. All the time at my disposal, after the performance of the daily toilet, was divided between school and attending on my father. I would only go out for an evening walk when he permitted me or when he was feeling better.

This was also the time when my wife was expecting a baby. Such a circumstance, as I can see to-day, meant a double shame for me. First of all, I did not restrain myself, as I should have done, whilst I was yet a student. And secondly, this carnal desire had got the better of what I regarded as my duty as a student, and of what was even a greater duty, my devotion to my parents. Every night, while my hands were busy massaging my father's legs, my mind was hovering about the bedroom, and that too at a time when religion, medical science, and common sense alike forbade sexual intercourse. I was always glad to be relieved from my duty, and went straight to the bedroom after doing obeisance to my father.

At the same time my father was getting worse every day. Ayurvedic physicians had tried all their ointments, Hakims [5] their plasters, and local quacks their remedies. An English surgeon had also used his skill. As the last and only resort he had recommended a surgical operation. But the family physician came in the way. He disapproved of an operation being performed at such an advanced age. This family physician was competent and well-known, and his advice prevailed. The operation was abandoned, and various medicines purchased for the purpose went to no account. I have an impression that if the family physician had allowed the operation to be performed the wound

[5] Ayurvedic medicine represents the Hindu form of medical treatment according to the Vedas. The Muhammadan treatment is called Yunani (Greek). Its practising doctors are called Hakims.

would have been easily healed. The operation also was to have been undertaken by a surgeon who was then of high repute in Bombay. But God had willed otherwise. When death is imminent, who can think of the right remedy? My father returned from Bombay with all the paraphernalia for the operation which were now useless. He despaired of living any longer. He was getting weaker and weaker, until at last he had to be asked to perform the necessary functions in bed. But up to the last he refused to do anything of the kind, always insisting on going through the strain of leaving his bed—the Vaishnava rules about external cleanliness are so inexorable.

Such cleanliness is quite essential no doubt, but Western medical science has taught that all the toilet functions, including a bath, can be done in bed with the strictest regard to cleanliness, and without any discomfort to the patient, the bed always remaining spotlessly clean. I should regard such cleanliness as quite consistent with the tenets of the Vaishnava religion. But my father's insistence on leaving the bed only struck me with wonder at that time, and I had nothing but admiration for him.

The dreadful night came at last. My uncle was then in Rajkot. I have a faint recollection that he had arrived after having received news that my father was getting worse. The brothers were deeply attached to each other. My uncle would sit near my father's bed the whole day, and would insist on sleeping by his bedside after sending us all to sleep. No one had dreamt that this was to be the fateful night. The danger of course was there all the while.

It was about 10:30 or 11 p.m. I was giving the massage. My uncle offered to relieve me. I was glad and went straight to the bedroom. My wife, poor thing, was fast asleep. But how could she sleep when I was there? I woke her up. In five or six minutes, however, the servant knocked at the door. I started with alarm. "Get up," he said, "Father is very ill." I knew of course that he was ill, and so I guessed what "very ill" meant at that moment. I sprang out of bed.

"What is the matter? Do tell me!"

"Father is no more."

So all was over! I had but to wring my hands. I felt deeply ashamed and miserable and ran to my father's room. If animal passion had not blinded me, I should have been spared the torture of separation from my father during his last moments and should have been massaging him. He would have died in my arms. But now it was my uncle who had been given this honour. He was so deeply devoted to his elder brother that he had earned the reward of doing him these last services. My father had forebodings of the coming event. He had made a sign for pen and paper, and written: "Prepare for the last rites." He had then snapped the amulet off his arm, and also his gold necklace of Tulasi-beads [6] and flung them aside. A moment after this he was no more.

The shame, to which I have referred above, was this shame of my carnal desire even at the critical hour of my father's death, which had demanded wakeful service. It is a blot I have never been able either to efface or to forget; and I have always thought, that although my devotion to my parents knew no bounds, so that I would have given up anything for it, yet it was weighed in the balance that hour and found unpardonably wanting, be-

[6] The Tulasi plant is sacred in India. The beads would be used as a kind of rosary.

cause my mind was in the grip of lust. I have therefore always regarded myself as a lustful, though a faithful husband. It took me long to get free from these shackles, and I had to pass through many ordeals before I could find release.

Before I close this chapter of my double shame, I may mention that the poor mite of a baby that was born to my wife scarcely breathed for more than three or four days. Nothing else could be expected. Let all those who are married be warned by my example.

CHAPTER III

EARLY YOUTH

FROM MY SIXTH OR SEVENTH YEAR up to my sixteenth I was at school, where I was taught all sorts of things except religion. I may say that I failed to get from the teachers what they could have given me without any effort on their part. And yet here and there I kept on picking up different religious ideas from my surroundings. The term "religion" I am using in its broadest sense, meaning thereby self-realization.

Being born in the Vaishnava faith, I had often to go to the family shrine. But temple worship never appealed to me. I did not like its glitter and pomp. Also I heard rumours of immorality being practised there and lost all interest in it.

But what I failed to get there I obtained from my nurse, an old servant of the family, whose affection for me I still recall. My nurse, Rambha (for that was her name) suggested as a remedy for my fear of ghosts the repetition of the name of Rama.[1] I had more faith in her than in her remedy, and so at a tender age I tried this method to cure my fear. It was of course short-lived; but the good seed sown in childhood was not sown in vain. I think it is due to the seed sown by that good woman Rambha that to-day the repetition of the name of Rama has become an infallible remedy for me in times of trouble.

[1] "Ramanama" is the word used for the constant repetition of the name Rama as an act of devotion to the Lord. Rama is the divine incarnation of the Supreme in human form as described in the Ramayana Epic of Tulasidas. This Epic poem in Hindi is based upon the original Sanskrit Epic of Valmiki.

Just about this time, a cousin of mine, who was a devotee of the Ramayana, arranged for my second brother and me to learn Rama Raksha.[2] We got it by heart, and made a rule to recite it every morning after the bath. The practice was kept up as long as we were in Porbandar. But as soon as we reached Rajkot it was forgotten. For I had not much belief in it and recited it partly because of my pride in being able to recite Rama Raksha with correct pronunciation. What, however, left a deep impression on me was the reading of the Ramayana of Tulasidas itself before my father. During part of his illness my father was in Porbandar. There, every evening, he used to listen to the Ramayana being recited. The reader was a great devotee of Rama, Ladha Maharaj of Bileshvar. It was said of him that he cured himself of his leprosy, not by any medicine, but by applying to the affected parts the leaves of a sacred tree which had been offered to the image of the Great God in Bileshvar temple, and by the regular repetition of the name of Rama. His faith, it was said, had made him whole. This may or may not be true. We at any rate believed the story. And it is a fact that when Ladha Maharaj began his reading of the Ramayana his body was entirely free from leprosy. He had a melodious voice and would sing couplets and quatrains, losing himself in the discourse and carrying his listeners along with him. I must have been thirteen at that time; but I quite remember being enraptured by his reading. That laid the foundation of my deep devotion to the Ramayana. To-day I regard the Ramayana of Tulasidas as the greatest book in all devotional literature.

[2] A recitation of sacred texts asking for the protection of Rama.

A few months after this we came to Rajkot. There was no Ramayana reading there. The Bhagavat,[3] however, used to be read there. Sometimes I attended the reading, but the reciter was uninspiring. To-day I see that the Bhagavat is a book which can evoke religious fervour. I had read it in Gujarati with intense interest. But when I heard portions of the original read by Pandit Madan Mohan Malaviya during my twenty-one days' fast at Delhi, I wished I had heard it in my childhood from such a devotee as he is, so that I could have formed a liking for it at an early age. Early impressions strike roots deep down into one's nature, and it is my perpetual regret that I was not fortunate enough to hear more good books of this kind read during that period.

In Rajkot, however, I got an early grounding in toleration for all branches of Hinduism and sister religions. For my father and mother would visit the family shrine, as also Shiva's and Rama's temples, and would take or send us youngsters there. Jain monks also would pay frequent visits to my father and would even go out of their way to accept food from us who were non-Jains. They would have talks with my father on subjects both secular and sacred. He had in addition Musalman and Parsi friends, who would talk to him about their own faiths; and he would listen to them always with respect, and often with interest. Being his nurse, I had a chance

[3] The Bhagavat is the most famous of the Puranas, or sacred legendary books of medieval Hinduism, which represent the religious ideal of Bhakti, or Devotion, in its concrete form. They tell the legends of the divine incarnations.

Mahatma Gandhi fasted as a penance for twenty-one days at Delhi in order to bring to an end the rioting between Hindus and Musalmans. I was present at the time that Pandit Madan Mohan Malaviya read this Purana and heard afterwards from Mahatma Gandhi what a spiritual help the reading had been to him.

to be present at these talks. These many things combined to inculcate in me a toleration for all faiths.

Only Christianity was at the time an exception. I developed a sort of dislike for it. And for a reason. In those days, Christian missionaries used to stand in a corner near the high school and hold forth, pouring abuse on Hindus and their gods. I could not stomach this. I must have stood there to hear them once only; but that was enough to dissuade me from repeating the experiment. About the same time, I heard of a well-known Hindu having been converted to Christianity. It was the talk of the town, that when he was baptised he had to eat beef and drink liquor; that he also had to change his clothes, and that henceforth he began to go about in European costume including a hat. These things got on my nerves. Surely, thought I, a religion that compelled one to eat beef, drink liquor and change one's own clothes did not deserve that name. I also heard that the new convert had already begun abusing the religion of his ancestors, their customs and their country. All these things created in me a dislike for Christianity.[4]

But the fact that I had learnt to be tolerant to other religions did not mean that I had any living faith in God. I happened to come across, about that time, Manusmriti,[5] which was amongst my father's collection. The story of the creation and similar things in it did not impress me

[4] This passage in the Autobiography was challenged by Mr. Scott, the missionary, who was living at Rajkot forty years ago. Mahatma Gandhi accepted Mr. Scott's repudiation and pointed out that he had stated simply what he, as a young boy, had *heard*. See "Mahatma Gandhi's Ideas," page 87.

[5] "Manusmriti" is a very ancient Hindu religious code authoritatively upholding the caste system and also containing legendary accounts of Creation and the origin of mankind.

very much and on the contrary made me incline somewhat toward atheism.

There was a cousin of mine for whose intellect I had great regard. To him I turned with my doubts, but he could not resolve them. He sent me away with this answer: "When you grow up, you will be able to solve these doubts yourself. These questions ought not to be raised at your age." I was silenced, but was not comforted. Chapters about diet and the like in Manusmriti seemed to me to run contrary to daily practice. To my doubts as to this also I got the same answer.

Manusmriti at any rate did not teach me Ahimsa. I have told the story of my meat-eating. Manusmriti seemed to support it. I also felt that it was quite moral to kill serpents, bugs and the like. I remember to have killed at that age bugs and such other insects, and to have regarded it as a duty.

But one thing took deep root in me—the conviction that morality is the basis of things, and that truth is the substance of all morality. Truth now became my sole objective. Truth began to grow in magnitude every day. Since then, also, my definition of Truth has been ever widening.

A Gujarati didactic stanza likewise gripped my mind and heart. Its precept—"return good for evil"—became my guiding principle. It became such a passion with me that I began numerous experiments in it. Here are those (for me) wonderful lines:

> For a bowl of water give a goodly meal;
> For a kindly greeting bow thou down with zeal;
> For a simple penny pay thou back with gold;
> If thy life be rescued, life do not withhold.

Thus the words and actions of the wise regard;
Every little service tenfold thy reward.
But the truly noble know all men as one,
And return with gladness good for evil done.

After I had passed my matriculation my elders wanted me to pursue my studies at college. There was a college at Bhavnagar in Kathiawar as well as in Bombay. Since the former was cheaper, I decided to go there and join the Samaldas College. I went, but found myself entirely at sea. Everything was difficult. I could not follow the professors' lectures. It was no fault of theirs. The professors in that college were regarded as first rate. But I was so raw. At the end of the first term I returned home.

We had in Mavji Dave, who was a shrewd and learned Brahman, an old friend and adviser of the family. He happened to visit us during my vacation. In conversation with my mother and elder brother, he inquired about my studies. Learning that I was at Samaldas College, he said: "The times are changed, and none of you can expect to succeed to your father's position as Diwan without having had a proper education. Now as this boy is still pursuing his studies, you should all look to him to continue the succession as Diwan. It will take him four or five years to get his B. A. degree, which will at best qualify him for an inferior post, not for a Diwanship. If, like my son, he went in for law it would take him still longer; by which time there would be a host of lawyers aspiring for a Diwan's post. I would far rather that you sent him to England. My son Kevalram says it is very easy to be a barrister. In three years' time he would return. Also expenses would not exceed four to five thousand rupees."

Joshiji,[6]—that is how we used to call old Mavji Dave, —turned to me with complete assurance and asked, "Would you not rather go to England than study here?" Nothing could have been more welcome to me. I was fighting shy of my difficult studies. So I jumped at the proposal and said that the sooner I was sent the better. It was no easy business to pass examinations quickly. Could I not be sent to qualify for the medical profession?

My brother interrupted me: "Father never liked it. He had you in mind when he said that we Vaishnavas should have nothing to do with the dissection of dead bodies. Father intended you for the Bar."

Joshiji chimed in: "A medical degree will not make a Diwan of you and I want you to be Diwan, or if possible something better. Only in that way could you undertake your large family responsibilities. The times are fast changing and getting harder. It is the wisest thing therefore to become a barrister."

Joshiji went away, and I began building castles in the air. My elder brother was greatly exercised in his mind. How was he to find the wherewithal to send me? And was it proper to trust a young man like me to go abroad alone? My mother was sorely perplexed. She did not like the idea of parting with me. This is how she tried to put me off: "Uncle," she said, "is now the eldest member of the family. He should first be consulted. If he consents we will consider the matter."

When I met my uncle I did obeisance and told him everything. He thought it over and said: "I am not sure whether it is in accordance with our religion. From all

[6] The suffix "ji," when added to a proper name, denotes kindly respect. It is constantly added when speaking as well as when writing, e. g. Gandhiji, Swamiji, etc.

I have heard, I have my doubts. When I meet these big barristers, I see no difference between their life and that of Europeans. They know no scruples regarding food. Cigars are never out of their mouths. They dress as shamelessly as Englishmen. All that would not be in keeping with our family tradition. I am shortly going on a pilgrimage and have not many years to live. At the threshold of death, how dare I give you permission to go to England, to cross the seas? But I will not stand in your way. It is your mother's permission which really matters. If she permits you, then Godspeed! Tell her I will not interfere. You will go with my blessings."

On returning to Rajkot I reported all that had happened. My mother, however, was still unwilling. She had begun making minute inquiries. Some one had told her that young men got morally lost in England. Some one else had said that they took to meat; and yet another that they could not live there without liquor. "How about all this?" she asked me. "Mother dear," I replied, "will you not trust me? I shall not lie to you. I swear that I shall not touch any of these things. If there were any such danger, would Joshiji let me go?"

"I can rely on you," she said. "But how can I trust you in a distant land? I am dazed and know not what to do. I will ask Becharji Swami."

Becharji Swami was by birth a Modh Bania,[7] but had now become a Jain monk. He too was a family adviser like Joshiji. He came to my help, and said: "I shall get the boy solemnly to take the three vows, and then he can be allowed to go." He administered the oath and I vowed to live a celibate life in England and never to touch wine

[7] He thus belonged to the same sub-caste (Modh Bania) as the Gandhi family.

or meat. This done, my mother gave her permission and her blessing.

With my mother's blessings, I set off exultantly for Bombay, leaving my wife with a baby of a few months. But on arrival there, friends told my brother that the Indian Ocean was rough in June and July; and as this was my first voyage, I should not be allowed to sail until November. Some one also reported that a steamer had just been sunk in a gale. This made my brother uneasy and he refused to take the risk of allowing me to sail immediately. Leaving me with a friend in Bombay, he returned to Rajkot to resume his duty. He put the money for my travelling expenses in the keeping of a brother-in-law, and left word with some friends to give me whatever help I might need. Time hung heavily on my hands in Bombay, and I dreamt continually of going to England.

Meanwhile my caste-people were agitated over my going abroad. No Modh Bania had been to England up to now, and if I dared to do so, I ought to be brought to book! A general meeting of the caste was called and I was summoned to appear. How I suddenly managed to muster up courage to go before it I do not know. Nothing daunted, and without the slightest hesitation, I came before the meeting. The Sheth—the headman of the community—who was distantly related to me and had been on very good terms with my father, thus accosted me:

"In the opinion of the caste, your proposal to go to England is not proper. Our religion forbids voyages abroad. We have also heard that it is not possible to live there without compromising our religion. One is obliged to eat and drink with Europeans!"

To which I replied: "I do not think it is at all against our religion to go to England. I intend going there for further studies. And I have already solemnly promised to my mother to abstain from three things you fear most. I am sure the vow will keep me safe."

"But we tell you," rejoined the Sheth, "that it is *not* possible to keep our religion there. You know my relations with your father and you ought to listen to my advice."

"I know those relations," said I. "And you are as an elder to me. But I am helpless in this matter. I cannot alter my resolve to go to England. My father's friend and adviser, who is a learned Brahman, sees no objection to my going to England and my mother and brother have also given me their permission."

"But will you disregard the orders of the caste?"

"I am really helpless. The caste should not interfere in the matter."

This incensed the Sheth. He swore at me, while I sat unmoved. So the Sheth pronounced his order: "This boy shall be treated as an outcaste from to-day. Whosoever helps him or goes to see him off at the dock shall be punishable with a fine of one rupee four annas."

The order had no effect on me, and I took my leave of the Sheth. But I wondered how my brother would take it. Fortunately he remained firm and wrote to assure me that I had his permission to go, the Sheth's order notwithstanding.

As I was thus worrying over my predicament, I heard that a Junagadh lawyer was going to England by a boat sailing on the fourth of September. I met the friends to whose care my brother had commended me. They also agreed that I should not let go the opportunity of travelling to England in such company. There was no time to be lost. I wired to my brother for permission, which he granted. Then I asked my brother-in-law to give me the money. But he referred to the order of the Sheth and said that he could not afford to lose caste. On this, I sought a friend of the family and requested him to accommodate me to the extent of my passage and sundries, and to recover the loan from my brother. The friend was not only good enough to accede to my request, but cheered me up as well.

With part of the money I at once purchased the passage. Then I had to equip myself for the voyage. There was another friend who had experience in the matter. He got clothes and other things ready. Some of the clothes I liked and some I did not like at all. The necktie, which I delighted in wearing later, I then abhorred. The short jacket I looked upon as immodest. But this dislike was nothing before the desire to go to England which was uppermost in my mind. Of provisions also I had enough and to spare for the voyage. A berth was reserved for me by my friends in the same cabin as that of the Junagadh lawyer. They also commended me to him. He was an experienced man of mature age and knew the world. I was yet a stripling of eighteen without any experience of the world.

We sailed at last from Bombay on the fourth of September, and reached Southampton towards the end of that month. On the boat I had worn a black suit, the white flannel one, which my friends had got me, having been kept especially for wearing when I landed. I had thought that white clothes would suit me better when I stepped ashore, and therefore I did so in white flannels. Those were the last days of September, and I found I was the only person wearing such clothes. I had left in charge of an agent of Grindlay and Co. all my kit, including the keys, seeing that many others also had done the same. The shame of being the only person in white clothes was too much for me. And when at the hotel I was told that I should not get my things from Grindlay's the next day, it being a Sunday, I was exasperated. Dr. Mehta, to whom I had wired from Southampton, called at about eight o'clock the same evening. He gave me a hearty greeting, but smiled at my being in flannels. As we were talking, I casually picked up his top-hat, and trying to see how smooth it was, passed my hand over it the wrong way and disturbed the fur. Dr. Mehta looked somewhat angrily at what I was doing and stopped me. But the mischief was done. The incident was a warning for the future. This was my first lesson in European etiquette.

I would continually think of my home and country. My mother's love always haunted me. At night the tears would stream down my cheeks and home memories of all sorts made sleep out of the question. It was impossible to share the misery with any one. And even if I could have done so, where was the use? I knew of nothing that would soothe me. Everything was strange—the people, their ways, and even their dwellings. I was a complete novice in the matter of English etiquette, and continually had to be on my guard. There was the additional inconvenience of the vegetarian vow. Even the dishes that I could eat were tasteless and insipid. I thus found myself in a dilemma. England I could not bear, but to return to India was not to be thought of. Now that I had come, I must finish the three years, said the inner voice.

CHAPTER IV

LIFE IN LONDON

DR. MEHTA INSPECTED MY ROOM and its appointments and shook his head in disapproval. "This place won't do," he said. "We come to England not so much for the purpose of studies as for gaining experience of English life and customs. And for this you need to live with a family. But before you do so, I think you had better serve a period of apprenticeship with a friend of mine who will look after you."

The suggestion was gratefully accepted and I removed to the friend's rooms. He was all kindness and attention, treating me as his own brother and initiating me into English ways. My food, however, became a serious question. I could not relish boiled vegetables cooked without condiments. The landlady was at a loss to know what to prepare for me. We had oatmeal porridge for breakfast, which was fairly satisfying, but I always went hungry at lunch and dinner. The friend continually reasoned with me to eat meat; but I pleaded my vow and remained silent. Both for lunch and dinner we had spinach and bread and jam. My appetite often became ravenous, but I was ashamed to ask for more than two or three slices of bread, because it did not seem correct to do so. There was no milk either for lunch or dinner. The friend once got disgusted with this state of things and said plainly: "Had you been my own brother, I would have sent you packing. What is the value of a vow made before an illiterate mother who is ignorant of conditions out here? Your vow is no vow at all. It would not be regarded as a vow in a court of law. It is pure superstition to stick to such a promise. This persistence will not help you to gain anything here. You confess to having eaten and relished meat. You took it when it was quite unnecessary, and will not take it where it is essential." But I remained adamant.

The friend would go on arguing, but I had an eternal negative to face him with. The more he argued, the more uncompromising I became. Daily I would pray for God's protection and get it. Not that I had any clear idea of God. It was faith that was at work, of which the seed had been sown by the good nurse, Rambha.

During my wanderings in the city, at last I hit on a vegetarian restaurant in Farringdon Street. The sight of it filled me with the same joy that a child feels on getting a thing after its own heart. Before I entered I noticed books for sale behind a glass window near the door and among them Salt's "Plea for Vegetarianism." This I purchased for a shilling and went straight to the dining room. There I had my first hearty meal since my arrival in England. God had come to my aid.

I read Salt's book from cover to cover and was very much impressed by it. From the date of reading this book, I may claim to have become a vegetarian by choice and now I blessed the day on which I had taken that vow before my mother. Formerly I had abstained from meat in the interests of truth and of the vow I had taken, but had wished at the same time that every Indian should be a meat-eater. Indeed, I had looked forward to the time when I should be one myself, freely and openly, and enlist others in the cause. But the choice was now made in favour of vegetarianism. To spread it henceforward became my mission.

The clothes which I had brought from Bombay now seemed to me to be unsuitable for English society, and I got new ones made at the Army and Navy Stores. Also I purchased a silk hat costing nineteen shillings. Not content with this, I wasted ten pounds on an evening dress suit made in Bond Street and got my good and noble-hearted brother to send me a double watch-chain of gold. It was not correct to wear a ready-made tie, and so I learnt the art of tying one for myself. While in India, the mirror had been a luxury, only permitted on the days when the family barber gave me a shave. Here I wasted ten minutes every day before a huge mirror watching myself arranging my tie and parting my hair in the correct fashion. My hair was by no means soft and every day it meant a regular struggle with the brush to keep it in position. Each time the hat was put on and off, the hand would automatically move towards the head to adjust the hair.

As if all this were not enough I began to direct my attention to other details that were supposed to go towards the making of an English gentleman. Thus I was informed that it was necessary for me to take lessons in dancing, French and elocution. I decided to take dancing lessons at a class and paid down three pounds as fees for a term for the first three weeks. I must have taken about six lessons. But it was beyond me to achieve anything like rhythmic motion; for I could not follow the piano and hence found it impossible to keep time. What then was I to do? The recluse in the fable kept a cat to keep away the rats, and then a cow to feed the cat with milk, and then a man to keep the cow and so on. My ambitions also grew like the family of that recluse. I thought I should learn to play the violin in order to cultivate an ear for Western music. So I invested three pounds in a violin and something more in fees, and then sought a third teacher to give me lessons in elocution and paid him a preliminary fee of a guinea. He recommended "Bell's Standard Elocutionist" as the textbook, which I purchased.

But Bell's textbook rang the bell of alarm in my ear and I awoke. After all, I said to myself, I had not to spend a lifetime in England. What then was the use of learning elocution? And how could dancing make a gentleman of me? The violin I could learn even in India. I was a student and ought to go on with my studies. If my character made a gentleman of me, so much the better. Otherwise, I should abandon such an ambition.

These and similar thoughts possessed me; and I expressed them in a letter which I addressed to the elocution teacher, requesting him to excuse me from further lessons. A similar letter was written to the dancing teacher, and I went personally to the violin teacher with a request to dispose of the violin for any price it might fetch. She was rather friendly to me; so I told her how I had discovered that I was pursuing a false ideal and she encouraged me in the determination to make a complete change. All this infatuation must have lasted about three months. The punctiliousness in dress persisted for years. But henceforward I became a student.

Let no one imagine that my experiments in dancing and the like marked a stage of self-indulgence in my life. Even then I had my wits about me and this period of infatuation was not unrelieved by a certain amount of introspection on my part. I kept account of every farthing

I spent. As I began to analyse my expenditure I could see that it was absolutely necessary to economise. I therefore decided to reduce my cost of living by half. My accounts showed numerous items spent on fares. Again my living with a family meant the payment of a regular weekly bill. It also included the courtesy of occasionally taking members of the family out to dinner, and likewise attending parties with them. All this involved heavy items for conveyances. If the friend was a lady, custom required that the man should pay all the expenses. Also dining out meant extra cost, as no deduction could be made from the regular weekly bill for meals not taken. It seemed to me that all these items could be saved, and likewise the drain on my purse, which had been caused through a false sense of propriety.

So I decided to take rooms on my own account, instead of living any longer in a family, and also to remove from place to place according to the work I had to do, thus gaining fresh experience at the same time. The rooms were so selected as to enable me to reach the place of business on foot in half an hour, and so save fares. Before this I had always taken some kind of conveyance whenever I went anywhere, and had to find extra time for walks. The new arrangement combined walks and economy, as it meant a saving of fares and gave me walks of eight and ten miles a day. It was mainly this habit of long walks that kept me practically free from illness throughout my stay in England and gave me a fairly strong body.

Soon after this, I happened to come across books on simple living and after reading them I abandoned the suite of rooms and rented one instead, invested in a stove, and began cooking my own breakfast at home. The process scarcely took me more than twenty minutes; for there was only oatmeal porridge to cook and water to boil for cocoa. I had lunch out, and for dinner had bread and cocoa at home. Thus I managed to live on a shilling and three pence a day. This was also a period of intensive study. Plain living saved me plenty of time and I passed my examination. This economy did not make my life by any means a dreary affair. On the contrary the change harmonised my inward and outward conduct. It was also more in keeping with the means of my family. My life became certainly more truthful and the joy within my soul was unbounded.

Forty years ago, there were comparatively few Indian students in England. It was a practice with them to affect the bachelor, even though they might be married. School or College students in England are all bachelors, the students' life being regarded as incompatible with marriage. We had that tradition in India in the good old days, but in modern times we have child marriages, a thing practically unknown in England. Indian youths in England therefore felt ashamed to confess that they were married. I too caught the contagion, and did not hesitate to pass myself off as a bachelor, though I was married and the father of a son. But I was none the happier for being a dissembler. Only my shyness and reticence saved me from going into deeper waters.

Once I was staying with a family at Ventnor during my vacation. It was customary in families like this for the daughter of the landlady to take out guests for a walk. My landlady's daughter took me one day to the lovely hills round Ventnor. I was no slow walker, but my companion walked even faster, dragging me after her and chattering away all the while. I responded to her chatter sometimes with a whispered "Yes" or "No," or at the most "Yes, how beautiful!" She was flying like a bird, while I was wondering when I should get back home. We thus reached the top of a hill. How to get down again was the question. In spite of her high-heeled boots this sprightly young lady of twenty-five darted down the hill like an arrow. I was shamefacedly struggling to get down. She stood at the foot smiling and cheering me and offering to come and drag me. With the greatest difficulty, and crawling at intervals, I somehow managed tc scramble to the bottom. She loudly laughed "Bravo" and shamed me all the more, as well she might.

But I could not escape unscathed altogether. For God wanted to rid me of the canker of untruth. I once went to Brighton and met there at a hotel an old widow of moderate means. This was my first year in England. The courses on the menu were all described in French, which I did not understand. I sat at the same table as the old lady. She saw that I was a stranger and puzzled, and immediately came to my aid. "You seem to be a stranger," she said, "and look perplexed. Why have you not ordered anything?" I thanked her, and explaining my difficulty, told her that I was at a loss to know which of the courses were vegetarian as I did not understand French.

"Let me help you," she said. "I shall explain the menu to you and show you what you may eat." This was the beginning of an acquaintance that ripened into friendship and was kept up all through my stay in England and long after. She gave me her London address and invited me to dine at her house every Sunday. On special occasions also she would introduce me to young ladies and draw me into conversation with them. Particularly marked out for these conversations was a young lady who stayed with her, and often we would be left entirely alone together.

I found all this very trying at first. I could not start a conversation, nor could I indulge in any jokes. But she put me in the way of doing so. I began to learn; and in course of time looked forward to every Sunday and came to like the conversation with the young friend.

The old lady went on spreading her net wider every day. She felt interested in our meetings. Possibly she had her own plans about us. I was in a terrible quandary. "How I wish I had told the good lady that I was married!" I said to myself. "She would then have not thought of an engagement between us. However, it is never too late to mend. If I declare the truth now, I may yet be saved more misery." With these thoughts in my mind, I wrote a letter to her somewhat to this effect:

"Ever since we met at Brighton you have been kind to me. You have taken care of me even as a mother of her son. You also think that I should get married and with that view you have been introducing me to young ladies. Rather than allow matters to go further, I must confess to you that I have been unworthy of your affection. I should have told you when I began my visits to you that I was married. I knew that Indian students in England dissembled the fact of their marriage and I followed suit. I now see that I should not have done so. I must also add that I was married while yet a boy and am the father of a son. I am pained that I should have kept this knowledge from you so long. But I am glad God has now given me the courage to speak out the truth. Will you forgive me? I assure you I have taken no improper liberties with the young lady you were good enough to introduce to me. I knew my limits. You, not knowing that I was married, naturally desired that we should be engaged. In order that things should not go beyond the present stage, I must tell you the truth.

"If on receipt of this, you feel that I have been unworthy of your hospitality, I assure you I shall not take it amiss. You have laid me under an everlasting debt of gratitude by your kindness and solicitude. If, after this, you do not reject me but continue to regard me as worthy of your hospitality, which I will spare no pains to deserve, I shall naturally be happy and count it a further token of your kindness."

This letter I must have drafted and redrafted many times over. But it lifted a burden that was weighing me down. Almost by return post came her reply somewhat as follows:

"I have your frank letter. We were both very glad and had a hearty laugh over it. The untruth you say you have been guilty of is pardonable. But it is well that you have acquainted us with the real state of things. My invitation still stands and we shall certainly expect you next Sunday and look forward to hearing all about your child-marriage and to the pleasure of laughing at your expense. Need I assure you that our friendship is not in the least affected by this incident?"

I thus purged myself of the canker of untruth and never thenceforward hesitated to talk of my married state wherever necessary.

Towards the end of my second year in England I came across two Theosophists, who were brothers and both unmarried. They talked to me about the Gita. They were reading Sir Edwin Arnold's translation—"The Song Celestial"—and they invited me to read the original with them. I felt ashamed, as I had neither read the Divine Song in Sanskrit nor in Gujarati. So I was constrained to tell them that I had not read the Gita, but that I would glady read it with them, and though my knowledge of Sanskrit was meagre, I hoped to be able to understand the original to the extent of telling where the translation failed to bring out the meaning. Thus I began reading the Gita with them. The following verses in the second chapter made a deep impression on me:

> If one
> Ponders on objects of the sense, there springs
> Attraction; from attraction grows desire;
> Desire flames to fierce passion; passion breeds
> Recklessness; then the memory—all betrayed—
> Lets noble purpose go, and saps the mind,
> Till purpose, mind and man are all undone.

The book struck me as one of priceless worth. This opinion of the Gita has ever since been growing on me with the result that I regard it to-day as the supreme book for the knowledge of Truth. It has afforded me invaluable help in my moments of gloom. I have read almost all the English translations of it and I regard Sir Edwin Arnold's as the best. He has been faithful to the text and yet it does not read like a translation. Though I read the Gita with these friends, I cannot pretend to have studied it then. It was only after some years that it became a book of daily reading.

They also recommended "The Light of Asia" by Sir

Edwin Arnold, whom I knew till then only as the author of "The Song Celestial," and I read it with even greater interest than I did the Bhagavad Gita. Once I had begun it I could not leave off. They also took me on one occasion to the Blavatsky Lodge and introduced me to Madame Blavatsky and Mrs. Besant. The latter had just then joined the Theosophical Society, and I was following with great interest the controversy about her conversion. The friends advised me to join the Society, but I politely declined, saying, "With my meagre knowledge of my own religion, I do not want to belong to any religious body." I recall having read, at the brothers' instance, Madame Blavatsky's *Key to Theosophy*. This book stimulated in me the desire to read books on Hinduism, and disabused me of the notion fostered by the missionaries that Hinduism was rife with superstition.

About the same time I met a good Christian from Manchester in a vegetarian boarding house. He talked to me about Christianity. I narrated to him my Rajkot recollections. He was pained to hear them. He said, "I am a vegetarian, I do not drink. Many Christians are meat-eaters and drink, no doubt; but neither meat-eating nor drinking is enjoined by Scripture. Do please read the Bible." I accepted his advice and he got me a copy. I have a faint recollection that he himself used to sell copies of the Bible, and I purchased from him an edition containing maps, concordance, and other aids. I began reading it, but I could not possibly read through the Old Testament. I read through the book of Genesis, and then the chapters that followed invariably sent me to sleep. But just for the sake of being able to say that I had read it, I plodded through the other books with much difficulty and without the least interest or understanding. I disliked reading the Book of Numbers.

But the New Testament produced a different impression, especially the Sermon on the Mount which went straight to my heart. I compared it with the Gita. The verses, "I say unto you, that ye resist not evil: but whosoever shall smite thee on thy right cheek, turn to him the other also. And if any man take away thy coat let him have thy cloak also," delighted me beyond measure and put me in mind of Shamal Bhatt's "For a bowl of water, give a goodly meal." My young mind tried to unify the teaching of the Gita, the Light of Asia, and the Sermon on the Mount. The idea of Renunciation as the highest form of religion appealed to me greatly.

This reading whetted my appetite for studying the lives of other religious teachers. A friend recommended Carlyle's "Heroes and Hero Worship." I read the chapter on the "Hero as a Prophet" and learnt of the Prophet of Islam's greatness and bravery and austere living.

Beyond this acquaintance with religion I could not go at the moment, because reading for the examination left me scarcely any time for outside subjects. But I took mental note of the fact that I should read more religious books and acquaint myself with all the principal religions.

And how could I help knowing something of atheism too? Every Indian knew Bradlaugh's name and his so-called atheism. I read some book about it, the name of which I forget. It had no effect on me; for I had already crossed the Sahara Desert of atheism. Mrs. Besant, who was then very much in the limelight, had turned to theism from atheism; and that fact also strengthened my aversion from atheism. I had read her book, "How I became a Theosophist."

It was about this time that Bradlaugh died. He was buried in the Woking Cemetery. I attended the funeral, as I believe every Indian residing in London did. A few clergymen also were present to do him the last honours. On our way back from the funeral we had to wait at the station for our train. A champion atheist from the crowd heckled one of these clergymen. "Well, sir, do you believe in the existence of God?"

"I do," said the good man in a low tone.

"You also agree that the circumference of the Earth is 28,000 miles," said the atheist, with a smile of self-assurance. "Pray tell me, then, the size of your God and where he may be."

"Well, if we but knew, He resides in the hearts of us both."

"Now, now, don't take me to be a child," said the champion with a triumphant look at us. The clergyman assumed a humble silence.

This talk still further increased my prejudice against atheism.

Just about this time Narayan Hemchandra came to England. I had heard of him as a writer. We met at the house of Miss Manning of the National Indian Association. When I went to her house, I used to sit tongue-tied, never speaking except when spoken to. She introduced me to Narayan Hemchandra. He did not know English. His dress was queer—a clumsy pair of trousers, a wrinkled, dirty, brown coat, after the Parsi fashion, no necktie or collar, a tasselled woollen cap and a long beard. He was lightly built and short of stature. His round face was scarred with smallpox, and he had a nose which was neither pointed nor blunt. Such a queer-looking and queerly-dressed person was bound to be singled out in fashionable society.

We met daily. There was a considerable amount of similarity between our thoughts and actions. Both of us were vegetarians. We would often have our lunch together. This was the time when I lived on seventeen shillings a week and cooked for myself. Sometimes I would go to his room, and sometimes he would come to mine. My cooking was in the English style. Nothing but Indian style would satisfy him. I would make soup of carrots and he would pity me for my taste. Once he somehow hunted out some dhal, (lentils) and cooked it and brought it to my place. I ate it with delight. This led on to a regular system of exchange between us. I would take my delicacies to him and he would bring his to me.

Cardinal Manning's name was then on every lip. The dock labourers' strike had come to an early termination owing to the efforts of John Burns and Cardinal Manning. I told Narayan Hemchandra of Disraeli's tribute to the Cardinal's simplicity. "Then I must see the sage," he said.

"He is a big man. How do you expect to meet him?"

"Why? I know how. I must get you to write to him in my name. Tell him I am an author and that I want to congratulate him personally on his humanitarian work, and also say that I shall have to take you as interpreter because I do not know English."

I wrote a letter to that effect. In two or three days came Cardinal Manning's card in reply giving us an appointment. So we both called on the Cardinal. I put on the usual visiting suit. Narayan Hemchandra was the same as ever, in the same coat and the same trousers. I tried to make fun of this, but he laughed me out and said:

"You civilised fellows are all cowards. Great men never look at a person's exterior. They think of his heart."

We entered the Cardinal's mansion. As soon as we were seated, a thin, tall old gentleman made his appearance and shook hands with us. Narayan Hemchandra thus gave his greetings:

"I do not want to take up your time. I had heard a lot about you and I felt I should come and thank you for the good work you have done for the strikers. It has been my custom to visit the sages of the world and that is why I have put you to this trouble." This was of course my translation of what he spoke in Gujarati.

"I am glad you have come," the Cardinal replied. "I hope your stay in London will agree with you and that you will get in touch with people here. God bless you." With these words he stood up and said good-bye.

Once Narayan Hemchandra came to my place in a shirt and dhoti,[1] such as we wear in India. The good landlady opened the door and came running to me in a fright. "A sort of a madcap," she said, "wants to see you." I went to the door and to my surprise found Narayan Hemchandra dressed in a dhoti. I was shocked. His face, however, showed nothing but his usual smile.

"But did not the children in the street jeer at you?"

"Yes, they ran after me, but I did not mind them and they were quiet."

Narayan Hemchandra went to Paris after a few

[1] A long piece of cotton cloth, worn round the waist and covering the lower part of the body.

months' stay in London. He began studying French and also translating French books. I knew enough French to revise his translation, so he gave it to me to read. It was not a translation; it was a fresh substance.

Finally he carried out his determination to visit America. It was with great difficulty that he succeeded in securing a deck ticket. While in the United States he was prosecuted for "being indecently dressed," because he once went out in a shirt and dhoti. I have a recollection that he was discharged.

It was easy enough to be called to the bar in England but it was difficult to practise. I had read Law as my subject, but I had not learnt how to practise. I had studied with interest "Legal Maxims," but did not know how to apply them in my profession.

Whilst I was studying law I was torn with doubts and confided my difficulties to some of my friends. One of them suggested that I should seek Dadabhai Naoroji's advice. Though I had brought an introduction to him from India, it seemed to me that I had no right to trouble such a great man for an interview. Whenever an address by him was announced, I would attend it, listen to him from a corner of the hall, and go away after having feasted my eyes and ears. In order to come in close touch with the students he had founded an association. I used to attend its meetings, and rejoiced at Dadabhai's solicitude for the students and their respect for him. In course of time at last I mustered up courage to present to him the letter of introduction. "You can come," he said, "and have my advice whenever you like." But I never availed myself of his offer.

I forget now whether it was the same friend who

recommended me to meet Mr. Frederick Pincutt. He was a Conservative, but his affection for Indian students was pure and unselfish. Many students sought his advice and I also applied to him for an appointment, which he granted. I can never forget that interview. He greeted me as a friend and laughed away my pessimism. "Rest assured," said he, "that it takes no exceptional skill to be an ordinary lawyer. Common honesty and industry are quite enough to enable him to make a living. All cases are not complicated. Well, let me know the extent of your general reading."

When I acquainted him with my little stock I could see he was rather disappointed. But it was only for a moment. Soon his face beamed with a pleasing smile and he said: "I understand your trouble. Your general reading is meagre. You have no knowledge of the world. You have not even read the history of your own country. A barrister ought to study human nature. And every Indian ought to know Indian history. This has no connexion with the practice of law, but you ought to have that knowledge. I see that you have not even read Kay and Malleson's 'History of the Mutiny.' Get hold of that at once and also read one or two books on human nature."

I was extremely grateful to this venerable friend for what he did for me. His advice itself did me very little direct service; but his affection stood me in good stead. His smiling open face stayed in my memory and I trusted his saying that great ability was not essential to the making of a successful lawyer; honesty and industry were enough. Since I had a fair share of these I felt somewhat reassured. I passed my Law examinations and my stay in England drew to an end.

CHAPTER V

RETURN TO INDIA

THE TIME HAD NOW ARRIVED for me to leave England and I booked my passage home on the *S.S. Assam* in June. The monsoon had already started when we reached the Arabian Sea and there was rough weather all the way to Bombay after we had passed Aden. Almost every passenger on the steamer was sea-sick but I remained perfectly well and greatly enjoyed staying on deck, watching the stormy surge and the splash of the waves. Since the greater number of the passengers were ill, there would be only two or three of us present for breakfast, eating our oatmeal porridge from plates carefully held on our laps lest the porridge itself should find a place there.

The outer storm was to me a symbol of the storm within. But even as the former left me unperturbed, I think I can say the same thing about the latter. There was stormy trouble with my own caste confronting me. There was also my utter helplessness in starting on my profession as a barrister. And again, since I was at heart a reformer, I was taxing myself as to how best certain reforms might be begun. But there was even more in store for me than I knew.

My elder brother had come down from Kathiawar to meet me at the dock. He had already made the acquaintance of Dr. Mehta and his brother; and as the latter insisted on putting us up at his house we went to stay there. Thus the acquaintance already begun in England continued in India and ripened into a permanent friendship between the two families. All through the voyage home I had been pining to see my mother. I did not know that she was no more in the flesh to receive me back into her bosom. The sad news was now given me, and I underwent the usual ablution. My brother had kept me all the while ignorant of her death, which took place when I was still in England. He wanted to spare me the blow in a foreign land. The news, however, was none the less a severe shock to me; but I must not dwell upon it. My grief was even greater than over my father's death. Most of my cherished hopes were shattered. But I remember that I did not give myself up to any wild expression of grief. I could even check the tears, and took to life just as though nothing had happened.

Dr. Mehta introduced me to several friends, one of them being his brother whose name was Revashankar Jagjivan. With him there grew up a lifelong friendship. But the introduction that I need particularly take note of at this time was that to the poet Raychand, the son-in-law of an elder brother of Dr. Mehta, and partner of the firm of jewellers conducted in the name of Revashankar Jagjivan. He was not above twenty-five years old; but my first meeting with him convinced me that he was a man of remarkable character and learning. He was also known as a *shatavadhani* (one having the faculty of remembering or attending to a hundred things simultaneously) and Dr. Mehta recommended me to see some of his memory feats. I exhausted my vocabulary of all the European tongues I knew, and asked the poet to repeat the words. He did so in the precise order in which I had given them. I envied his gift without however coming under its spell. The things, however, that did cast their spell over me were his wide knowledge of the scriptures, his spotless character, and his burning passion for self-realisation. I saw that this last was the only object for which he lived. The following lines of Muktanand were always on his lips and engraved on the tablets of his heart:

> I shall think myself blessed only when I see Him in every
> one of my daily acts;
> Verily He is the thread,
> which supports Muktanand's life.

Raychandbhai's[1] commercial transactions covered hundreds of thousands of rupees. He was a connoisseur of pearls and diamonds. No knotty business problem was too difficult for him. But all these things were not the centre round which his life revolved. The centre was the passion to see God face to face. Amongst other things on his business table there were invariably to be found some religious book and also his diary. The moment he finished his business he opened the religious book or the diary. Much of his published writing is a reproduction from this diary. The man who immediately on finishing important business transactions could begin to write about the hidden things of the spirit was evidently not a business man at all, but a real seeker after Truth. And I watched him thus absorbed in these spiritual pursuits in the midst of business, not once or twice, but very often. I never saw him lose his balance of mind on any occasion. There was no worldly tie that bound him to me, and yet I enjoyed the closest fellowship with him. I was but a briefless barrister; nevertheless whenever I saw him he would engage me in conversations of a seriously religious nature. Though I

[1] It is the custom in Gujarat and other parts of India to add the word "bhai" (meaning "brother") to the proper name of a friend.

was then groping and could not be said to have any serious concern for religious discussion, I always found his talk of absorbing interest. Since then, I have visited many religious teachers and have tried to meet the heads of various religious faiths; but no one else has ever made on me the same impression that Raychandbhai did. His words went straight home to me. His intellect compelled as high a regard from me as his moral earnestness; and deep down in me was the conviction that he would never willingly lead me astray but would always confide to me his innermost thoughts. Therefore, in moments of spiritual crisis, he was constantly my refuge.

Nevertheless, in spite of my deep regard for him, I could not enthrone him in my heart as my Guru.[2] That throne has remained vacant and my search still continues. I believe in the Hindu theory of the Guru and his importance in spiritual realisation. I think there is a great deal of truth in the doctrine that true knowledge is impossible without a Guru. An imperfect teacher in mundane matters may be tolerable, but not so an imperfect one in spiritual matters. Only a perfect Master of spiritual wisdom deserves to be enthroned as Guru. There must, therefore, be always ceaseless striving after perfection. For one gets the Guru that one deserves. Infinite striving after perfection is our human right. It carries with it its own reward. The rest is in the hands of God. Thus, though I could not place Raychandbhai on the throne of my heart as my Guru, he was on many occasions my guide and helper. Three moderns have left a deep impress on my life and captivated me,—Raychandbhai by his living con-

[2] Spiritual Teacher.

tact; Tolstoy by his book, "The Kingdom of God Is within You"; and Ruskin by his "Unto This Last."

My elder brother had built high hopes on me. The desire for wealth and name and fame was strong in him. He had a large heart and was generous to a fault. This, combined with his simple nature, had attracted to him many friends, and through them he expected to get me many briefs. He had also assumed that I should soon have a large practice, and in that expectation had allowed the household expenses to become excessive. He had also left no stone unturned in preparing the field for my work at the bar as a lawyer.

The storm in my caste over my foreign voyage was still brewing when I returned. It had divided the caste into two camps, one of which immediately readmitted me to the caste, while the other was bent upon keeping me out. To please the former my brother took me to Nasik before going to Rajkot, gave me a bath in the sacred river, and on reaching Rajkot provided a caste-dinner as an expiation. I did not like all this. But my brother's love for me was boundless and my devotion to him was in proportion to it; therefore I mechanically acted as he wished, taking his will to be law. The trouble about re-admission to the caste was thus practically over.

I never tried to seek admission to the section that had refused it to me. Nor did I feel even mental resentment against any of the headmen of that section. Some of these regarded me with dislike, but I scrupulously avoided hurting their feelings. I fully respected the caste regulations about excommunication. According to these, none of my relations, including my father-in-law and mother-in-law, and even my sister and brother-in-law, could entertain me; and I would not so much as drink water at their house. They were prepared secretly to evade the prohibition, but it went against the grain with me to do a thing in secret that I would not do in public.

The result of my scrupulous conduct was that I never had occasion to be troubled by the caste; nay, I have experienced nothing but affection and generosity from the general body of the section that still regards me as excommunicated. They have even helped me in my work, without ever expecting me to do anything for the caste. It is my conviction that all these good things are due to my non-resistance. Had I agitated for being admitted to the caste; had I attempted to divide it into more camps; had I provoked the caste leaders, they would surely have retaliated. Instead of steering clear of the storm, I should on my arrival from England have found myself in a whirlpool of agitation and perhaps have been obliged to become party to dissimulation.

My relations with my wife were still not as I desired. Even my stay in England had not cured me of my jealousy. I continued my suspiciousness in respect of every little thing, and hence all my cherished desires remained unfulfilled. I had decided that my wife should learn reading and writing and that I should help her in her studies, but my lust came in the way and she had to suffer for my own shortcoming. Once I went the length of sending her away to her father's house, and consented to receive her back only after I had made her thoroughly miserable. Later on I saw that all this was pure folly on my part.

I had planned reform in the education of children. My brother had children, and my own child which I had left at home when I went to England was now a boy of nearly four. It was my desire to teach these little ones physical exercise and make them hardy, and also to give them the benefit of my personal guidance. In this I had my brother's support and I succeeded in my efforts more or less. The company of children was always a joy to me, and the habit of playing and joking with them has stayed with me till to-day. I have ever since thought that I should make a good teacher of children.

The necessity for food "reform" was obvious. Tea and coffee had already found their place in the house. My brother had thought fit to keep some sort of English atmosphere ready for me on my return; and to that end, crockery and such other things, which used to be kept in the house only for special occasions, were now in general use. My "reforms" put the finishing touch to all these innovations. I introduced oatmeal porridge, and cocoa was to replace tea and coffee. But in truth it became an addition to tea and coffee. Boots and shoes were already there, and I completed the Europeanisation by adding the European dress.

Expenses thus went up. New things were added every day. We had succeeded in tying up a white elephant at our door. But how was the wherewithal to be found? To start legal practice in Rajkot would have meant sure ridicule. I had hardly the knowledge of a qualified vakil,[3] and yet I expected to be paid ten times his fee! No client would be fool enough to engage me. And even if such a one was to be found, should I add arrogance and fraud to my ignorance, and increase the burden of debt I owed to the world?

[3] A vakil is the Indian name for a barrister who has passed his law examinations in India.

Friends advised me to go to Bombay for some time in order to gain experience of the High Court, to study Indian law and get what briefs I could. I took up the suggestion and went. In Bombay I started a household with a cook as incompetent as myself. He was a Brahman, called Ravishankar. I did not treat him as a servant but as a member of the household. He would pour water over himself but never wash. His dhoti was dirty, as also his sacred thread, and he was completely innocent of any knowledge of the Hindu scriptures. But how was I to get a better cook?

"Well, Ravishankar," I would ask him, "you may not know cooking, but don't you even know your *sandhya* (daily worship)?"

"Sandhya, sir! The plough is our sandhya and the spade our daily ritual. That is the type of Brahman I am. I must live on your mercy. Otherwise agriculture will be my occupation."

So I had to be Ravishankar's teacher. Time was hanging idly on my hands, so I began to do half the cooking myself and introduced English experiments in vegetarian cookery. I invested in a stove, and with Ravishankar began to run the kitchen. Personally I had no scruples about inter-dining, and Ravishanker also came to have none. So we went on merrily together. There was only one obstacle. Ravishankar had sworn to remain dirty and he would keep the food unclean.

But it was impossible for me to get along in Bombay for more than four or five months because there was no income to meet my expenditure. Therefore, after becoming disappointed about getting practice in Bombay, I left that city and went back to Rajkot where I set up my own office. Here I got along moderately well. Drafting applications and memorials brought me in, on an average, three hundred rupees a month. For this work I had to thank influence rather than my own ability, for my brother's partner had a settled practice. All applications which were of an important character, he sent to big barristers. To my lot fell the applications to be drafted on behalf of his poor clients.

I must confess that at this time I had to compromise with the principle I had already decided upon of giving no commission. I was told that conditions were different; that whilst in Bombay commissions had to be paid to touts, here they had to be paid to vakils who briefed you; that here, as in Bombay, all barristers, without exception, paid a percentage of their fees as commission. The argument of my brother was in my own case unanswerable. "You see," he said, "that I am in partnership with another vakil. I shall always be inclined to make over to you all our cases with which you can possibly deal, and if you refuse to pay a commission to my partner, you are sure to embarrass me. As you and I have a joint establishment, your fee comes to our common purse, and I automatically get a share. But what about my partner? Supposing he gave the same case to some other barrister, he would certainly get his commission from him." I was taken in by this plea, and felt that, if I was to practice as a barrister, I could not press my principle regarding commissions in such cases. That is how I argued with myself, or to put it bluntly, how I deceived myself. Let me add, however, that I do not remember ever to have given a commission in respect of any other case.

Though I thus began to make both ends meet, I got the first shock of my life about this time. I had heard before what a British officer was like, but up to now had never been face to face with one.

My brother had been secretary and adviser to the late Rana of Porbandar, and hanging over his head at this time was the charge of having given wrong advice when in that office. The matter had gone to the Political Agent who was prejudiced against my brother. Now I had known this officer when in England and he might be said to have been fairly friendly to me. My brother thought that I should avail myself of the friendship by putting in a good word on his behalf. Thus, he said, I might try to disabuse him of his prejudice. I did not at all like this idea, because I did not think it right to try to take advantage of a trifling acquaintance in England. If my brother was really at fault, what use was my recommendation? If he was innocent, he should submit a petition in the proper course and face the result. But my brother did not relish this advice. "You do not know Kathiawar," he said, "and you have yet to know the world. Only influence counts here. It is not proper for you, a brother, to shirk from fulfilling your duty, when you can clearly put in a good word about me to an officer whom you know."

It was impossible for me to refuse him; so I went to the officer much against my will. I knew I had no right to approach him and was fully conscious that I was compromising my self-respect. Nevertheless, I sought an appointment and got it. I reminded him of the old acquaintance, but saw immediately that Kathiawar was different from England; that an officer on leave was not the same as an officer on duty. The Political Agent owned the

acquaintance, but the reminder seemed to stiffen him. "Surely you have not come here to abuse that acquaintance, have you?" appeared to be the meaning of that stiffness. Nevertheless, I opened my case. He became impatient. "Your brother is an intriguer," he said. "I want to hear nothing more from you. I have no time. If your brother has anything to say, let him apply through the proper channel." The sharp answer was perhaps deserved. But selfishness is blind and I went on with my story. The Sahib got up and said: "You must go now."

"But please hear me out," said I. That made him all the more angry. He called his servant and ordered him to show me the door. I was still hesitating when the servant came in, placed his hands on my shoulders and put me out of the room.

At once I wrote out and sent over a note to this effect: "You have insulted me. You have assaulted me through your servant. If you make no amends, I shall have to proceed against you."

Quick came the answer through his orderly:

"You were rude to me. I asked you to go and you would not. I had no option but to order my servant to show you the door. Even after he asked you to leave the office, you did not do so. He therefore had to use just enough force to put you out. You are at liberty to proceed as you wish."

With this answer in my pocket, I came home crestfallen, and told my brother all that had happened. He was grieved, but was at a loss how to console me. He spoke to his vakil friends. For I did not know how to proceed against the Sahib. Sir Phirozeshah Mehta happened to be

in Rajkot at this time, having come down from Bombay for some case. But how could a junior barrister like me dare to see him? So I sent him the papers of my case, through the vakil who had engaged him, and begged for his advice. "Tell Gandhi," he said, "such things are common experience. He is still fresh from England and hot-blooded. He does not know British officers. If he would earn something and have an easy time here, let him tear up the note and pocket the insult. He will gain nothing by proceeding against the Sahib, and on the contrary will very likely ruin himself. Tell him he has yet to know life."

The advice was as bitter as poison to me, but I had to swallow it. I pocketed the insult, but also profited by it. "Never again," said I to myself, "shall I place myself in such a false position; never again shall I try to exploit friendship in this way." Since that time, I have never been guilty of a breach of the determination which I then made. This shock changed the whole course of my life.

No doubt I was at fault in having gone to the Political Agent. But his impatience and overbearing anger were out of all proportion to my mistake. It did not warrant such an expulsion. Indeed, I can scarcely have taken up more than five minutes of his time. But he simply could not endure my talking. He could have politely asked me to go; but power had intoxicated him to an inordinate extent. Later I came to know that patience was not one of his virtues.

If I were to continue to practice in that place, most of my work would naturally be in his court. Yet it was beyond me to conciliate him and I had no desire to curry favour with him. Indeed, having once threatened to pro-

ceed against him, I did not like to remain silent. Meanwhile I began to learn something of the petty politics of the country. Kathiawar, being a conglomeration of small States, naturally had its rich crop of political adventurers. Petty intrigues between states and conspiracies of officers for power were the order of the day. The Princes themselves were always at the mercy of others and ready to lend their ears to sycophants. Such an atmosphere appeared to me to be poisonous, and how to remain unscathed was a perpetual problem. In the end, I was thoroughly depressed and my brother clearly saw it. We both felt, that if I could secure some post elsewhere I should be free from all this atmosphere of intrigue. But without underhand methods a ministership or judgeship was out of the question. And this quarrel with the Political Agent stood in the way of my practice.

Porbandar was then under administration, and I had some work there in the shape of securing more powers for the Prince. Also I had to see the Administrator with regard to the heavy land rent exacted from the tenants; but I found this administrative officer, though an Indian, to be even worse than the Sahib in arrogance. So even in this mission I was comparatively disappointed. It seemed to me that justice was not done to my clients, and yet I had not the means to secure it. At the most, I could have appealed to the Political Agent, or to the Governor, who would have dismissed the appeal saying, "We decline to interfere." If there had been any rule or regulation governing such decisions, it would have been something; but here the Sahib's will was law. In the end, I became exasperated and wished to get away from the whole intriguing surroundings.

It was at this juncture that a business firm from Porbandar wrote to my brother making the following offer: "We have business in South Africa. Ours is a large firm, and we have an important case there in the Court, our claim being forty thousand pounds. The suit has been going on for a long time. We have engaged the services of the best vakils and barristers. If you sent your brother there, he would be useful to us and also to himself. He would be able to instruct our counsel better than ourselves. And he would have the advantage of seeing a new part of the world and of making new acquaintances."

My brother discussed the new proposition with me. I could not clearly make out whether I had simply to instruct the counsel or to appear in Court. But I was tempted to accept the offer. My brother introduced me to the late Sheth Abdul Karim Jhaveri, a partner of Dada Abdulla and Co., the business firm in question. "It won't be a difficult job," the Sheth assured me. "We have Europeans as our friends, whose acquaintance you will make. You can be useful to us in our shop. Much of our correspondence is in English and you can help us with that too. You will, or course, be our guest and hence will have no expense whatever."

"How long do you require my services?" I asked. "And what will be the payment?"

"Not more than a year. We will pay you a first class return fare and a sum of one hundred and five pounds, all found."

This hardly implied going out there as a barrister. Indeed it was rather like going out as a servant of the firm. But I wanted somehow to leave India. There was the tempting opportunity of seeing a new country and of having new experience. Also I could send one hundred and five pounds to my brother and thus help in the expenses of the household. So I closed with the offer without any bargaining and got ready to go to South Africa forthwith.

CHAPTER VI

ARRIVAL IN NATAL

ABDULLA SHETH WAS WAITING at Durban to receive me. The ship arrived at the quay. I noticed the people coming on board to meet their friends, and I observed that the Indians were not held in respect. I could not fail to notice a sort of snobbishness about the manner in which those who knew Abdulla Sheth behaved towards him, and it stung me. Abdulla Sheth had got used to it. Those who looked at me did so with a certain amount of curiosity. My dress marked me out from other Indians. I had a frock-coat and a small turban.

Abdulla Sheth was practically unlettered, but he had a rich fund of experience. He had an acute intellect and was conscious of it. By practice he had picked up just sufficient English for conversational purposes, but that served him for carrying on all his business, whether it was dealing with bank managers and European merchants or explaining his case to his counsel. The Indians held him in very high esteem. His firm was then the biggest, or at any rate one of the biggest, of the Indian firms. With all these advantages he had one disadvantage,—he was by nature suspicious.

He was proud of Islam and loved to discourse on Islamic philosophy. Though he did not know Arabic, his acquaintance with the Holy Koran and Islamic literature in general was fairly good. Illustrations he had in plenty, always ready at hand. Contact with him gave me a fair amount of practical knowledge of Islam. When we came closer to each other, we had long discussions on religious topics.

On the second or third day of my arrival he took me to see the Durban court. There he introduced me to several people and seated me next to his attorney. The magistrate kept staring at me and finally asked me to take off my turban, which I refused to do and left the court. So here too there was fighting in store for me. Abdulla Sheth explained to me why some Indians were required to take off their turbans. Those wearing the Musalman costume might, he said, keep their turbans on; but the other Indians on entering a court had to take theirs off as a rule.

I must enter into some details in order to make this nice distinction intelligible. In the course of these two or three days, I could see that the Indians were divided into different groups. One was that of Musalman merchants, who would call themselves "Arabs." Another was that of Hindu and yet another of Parsi clerks. The Hindu clerks were neither here nor there, unless they cast in their lot with the "Arabs." The Parsi clerks would call themselves Persians. These three classes had some social relations with one another. But by far the largest class was that composed of Tamil, Telugu and North Indian indentured and freed labourers. The indentured labourers were those who had gone to Natal on an agreement to serve for five years. The other three classes had none but business relations with this class. Englishmen called them "coolies," and as the majority of Indians belonged to the labouring class, all Indians were called "coolie" or "Sammy." [1]

[1] Sammy is a corruption of Swami, which is an ending of many Tamil proper names.

For this reason I became known as a "coolie barrister." The merchants were known as "coolie merchants." The original meaning of the word "coolie" was thus forgotten, and it became a common appellation for all Indians. The Musalman merchant would resent this and say: "I am not a coolie, I am an Arab," or "I am a merchant," and the Englishman, if courteous, would apologise to him.

The question of wearing the turban had a great importance in such a state of things. Taking off one's Indian turban would be like pocketing an insult. So I thought I had better bid good-bye to the Indian turban and begin wearing an English hat, which would save me from the insult and the unpleasant controversy. But Abdulla Sheth disapproved of the idea. He said, "If you do anything of the kind it will have a very bad effect. You will compromise those insisting on wearing Indian turbans. And an Indian turban sits well on your head. If you wear an English hat you will pass for a waiter."

There was practical wisdom, patriotism, and a little bit of narrowness in this advice. The wisdom was apparent, and he would not have insisted on the Indian turban except out of patriotism; the slighting reference to the waiter betrayed a kind of narrowness. Amongst the indentured Indians there were Hindus, Musalmans, and Christians. The last were the children of indentured Indians who had become converts to Christianity. Even in 1893 their number was large. They wore the English costume, and the majority of them earned their living by service as waiters in hotels. Abdulla Sheth's criticism of the English hat was with reference to this class. It was considered demeaning to serve as a waiter in a hotel.

On the whole I liked Abdulla Sheth's advice. I wrote

to the press about the incident and defended the wearing of my turban in the court. The question was much discussed in the papers which described me as an "unwelcome visitor." Thus the incident gave me an unexpected advertisement in South Africa within a few days of my arrival. Some supported me, while others severely criticised my temerity.

On the seventh or eighth day after my arrival, I left Durban. A first class seat was booked for me. It was usual to pay five shillings extra if one needed bedding. Abdulla Sheth insisted that I should book one bedding; but out of obstinacy and pride, and with view to economy, I declined. Abdulla Sheth warned me. "Look, now," said he, "this is a different country from India. Thank God, we have enough and to spare. Please do not stint yourself in anything that you may need."

The train reached Maritzburg, the capital of Natal, at about 9 p.m. Bedding used to be provided at this station. A railway servant came and asked me if I wanted one. I declined and he went away. But a passenger came next and looked me up and down. He saw that I was a "coloured" man. This disturbed him. Out he went and came in again with one or two officials. They all kept quiet, when another official came to me and said, "Come along, you must go to the van compartment."

"But I have a first class ticket," I said.

"That doesn't matter," rejoined the other. "I tell you, you must go to the van compartment."

"I was permitted to travel in this compartment at Durban, and I insist on going on in it."

"No, you won't," said the official. "You must leave this

compartment, or else I shall have to call a police constable to push you out."

"Yes, you may," I replied. "I refuse to get out voluntarily."

The constable came. He took me by the hand and pushed me out. My luggage was also taken out. I refused to go to the other compartment and the train steamed away. I went and sat in the waiting room, keeping my handbag with me and leaving the other luggage where it was. The railway authorities had taken charge of it.

It was winter, and winter in the higher regions of South Africa can be severely cold. Maritzburg being at a high altitude, the cold was extremely bitter. My overcoat was in my luggage, but I did not dare to ask for it lest I might be insulted again, so I sat and shivered. There was no light in the room. A passenger came in at about midnight and possibly wanted to talk to me. But I was in no mood to talk.

I began to think of my duty. Should I fight for my rights or go back to India; or should I go on to Pretoria without minding the insults, and return to India after finishing the case? It would be cowardice to run back to India without fulfilling my obligation. The hardship, to which I was subjected, was only superficial. It was only a symptom of the deep disease of colour prejudice. I should try, if possible, to root out the disease and suffer hardship in the process. Redress for wrongs I should seek only to the extent that would be necessarv for the removal of the colour prejudice.

So I decided to take the next available train to Pretoria and on the following morning sent a long telegram to the general manager of the railway, and also telegraphed to

Abdulla Sheth, who immediately met the general manager. The manager justified the conduct of the railway authorities, but informed him that he had already instructed the station master to see that I reached my destination safely. Abdulla Sheth wired to the Indian merchants in Maritzburg and to friends in other places to meet me and look after me. The merchants came to see me at the station and tried to comfort me by narrating their own hardships and explaining that what had happened to me was nothing unusual. They also said, that Indians travelling first or second class had to expect trouble from railway officials and white passengers. The day was thus spent in listening to these tales of woe. The evening train arrived. There was a reserved berth for me. I now purchased at Maritzburg the bedding ticket I had refused to book at Durban.

The train reached Charlestown in the morning. There was no railway in those days between Charlestown and Johannesburg, but only a stage-coach, which halted at Standerton for the night. I possessed a ticket for the coach, which was not cancelled by the break of the journey at Maritzburg for a day; besides Abdulla Sheth had sent a wire to the coach agent at Charlestown.

But the agent only needed a pretext for putting me off, and so, when he discovered me to be a stranger, he said, "Your ticket is cancelled." I gave him the proper reply. The reason at the back of his mind was not want of room, but quite another. Passengers had to be accommodated inside the coach, but as I was regarded as a "coolie" and looked a stranger, it would not be proper, thought the conductor, to seat me with the white passengers. There were seats on either side of the coachbox. The conductor sat on one of these as a rule. To-day he sat inside and gave me his seat. I knew it was sheer injustice and an insult, but I thought it better to pocket it. I could not have forced myself inside; and if I had raised a protest, the coach would have gone off without me. This would have meant the loss of another day, and Heaven only knows what would have happened the next day! So, much as I fretted within myself, I prudently sat next to the coachman.

At about three o'clock the coach reached Pardekop. The conductor now desired to sit where I was seated, as he wanted to smoke and possibly to have some fresh air. So he took a piece of dirty sack-cloth from the driver, spread it on the foot-board and addressing me said, "Sammy, you sit on this; I want to sit near the driver." The insult was more than I could bear. In fear and trembling, I said to him, "It was you who seated me here, though I should have been accommodated inside. That insult I put up with. Now that you want to sit outside and smoke, you would have me sit at your feet. I refuse to do so, but I am prepared to sit inside."

As I was struggling through these sentences, the man came for me and began heavily to box my ears. He seized me by the arm and tried to drag me down. I clung to the brass rails of the coachbox and was determined to keep my hold even at the risk of breaking my wristbones. The passengers were witnessing the scene,—the man swearing at me, dragging and belabouring me, and I remaining still. He was strong and I was weak. Some of the passengers were moved to pity and exclaimed: "Man, let him alone. He is right. If he can't stay there, let him come and sit with us." "No fear," cried the conductor. But by this time he seemed somewhat crestfallen and stopped beating me. He let go my arm, swore at me a little more, and asking the Hottentot servant who was seated on the other side of the coachbox to sit on the footboard, took the seat so vacated.

The passengers took their seats; and, the whistle given, the coach rattled away. My heart was beating fast within my breast, and I was wondering whether I should ever reach my destination alive. The man cast an angry look at me now and then, and pointing his finger at me growled: "Take care, let me once get to Standerton and I'll show you." I sat speechless and prayed to God to help me.

After dark we reached Standerton and I heaved a sigh of relief on seeing some Indian faces. As soon as I got down, these friends said: "We are here to receive you and take you to Isa Sheth's shop. We have had a telegram from Dada Abdulla." I was very glad and we went to Sheth Isa Haji Sumar's shop. The Sheth and his clerks gathered round me. I told them all that I had gone through. They were very sorry to hear it, and comforted me by relating to me their own bitter experiences.

I wanted to inform the agent of the coach company of the whole affair. So I wrote him a letter, narrating everything that had happened, and drawing his attention to the threat his man had held out. I also asked for an assurance, that he would accommodate me along with the other passengers inside the coach, when we started the next morning. To which the agent replied to this effect: "From Standerton we have a bigger coach with different men in charge. The conductor complained of will not be there to-morrow, and you will have a seat with the other passengers." This somewhat relieved me. I had, of course, no intention of proceeding against the man who had assaulted me, and so the chapter of the assault closed there.

In the morning Isa Sheth's man took me to the coach. I got a good seat and reached Johannesburg quite safely that night.

Standerton is a small village and Johannesburg a big city. Abdulla Sheth had wired to Johannesburg also, and given me the name and address of Muhammad Kasam Kamruddin's firm there. Their servant had come to receive me at the stage, but neither did I see him nor did he recognise me. So I decided to go to a hotel. Taking a cab I asked to be driven to the Grand National Hotel. I saw the manager and asked for a room. He eyed me for a moment, and said politely: "I am sorry, we are full up." So I asked the cabman to drive to Muhammad Kasam Kamruddin's shop. Here I found Abdul Gani Sheth expecting me and he gave me a cordial greeting. He had a hearty laugh over the story of my experience at the hotel. "How ever did you expect," he said, "to be admitted to a hotel?"

"Why not?" I asked.

"You will come to know after you have stayed here a few days. We can only live in a land like this on sufferance. For the sake of making money we have not to mind pocketing insults. So here we are!" With this, he narrated to me the story of the hardships of Indians in South Africa.

Later on, he said to me: "This country is not for men like you. Look, now, you have to go to Pretoria to-morrow. You will have to travel third class. Conditions in the Transvaal are worse than in Natal. First and second class tickets are never issued to Indians."

"You cannot have made any persistent effort in this direction."

"We have sent representations; but I confess, our own

men do not want as a rule to travel first or second class."

I sent for the railway regulations and read them through. There was a loophole. The language of the old Transvaal enactments was not very exact or precise; that of the railway regulations was even less so.

I said to the Sheth: "I wish to go first class, and if I cannot, I prefer to take a cab to Pretoria, a matter of only thirty-seven miles."

Sheth Abdul Gani drew my attention to the extra time and money this would mean, but agreed to my proposal to travel first class, and accordingly we sent a note to the station master. I mentioned in my note, that I was a barrister and that I always travelled first. I also stated in the letter, that I needed to reach Pretoria as early as possible; and as there was no time to await his reply, I would receive it in person at the station. There was of course a purpose behind asking for the reply in person. I had thought, that if the station master gave a written reply, he would certainly say "No," especially because he would have his own notion of a "coolie" barrister. I would therefore appear before him in faultless English dress, talk to him and possibly persuade him to issue a first class ticket. So I went to the station in a frock-coat and necktie, placed a sovereign for my fare on the counter and asked for a first class ticket.

"You sent me that note?" he asked.

"That is so. I shall be much obliged if you will give me a ticket. I must reach Pretoria to-day."

He smiled and said kindly. "I am not a Transvaaler but a Hollander and so I appreciate your feelings, and you have my sympathy. I will give you a ticket, but on one condition, that if the guard should ask you to shift to the third class, you will not involve me in the affair; by which I mean that you will not proceed against the railway company. I wish you a safe journey. I can see you are a gentleman."

With these words he booked the ticket. I thanked him and gave him the necessary assurance.

Sheth Abdul Gani had come to see me off at the station. The incident gave him an agreeable surprise; but he warned me, saying: "I shall be thankful if you reach Pretoria all right. But I am afraid the guard will not leave you at rest in the first class; and even if he does, the passengers will not."

So I took my seat in a first class compartment and the train started. At Germiston, the guard came to examine the tickets. He was angry to find me there and signalled to me with his finger to go to the third class. I showed him my first class ticket. "That doesn't matter," he said. "Go up into the third class."

There was only one English passenger in the compartment. He took the guard to task. "What do you mean," he said, "troubling the gentleman? Don't you see he has a first class ticket? I do not mind in the least his travelling with me." Then, addressing me, he said, "Make yourself comfortable where you are."

The guard muttered: "If you want to travel with a 'coolie,' what do I care?" and went way.

At about eight o'clock in the evening the train reached Pretoria.

I had expected some one on behalf of Dada Abdulla's attorney to meet me at the station. Since I had particularly promised not to put up at an Indian house, I knew that no Indian would be there. But the attorney had sent no one.

I understood later that as I had arrived on a Sunday he could not have sent any one without inconvenience. I was perplexed and wondered where to go, as I feared that no hotel would accept me.

Pretoria Station, in 1893, was quite different from what it is now. The lights were burning dimly. The travellers were few. I let all the other passengers go, and thought that, as soon as the ticket collector was fairly free, I would hand him my ticket and ask him if he could direct me to some small hotel, or any other such place where I might go; otherwise I would spend the night at the station. I must confess I shrank from asking him even this; for I was afraid of being insulted.

The station became clear of all passengers. I gave my ticket to the ticket collector and began my enquiries. He replied to me courteously; I saw, however, that he could not be of any help. But an American negro, who was standing near by, broke into the conversation.

"I see," said he, "that you are an utter stranger here, without any friends. If you will come with me, I will take you to a small hotel where the proprietor is an American, who is very well known to me. I think he will accept you."

I had my own doubts about the offer, but I thanked him and accepted his suggestion. He took me to Johnston's Family Hotel. He drew the manager aside to speak to him, and the latter agreed to accommodate me for the night, on condition that I should have my dinner served in my room.

"I assure you," said he, "that I have no colour prejudice. But I have only European custom; and if I allowed you to eat in the dining room, my guests might be offended and even go away."

"Thank you," said I, "even for accommodating me for the night. I am now more or less acquainted with the conditions here, and I understand your difficulty. I do not mind your serving the dinner in my room, and I hope to be able to make some other arrangements to-morrow."

I was shown into a room, where I now sat, waiting for the dinner and musing, as I was quite alone. There were not many guests in the hotel, and I had expected the waiter to come very shortly with the dinner. Instead Mr. Johnston himself appeared. "I was ashamed," he said, "at having to ask you to have your dinner here. So I spoke to the other guests about you, and asked them if they would mind your having your dinner in the dining room. They said they had no objection and that they did not mind your staying here as long as you like. Please, therefore, come down to the dining room and stay here as long as you wish."

I thanked him again, went to the dining room and had a hearty dinner.

CHAPTER VII

AT PRETORIA

NEXT MORNING I CALLED on Mr. A. W. Baker, the attorney. Abdulla Sheth had given me some description of him; so his cordial reception did not surprise me. He received me very warmly and made kind enquiries. "We have no work," he said, "for you here as barrister; for we have engaged the best counsel. The case is a complicated one; so I shall take your assistance only to the extent of getting necessary information. You will be able to make my own intercourse with our client easy for me, because I shall now ask for all the information I want from him through you. That is certainly an advantage. There is a fearful amount of colour prejudice here, and therefore it is not easy to find lodgings for such as you. But I know a poor woman who is the wife of a retail trader. I think she will take vou in and thus add to her income."

So he took me to her house and spoke with her privately about me, and she agreed to accept me as a boarder on thirty-five shillings a week.

Mr. Baker was a staunch Christian lay preacher. He is still alive and now engaged in purely missionary work, having given up the legal profession. He is quite well-to-do. He has continued to keep up correspondence with me and in his letters always dwells on the same theme. He upholds the excellence of Christianity and contends that it is impossible to find eternal peace unless one accepts Jesus as the only Son of God and the Saviour of mankind.

During the very first interview, Mr. Baker ascertained from me my own religious views. "By birth I am a Hindu," I said to him, "and yet I do not know much about Hinduism; and I know still less of other religions. In fact, I hardly know where I am in religious matters and what is and what should be my belief. I intend to make a careful study of my own religion and as far as I can of other religions as well."

Mr. Baker was glad to hear all this. "I am one of the directors," he said, "of the South Africa General Mission and have built a church at my own expense and deliver sermons in it regularly. I am free from colour prejudice. There are some co-workers of mine and we meet at one o'clock, every day, for a few minutes and pray for peace and light. I shall be glad if you will join us there and I will introduce you to my co-workers, who will be happy to meet you; and I dare say you will like their company. Also I would like to give you some religious books to read, though of course the Book of Books is the Holy Bible, which I would specially recommend to you." I thanked Mr. Baker and agreed to attend the one o'clock prayers as regularly as possible. "So I shall expect you here to-morrow at one o'clock, and we shall go together to pray," added Mr. Baker, and we said good-bye.

I had little time for reflection just yet. I went to Mr. Johnston, paid the bill and removed to the new lodgings, where I had my lunch. The landlady was a good woman. She had cooked a vegetarian meal for me. It was not long before I made myself quite at home with the family. After this, I went to see the friend to whom Dada Abdulla had given me a note. From him I learnt more about the hardships of Indians in South Africa. He insisted that I should stay with him. I thanked him, and told him that I had already made my arrangements. He urged me not to hesitate to ask for anything I needed.

It was now dark. I returned home, had my dinner, went to my room and lay there absorbed in deep thought. There was not any immediate work for me to do. What, I wondered, could be the meaning of Mr. Baker's deep interest in me? What should I gain from his religious co-workers? How far should I undertake the study of Christianity? How was I to understand Christianity in its proper perspective without thoroughly knowing my own Hindu religion? I could come to only one conclusion: I should make a dispassionate study of all that came to me and deal with Mr. Baker's group as God might guide me; I should not think of embracing another religion before I had fully understood my own. Thus musing, I fell asleep.

The next day at one o'clock I went to Mr. Baker's prayer-meeting. There I was introduced to Miss Harris, Miss Gabb, Mr. Coates and others. Every one knelt down to pray and I followed their example. The prayers were supplications to God for various things, according to each other's needs. Thus the usual forms were for the day to be passed peacefully and for God to open the doors of the heart. An earnest prayer was now added for my welfare: "Lord, show the path to this new brother, who had come amongst us. Give him, Lord, the peace that Thou hast given us. May the Lord Jesus who has saved us save him too. We ask all this in the name of Jesus." There was no singing of hymns or other music at these meetings. After the supplication for something special every day, we dispersed, each going to his lunch, that being the hour for it. The prayer did not take more than about five minutes.

The Misses Harris and Gabb were both elderly maiden ladies. Mr. Coates was a Quaker. The two ladies lived together, and they gave me a standing invitation to four o'clock tea, at their house, every Sunday. When we met on Sundays, I used to give Mr. Coates my religious diary for the week and discuss with him the books I had read and the impression they had left on me. The ladies used to narrate their sweet experiences and talk about the peace they had found. Mr. Coates was a frank-hearted staunch young man. We went out for walks together, and he also took me to other Christian friends. As we came closer to each other, he began to give me books of his own choice, until my shelf was filled with them. In pure faith I consented to read all those books; and as I went on reading them, we discussed them.

Just as he introduced me to different books, so he introduced me to several friends whom he regarded as staunch Christians. One of these introductions was to a family which belonged to the Plymouth Brethren. Many of the contacts for which Mr. Coates was responsible were good. Most of them struck me as being God-fearing. But during my contact with this family, one of the Plymouth Brethren confronted me with an argument for which I was not prepared:

"You cannot understand the beauty of our religion. From what you say it appears, that you must be brooding over your transgressions every moment of your life, always mending them and atoning for them. How can this ceaseless cycle of action bring you redemption? You can never have peace. You admit that we are all sinners. Now look at the perfection of our belief. Our own attempts at improvement and atonement are futile; and yet redemption we must have. How can we bear the burden of sin? We can but throw it on Jesus. He is the only sinless Son of God. It is His word, that those who believe in Him shall have everlasting life. Therein lies God's infinite mercy. And as we believe in the atonement of Jesus, our own sins do not bind us. Sin we must; it is impossible to live in this world sinless. And therefore Jesus suffered and atoned for all the sins of mankind. Only he who accepts His great redemption can have eternal peace. Think what a life of restlessness is yours, and what a promise of peace we have."

The argument utterly failed to convince me. I humbly replied: "If this be Christianity I cannot accept it. I do not seek redemption from the consequences of my sin. I seek to be redeemed from sin itself, or rather from the very thought of sin. Until I have attained that end, I shall be content to be restless."

To which the Plymouth Brother rejoined: "I assure you, your attempt is fruitless. Think again over what I have said."

And the Brother proved as good as his word. He voluntarily committed transgressions, and showed me that he was undisturbed by the thought of them.

But I already knew before meeting with these friends, that all Christians did not believe in such a theory of atonement. Mr. Coates himself walked in the fear of God. His heart was pure, and he believed in the possibility of self-purification. The two ladies also shared this belief. Some of the books that came into my hands were full of devotion. So, although Mr. Coates was very much disturbed by this latest experience of mine, I was able to reassure him and tell him that the distorted belief of a Plymouth Brother could not prejudice me against Christianity. My difficulties lay elsewhere. They were with regard to the Bible and its accepted interpretation.

Before writing further about Christian contacts, I must record other experiences of the same period. Sheth Tyeb Haji Khan Muhammad had in Pretoria the same position as was enjoyed by Dada Abdulla in Natal. There was no public movement that could be conducted without him. I made his acquaintance during the very first week I was in Pretoria, and told him of my intention to get in touch with every Indian there. My first step was to call a meeting, which was principally attended by Meman [1] merchants, although there was a sprinkling of Hindus as well. The Hindu population in Pretoria was, as a matter of fact, very small.

My speech at this meeting may be said to have been the first public speech in my life. I went fairly prepared with my subject, which was about observing truthfulness in business. I had always heard the merchants say that truth was not possible in business. I did not think so then, nor do I now. Even to-day there are merchant friends, who contend that truth is inconsistent with business. Business, they say, is a very practical affair, and truth a matter of religion; and they argue that practical affairs are one thing while religion is quite another. I strongly contested the position in my speech, and awakened the merchants to a sense of their duty.

I had found our people's habits to be insanitary as

[1] The Meman Community is a peculiar sect of Islam which is found chiefly along the West Coast of India. They are merchants and traders.

compared with those of the Englishmen around them, and drew their attention to this. I laid stress on the necessity of forgetting all racial and religious distinctions. In conclusion, I suggested the formation of an association to approach the authorities concerned in respect of the hardships of the Indian settlers. I offered to place at its disposal as much of my time and service as was available.

I was satisfied with the result of the meeting. It was decided to hold such meetings, as far as I remember, once a week. These were held more or less regularly, and on these occasions there was a free exchange of ideas. The result was that there was now in Pretoria no Indian I did not know, or whose condition I was not acquainted with. This prompted me in turn to make the acquaintance of the British Agent in Pretoria, Mr. Jacobus de Wet. He had sympathy for the Indians, but he had very little influence. However, he agreed to help us as best he could, and invited me to meet him whenever I wished.

I now communicated with the railway authorities and told them that even under their own regulations, the disabilities about travelling, under which the Indians laboured, could not be justified. I got a letter in reply to the effect that first and second class tickets would be issued to Indians who were properly dressed. This was far from giving adequate relief, as it rested with the Station Master to decide who was "properly dressed." The British Agent showed me some papers dealing with Indian affairs. Tyeb Sheth had also given me similar papers. I learnt from them how cruelly the Indians were hounded out from the Orange Free State. Thus, my stay in Pretoria enabled me to make a study of the condition of the Indians in the Transvaal and the Orange Free

State. I had no idea that this study was to be of invaluable service to me in the future. For I had thought of returning home by the end of the year, or even earlier, if the case was finished before the year was out. But God had disposed otherwise.

The year's stay in Pretoria was a most valuable experience in my life. Here it was that I had opportunities of learning public work, and acquired some measure of my capacity for it. Here it was that the religious spirit within me became a living force, and here too I acquired a true knowledge of legal practice. Here I learnt the things that a junior barrister learns in a senior barrister's chamber, and here also I gained confidence that I should not after all fail as a lawyer. It was likewise here that I learnt the secret of success as a lawyer.

Dada Abdulla's case was no small one. The suit was for forty thousand pounds. Arising as it did out of business transactions, it was full of intricacies of accounts. Part of the claim was based on promissory notes, and part on the specific performance of a promise to deliver promissory notes. The defence was that the promissory notes were fraudulently taken.

I took the keenest interest in the case, and read all the papers pertaining to the transactions. My client was a man of great ability and reposed absolute confidence in me, and this rendered my work easy. I made a fair study of bookkeeping. My capacity for translation was improved by having to translate the correspondence which was for the most part in Gujarati.

Although, as I have said before, I took a keen interest in religious communion and in public work, and always gave some of my time to them, they were not then my first consideration. The preparation of the case was my primary interest. Reading of law and looking up law cases, when necessary, had always a prior claim on my time. As a result, I acquired such a grasp of the facts of the case as perhaps was not possessed even by the parties themselves, inasmuch as I had with me the papers of both the parties.

I recalled Mr. Pincutt's advice that facts are three fourths of the law. At a later date it was amply borne out by that famous barrister of South Africa, the late Mr. Leonard. In a certain case in my charge I saw that though justice was on the side of my client, the law seemed to be against him. In despair I approached Mr. Leonard for help. He also felt that the facts of the case were very strong. He exclaimed, "Gandhi, I have learnt one thing, and it is this, that if we take care of the facts of a case, the law will take care of itself. Let us dive deeper into the facts of this case." With these words he asked me to study the case further and then see him again. On a reëxamination of the facts I saw them in an entirely new light and I also hit upon an old South African case bearing on the point. I was delighted and went to Mr. Leonard and told him everything. "Right," he said, "we shall win the case. Only we must bear in mind which of the judges takes it."

When I was making preparation for Dada Abdulla's case, I had not fully realised this paramount importance of facts. Facts mean truth, and once we adhere to truth, then the law comes to our aid naturally. I saw that the facts of Dada Abdulla's case made it very strong indeed and that the law was bound to be on his side. But I also saw that the litigation, if it were persisted in, would ruin the plaintiff and the defendant, who were relatives and both belonged to the same city. No one knew how long the case might go on. Should it be allowed to continue to be fought out in court, it might go on indefinitely, and to no advantage of either party. Both therefore desired an immediate termination of the case if possible.

I approached Tyeb Sheth and advised him to go to arbitration. I recommended him to see his counsel and suggested to him that if an arbitrator commanding the confidence of both parties could be appointed, the case would be quickly finished. The lawyers' fees were so rapidly mounting up that they were enough to devour all the resources of the clients, big merchants as they were. The case occupied so much of their attention, that they had no time left for any other work. In the meantime mutual ill-will was steadily increasing. They strained every nerve to bring about a compromise. At last Tyeb Sheth agreed. An arbitrator was appointed, the case was argued before him, and Dada Abdulla won.

But that did not satisfy me. If my client were to seek immediate execution of the award, it would be impossible for Tyeb Sheth to meet the whole of the awarded amount, and there was an unwritten law among the Porbandar Memans living in South Africa that death should be preferred to bankruptcy. It was impossible for Tyeb Sheth to pay down the whole sum of about thirty-seven thousand pounds and costs. He meant to pay not a pie less than the amount, and he did not want to be declared bankrupt. There was only one way. Dada Abdulla should allow him to pay in moderate installments. He was equal to the occasion, and granted Tyeb Sheth installments, spread over a very long period. It was more difficult for me to secure this concession of payment by installments than to get the parties to agree to arbitration. But both were happy over the result, and both rose in the public estimation. My joy was boundless. I had learnt the true practice of law, namely, to find out the better side of human nature and to enter men's hearts. I realised that the true function of a lawyer was to unite parties driven asunder. The lesson was so indelibly burnt into me that a large part of my time during the twenty years of my practice as a lawyer was occupied in bringing about private compromises of hundreds of cases. I lost nothing thereby,—not even money, certainly not my soul.

During this time in Pretoria I often went out at night for a walk with Mr. Coates, and we rarely got back home much before ten o'clock. But there was a law for coloured people in the Transvaal by which Indians were not allowed to walk on the footpath or move out of doors after 9 p.m. without a permit. What if the police arrested me? Mr. Coates was more concerned about this than I. He had to issue passes to his negro servants. But how could he give one to me? Only a master might issue a permit to a servant. If I had wanted one, and even if Mr. Coates had been ready to give it, he could not have done so, for it would have been fraud.

So Mr. Coates or some friend of his took me to the State Attorney, Dr. Krause. We turned out to be barristers of the same Inn. The fact that I needed a pass to enable me to be out of doors after 9 p.m. was too much for him. He expressed sympathy for me. Instead of ordering for me a pass, he gave me a letter authorising me to be out of doors at all hours without police interference. I always kept this letter on me whenever I went out. The fact that I never had to make use of it was a mere accident.

The consequences of the regulation regarding the use of footpaths were rather serious for me. I always went out for a walk through President Street to an open plain. President Kruger's house was in this street—a very modest, unostentatious building without a garden, and not distinguishable from other houses in its neighbourhood. The houses of many of the rich men in Pretoria were far more pretentious, and were surrounded by gardens. Indeed President Kruger's simplicity was proverbial. Only the presence of a police patrol before the house indicated that it belonged to some official. I nearly always went along the footpath past this patrol without the slightest hitch or hindrance.

Now the man on duty used to be changed from time to time. Once one of these men, without even having asked me to leave the footpath, pushed and kicked me into the street. I was dismayed. Before I could question him as to his behaviour, Mr. Coates, who happened to be passing the spot on horseback, hailed me and said:

"Gandhi, I have seen everything. I shall gladly be your witness in court if you proceed against the man. I am very sorry you have been so rudely assaulted."

"You need not be sorry," I said. "What does the poor man know? All coloured people are the same to him. He no doubt treats negroes just as he has treated me. I have made it a rule not to go to court in respect of any personal grievance. So I do not intend to proceed against him."

"That is just like you," said Mr. Coates, "but do think it over again. We must teach such men a lesson." He then spoke to the policeman and reprimanded him. I could not follow their talk, as it was in Dutch, the policeman being a Boer. But he apologised to me, for which there was no need. I had already forgiven him.

But I never again went along this street. There would be other men coming in this man's place, and ignorant of the incident, they would behave likewise. Why should I unnecessarily court another kick? I therefore selected a different walk.

The incident deepened my feeling for the Indian settlers. I discussed with them the advisability of making a test case, if it were found necessary to do so, after having seen the British Agent in the matter of these regulations.

I thus made an intimate study of the hard condition of the Indian settlers, not only by reading and hearing about it, but by personal experience. Thus I saw that South Africa was no country for a self-respecting Indian, and my mind became more and more occupied with the question as to how this state of things might be improved.

Mr. Baker was getting anxious about my future. He took me to the Wellington Convention. The Protestant Christians organise such gatherings every few years for religious enlightenment, or in other words, self-purification. One may call this religious revival. The Wellington Convention was of this type. The chairman was the famous divine, the Reverend Andrew Murray. Mr. Baker had hoped that the atmosphere of religious exaltation at the Convention and the enthusiasm and earnestness of the people attending it would inevitably lead me to embrace Christianity.

But his final hope was the efficacy of prayer. He had

an abiding faith in prayer. It was his firm conviction that God could not but listen to prayer fervently offered. He would cite the instances of men like George Muller of Bristol, who depended entirely on prayer even for his temporal needs. I listened to his discourse on the efficacy of prayer with unbiassed attention, and assured him that nothing could prevent me from embracing Christianity, should I feel the call. I had no hesitation in giving him this assurance, as I had long since taught myself to follow the inner voice. Therefore I delighted in submitting myself to it. To act against it would be difficult and painful to me.

So we went to Wellington. Mr. Baker was hard put to it in having "a coloured man" like me for his companion. He had to suffer inconveniences on many occasions entirely on account of me. We had to break the journey on the way, as one of the days happened to be a Sunday, and Mr. Baker and his party would not travel on the sabbath. Though the manager of the station hotel agreed to take me in, after much altercation, he absolutely refused to admit me to the dining room. Mr. Baker was not the man to give way easily. He stood by the rights of the guests of a hotel. But I could see his difficulty. At Wellington also I stayed with Mr. Baker. In spite of his best efforts to conceal the little inconveniences he was put to, I could see them all.

This Convention was an assemblage of devout Christians. I was delighted at their faith. Here I met personally the Reverend Andrew Murray and saw that many were praying for me. Some of their hymns I like; they were very sweet.

The Convention lasted for three days. I could understand and appreciate the devoutness of those who attended it. But I saw no reason for changing my belief. It was impossible for me to believe that I could go to heaven or attain salvation only by becoming a Christian. When I frankly said so to some of the good Christian friends, they were shocked. But there was no help for it. My difficulties lay deeper. It was more than I could believe, that Jesus was the only incarnate son of God, and that only he who believed in Him would have everlasting life. If God could have sons, all of us were his sons. If Jesus was like God, or God Himself, then all men were like God and could be God Himself. My reason was not ready to believe literally that Jesus by his death and by his blood redeemed the sins of the world. Metaphorically, there might be some truth in it. Again, according to Christianity only human beings had souls, and not other living beings, for whom death meant complete extinction; while I held a contrary belief. I could accept Jesus as a martyr, an embodiment of sacrifice, and a divine teacher, but not as the most perfect man ever born. His death on the Cross was a great example to the world, but that there was anything like a mysterious or miraculous virtue in it my heart could not accept. The pious lives of Christians did not give me anything that the lives of men of other faiths had failed to give. I had seen in other lives just the same reformation that I heard of amongst Christians. Philosophically there was nothing extraordinary in Christian principles. From the point of view of sacrifice, it seemed to me that the Hindus greatly surpassed the Christians. It was impossible for me to regard Christianity as a perfect religion or the greatest of all religions.

I shared this mental churning with my Christian

friends whenever there was an opportunity, but their answers could not satisfy me. Thus if I could not accept Christianity either as a perfect or the greatest religion, neither was I then convinced of Hinduism being such. Hindu defects were pressingly visible to me. If untouchability could be a part of Hinduism, it could only be a rotten part or an excrescence. I could not understand the meaning of a multitude of sects and castes. What was the meaning of saying that Vedas were the inspired Word of God? If they were inspired, why not also the Bible and the Koran?

As Christian friends were endeavouring to convert me, even so were Musalman friends. Abdulla Sheth had kept on inducing me to study Islam, and of course he had always something to say regarding its beauty.

I expressed my difficulties in a letter to Raychandbhai and I also corresponded with other religious authorities in India and received answers from them. Raychandbhai's letter somewhat pacified me. He asked me to be patient and to study Hinduism more deeply. One of his sentences was to this effect: "On a dispassionate view of the question, I am convinced that no other religion has the subtle and profound thought of Hinduism, its vision of the soul, or its charity."

I purchased Sale's translation of the Koran and began reading it and also obtained other books on Islam. Furthermore I communicated with Christian friends in England. One of them introduced me to Edward Maitland, with whom I opened correspondence. He sent me "The Perfect Way," a book he had written in collaboration with Anna Kingsford. The book was a repudiation of the current Christian belief. He also sent me another book, "The New Interpretation of the Bible." I liked both. They seemed to support Hinduism. Tolstoy's "The Kingdom of God Is within You" overwhelmed me. It left an abiding impression on me. Before the independent thinking, profound morality, and the truthfulness of this book, all the books given by Mr. Coates to me seemed to pale into insignificance.

If I found myself at this time becoming more and more absorbed in the service of the Indian community, the reason behind it was my desire for self-realisation. I had made the religion of service my own, as I felt that God could be realised only through service. And service for me was the service of India, because it came to me without my seeking and I had an aptitude for it. I had gone to South Africa in order to find an escape from Kathiawar intrigues and to gain my own livelihood. But as I have said, I found myself all the while in search of God and striving for self-realisation.

Christian friends had whetted my appetite for knowledge, which had become almost insatiable; they would not leave me in peace, even if I desired to be indifferent. In Durban Mr. Spencer Walton, the head of the South Africa General Mission, found me out. I became almost a member of his family. At the back of this acquaintance was of course my contact with Christians in Pretoria. Mr. Walton had a manner all his own. I do not recollect his ever having invited me to embrace Christianity. But he placed his life as an open book before me, and let me watch all his movements. Mrs. Walton was a very gentle and talented woman. I liked the attitude of this couple. We knew the fundamental differences between us. Any amount of discussion could not efface them. Yet even differences prove helpful, where there is tolerance, charity and truth. I liked Mr. and Mrs. Walton's humility, perseverance and devotion to work, and we met very frequently.

This friendship kept alive my interest in religion. It was impossible now to get the leisure that I used to have in Pretoria for my religious studies. But what little time I could spare I turned to good account. My religious correspondence continued. Raychandbhai was guiding me. Some friend sent me Narmadashankar's book, "Dharma Vichar." Its preface proved very helpful. I had heard about the Bohemian way in which the poet had lived, and a description, in the preface, of the revolution effected in his life by his religious studies captivated me. I came to like the book, and read it from cover to cover with attention. I read with interest Max Muller's book, "India—What Can It Teach Us?" and the translation of the "Upanishads" published by the Theosophical Society. All this enhanced my regard for Hinduism, and its beauties began to grow upon me. It did not, however, prejudice me against the other religions. I read Washington Irving's "Life of Mahomet and His Successors" and Carlyle's panegyric on the Prophet. These books raised Muhammad in my estimation. I also read a book called "The Sayings of Zarathustra."

Thus I gained more knowledge of the different religions. The study stimulated my self-introspection, and fostered in me the habit of putting into practice whatever appealed to me in my studies. Thus I began some of the Yogic practices, as well as I could understand them from a reading of the Hindu books. But I could not get on very far, and decided to follow them with the help of some expert, when I returned to India. The desire has never been fulfilled.

I made too an intensive study of Tolstoy's books. "The Gospels in Brief," "What to Do" and other books of his made a deep impression on me. I began to realise more and more the infinite possibilities of universal love.

About the same time I came in contact with another Christian family. At their suggestion, I attended the Wesleyan church every Sunday, for these days I also had their standing invitation to dinner. The church did not make a favourable impression on me. The congregation did not strike me as being particularly religious. They were not an assembly of devout souls; they appeared rather to be worldly minded people going to church for recreation and in conformity to custom. Here, at times, I would involuntarily doze. I was ashamed, but some of my neighbours, who were in no better case, lightened the shame. I could not go on long like this, and soon gave up attending the service.

My connexion with the family I used to visit every Sunday was abruptly broken. In fact, it may be said that I was warned to visit it no more. It happened thus. My hostess was a good and simple woman, but somewhat narrow-minded. We always discussed religious subjects. I was then reading over again Arnold's "Light of Asia." Once we began to compare the life of Jesus with that of Buddha. "Look at Gautama's compassion!" said I. "It was not confined to mankind, it was extended to all living beings. Does not one's heart overflow with love to think of the lamb joyously perched on his shoulders? One fails to notice this love for all living beings in the life of Jesus." The comparison pained the good lady. I could understand her feelings. I cut the matter short, and we went to the dining room. Her son, a cherub aged scarcely five, was also with us. I am the happiest when in the midst of children, and this youngster and I had been friends. I spoke derisively of the piece of meat on his plate and in high praise of the apple on mine. The innocent boy was carried away and joined in my praise of the fruit.

But the mother? She was dismayed. I was warned. I checked myself and changed the subject. The following week I visited the family as usual, but not without trepidation. I did not see that I should stop going there, I did not think it proper either. But the good lady made my way easy.

"Mr. Gandhi," she said, "please don't take it ill if I feel obliged to tell you that my boy is none the better for your company. Every day he hesitates to eat meat and has asked for fruit, reminding me of your argument. This is too much. If he gives up meat, he is bound to get weak, if not ill. How could I bear it? Your discussions should henceforth be only with us elders. They are sure to react badly on children."

"I am sorry," I replied, "I can understand your feelings as a parent, for I too have children. We can very easily end this unpleasant state of things. What I eat and omit to eat is bound to have a greater effect on the child than what I say. The best way, therefore, is for me to stop these visits. That certainly need not affect our friendship."

"I thank you," she said with evident relief.

Though I took a path my Christian friends had not intended for me, I have remained forever indebted to them for the religious quest that they awakened in me. I shall always cherish the memory of their contact. The years that followed had more, not less, of such sweet and sacred contacts in store for me.

CHAPTER VIII

MOB VIOLENCE IN DURBAN

IN THE MIDDLE OF THE YEAR 1896 I returned to India. As steamers from Natal were then more easily available for Calcutta than for Bombay, I went on board one bound for that city, for the indentured labourers embarked from Calcutta or Madras. While proceeding to Bombay from Calcutta, I missed my train on the way and had to stop in Allahabad for a day. My work of explaining about South Africa commenced there. I saw Mr. Chesney of the "Pioneer." He talked with me courteously, but told me frankly that his sympathies were with the colonials. He, however, promised that if I wrote anything, he would read it and notice it in his paper. This was good enough for me.

While in India, I wrote a pamphlet on the condition of Indians in South Africa. It was noticed by almost all newspapers and it passed through two editions. Five thousand copies were distributed in various places in India. It was during this visit that I had the privilege of seeing the Indian leaders, and there were opportunities to deliver speeches in Bombay, Poona and Madras. I do not propose to deal with these things in detail; for while a public meeting was being arranged in Calcutta, I received a cablegram from Natal asking me to return at once, and this cut short my visit. From the cable I concluded that some movement hostile to the Indians must be on foot and therefore left my work at Calcutta incomplete and went to Bombay, where I took the first available steamer with my family. The *S.S. Courland* had been purchased by Messrs. Dada Abdulla and represented one more enterprise of that very adventurous firm which had decided to run a steamer between Porbandar and Natal. The *Naderi*, a steamer of the Persian Steam Navigation Company, left from Bombay for Natal immediately after. The total number of passengers on the two steamers was about eight hundred.

The agitation in India had reached enough importance as news for the principal Indian newspapers to notice it in their columns and for Reuter to send cablegrams about it to England. This I came to know only on reaching Natal. Reuter's representative in England had sent a brief cablegram to South Africa, containing an exaggerated summary of my speeches in India. Such a thing is not an unusual experience and the exaggeration is not always intentional. Very busy people with prejudices and prepossessions of their own read something superficially and then prepare a summary, which is sometimes partly a product of imagination. This summary, again, is differently interpreted in different places. Distortion thus takes place without any one's intending it. This is the risk always attending public activities and this is also their limitation.

While in India I had criticised the Europeans of Natal. I had spoken very strongly against the three pound tax on indentured labourers. I had given a vivid account of the sufferings of one indentured labourer, named Subrahmanyam, who had been assaulted by his master, whose wounds I had seen and whose case was in my hands. When the Europeans in Natal read the distorted summary of my speeches, they were greatly exasperated against me. The fact, however, was that what I had actually written in Natal about this when I was there was more severe and detailed than what I afterwards spoke in India. Indeed my speeches in India were carefully guarded against exaggeration. Since I knew from experience that if we describe an event to a stranger he sees more in it than what we intend to convey, I had deliberately described the South African situation in India less forcibly than the facts warranted. But very few Europeans would read what I wrote in Natal, and still fewer would care for it. The case, however, was obviously different with my speeches and writings in India. Thousands of Europeans read Reuter's summaries. Moreover, a subject which is considered worthy of being communicated by cablegram becomes invested with an importance it does not intrinsically possess. The Europeans of Natal thought that my work in India carried the weight attributed to it by them and that therefore the system of indentured labour would perhaps come to an end, and hundreds of European planters would suffer in consequence. Besides, they felt blackened before India.

While the Europeans of Natal were thus in an excited state of mind, they heard that I was returning to Natal with my family by *S.S. Courland*, that it carried from three hundred to four hundred Indian passengers, and that the *S.S. Naderi* was also arriving at the same time with an equal number of Indians. This inflamed them all the more and there was a great explosion of feeling. The Europeans of Natal held large meetings, which were attended by almost all the prominent members of the community. The Indian passengers in general and myself in particular came in for a great deal of severe criticism. The expected arrival of the *Courland* and the *Naderi*

(*Photo by Gabriel, Durban.*)

MR. GANDHI AS A BARRISTER AT DURBAN, ABOUT 1903

was represented as an "invasion" of Natal. The speakers said that I had brought those eight hundred passengers to Natal and that this was my first step towards flooding Natal with free Indians. A unanimous resolution was passed that the passengers of both the steamers, including myself, should be prevented from landing in Natal. If the Government of Natal would or could not prevent the passengers from landing, the Committee appointed at the meeting was to take the law into its own hands and prevent the Indians from landing by main force. Both the steamers reached Durban on the same day.

The bubonic plague had made its first appearance in India in 1896. This fact was utilised at the present juncture in their effort to prevent our landing, the Government of Natal was hampered by legal difficulties as the Immigration Restriction Act had not yet come into being. Otherwise, their sympathies were entirely with the Committee of Europeans. Mr. Escombe, a member of the Government, took a prominent part in the proceedings of that Committee. There is a rule in force at all ports that if a case of contagious disease occurs on board a steamer, or if a steamer is coming from an infected port, it is detained in quarantine for a certain period. This restriction can be imposed only on sanitary grounds, and under orders from the Health Officer of the Port. The Government of Natal abused their power by enforcing the above rule for a political purpose. Although there was no contagious disease on board, both the steamers were detained, far beyond the usual time limit, for as many as twenty-three days. Meanwhile, the Committee of Europeans continued their activities. Messrs. Dada Abdulla, who were the owners of the *Courland* and the agents for the *Naderi*, were subjected to a severe hectoring by them. Inducements were offered to them if they agreed to take back the passengers, and they were threatened with loss of business if they refused to do so. But the partners of the firm were no cowards. They said they did not care if they were ruined; they would fight to the bitter end, but would not be coerced into committing the crime of sending away those helpless but innocent passengers; they were no strangers to patriotism. The old advocate of the firm, Mr. F. A. Laughton, K.C., was also a brave man.

As luck would have it, the late Sjt. Mansukhlal Hiralal Nazar, a Kayastha gentleman from Surat and a nephew of the late Mr. Justice Nanabhai Haridas, reached Africa about the same time. I did not know him, nor was I aware of his going. I need scarcely say that I had no hand in bringing the passengers who arrived by the *Naderi* and the *Courland*. Most of them were old residents of South Africa. Many of them again were bound for the Transvaal. Threatening notices were served by the Committee of Europeans even upon these passengers. The captains of the steamers read them out to the passengers. The notices expressly stated that the Europeans of Natal were in a dangerous temper, and said in effect that if in spite of the warning the Indian passengers attempted to land, the members of the Committee would attend at the port and push every Indian into the sea. I interpreted this notice to the passengers on the *Courland*. An English speaking passenger on board the *Naderi* did the same for his fellow passengers. The passengers on both the steamers flatly declined to go back and added that many of them were proceeding to the Transvaal, that some of the rest were old residents of Natal, that in any case every one of them was legally entitled to land and that, the threats of the Committee notwithstanding, they were determined to land in order to test their right to do so.

The Government of Natal was at its wits' end. How long could an unjust restriction be enforced? Twenty-three days had passed already. Neither did Dada Abdulla flinch, nor did the passengers. The quarantine was thus lifted after twenty-three days and the steamers were permitted to steam into the harbour. Meanwhile, Mr. Escombe pacified the excited Committee of Europeans. At a meeting which was held, he said, "The Europeans in Durban have displayed commendable unity and courage. You have done all you could. Government has also helped you. The Indians have been detained for twenty-three days. You have given sufficient expression to your sentiments and your public spirit. That will make a profound impression on the Imperial Government. Your action has made the path of the Government of Natal easy. If you now prevent by force a single Indian passenger from landing, you will injure your own interests and place the Government in an awkward position. And even then you will not succeed in preventing the Indians from landing. The passengers are not at all to blame. There are women and children among them. When they embarked at Bombay, they had no idea of your feelings. I would therefore advise you to disperse and not to obstruct these people. I assure you, however, that the Government of Natal will obtain from the Legislative Council the requisite powers to restrict future immigration." This is only a summary of Mr. Escombe's speech. His audience was dissappointed, but he had great influence over the Europeans of Natal.

They dispersed in consequence of his advice and both the steamers came into port.

A message reached me from Mr. Escombe advising me not to land with the others, but to wait until evening, when he would send the Superintendent of the Harbour Police to escort me home, adding that my family were free to land at any time. This was not an order, according to law, but was by way of advice to the captain not to allow me to land and of warning to me of the danger that was hanging over my head. The captain had not the power forcibly to prevent me from landing. But I came to the conclusion that I should accept this suggestion. I sent my family to the residence of my old friend and client, Parsee Rustomji, and told them that I would meet them there. When the passengers had disembarked, Mr. Laughton, counsel for Dada Abdulla and a personal friend of mine, came up and met me. He asked me why I had not yet landed. I told him about Mr. Escombe's letter. He said that he did not like the idea of my waiting till evening and then entering the city like a thief or offender; that if I was not afraid I should accompany him and we would walk to the town as if nothing had happened. I replied that it was not a question of fear with me but only one of propriety, whether or not I should accept Mr. Escombe's suggestion. And we had also to consider whether the captain of the steamer was responsible in the matter. Mr. Laughton smiled and said: "What has Mr. Escombe done for you that you must needs heed his suggestion? And what reason have you to believe that he is actuated by kindliness and not by some ulterior motive? I know more than you what has happened in the town, and what hand Mr. Escombe had in the happenings there." I interrupted him with a shaking of the head.

"We might assume," continued Mr. Laughton, "that he is actuated by the best motives. But if you comply with his suggestion, you will stand humiliated. I would, therefore, advise you, if you are ready, to accompany me now. The captain is our man, and his responsibility is our responsibility. He is accountable only to Dada Abdulla. I know what they will think of the matter, as they have displayed great courage in the present struggle." I replied: "Let us go, then. I have no preparations to make. All I have to do is to put on my turban. Let us inform the captain and start." We took the captain's leave.

Mr. Laughton was an old and well-known advocate of Durban with whom I had already come into intimate contact, and I was accustomed to consult him in difficult cases and often to engage him as my senior. He was a brave and powerfully built man. Our road lay through the principal street of Durban. It was about half past four in the evening when we started. The sky was slightly overcast and the sun was not to be seen. It would take a pedestrian at least one hour to reach Parsee Rustomji's house. The number of persons present about the wharf was not larger than what is to be usually seen there. As soon as we landed, some young lads saw us. As I was the only Indian who wore a turban of a particular type, they at once recognised me, began to shout, "Here's Gandhi, here's Gandhi! Thrash him! Surround him!" and they came up towards me. Some began to throw stones. Then a few older Europeans joined the boys, and gradually the party of rioters began to grow. Mr. Laughton thought that there was danger in our going on foot. He therefore beckoned for a rickshaw. Up to now I had never sat in a rickshaw, as it was thoroughly disgusting to me to sit in a vehicle pulled by human beings. But I then felt that it was my duty to use that vehicle. Five or six times in my life I have experienced that one whom God wishes to save cannot fall even if he will. If I did not fall at that moment I cannot take any credit for it to myself. These rickshaws are pulled by Zulus. The older Europeans and the young lads threatened the rickshaw puller that if he allowed me to sit in his rickshaw, they would beat him and smash his rickshaw to pieces. The rickshaw boy, therefore, said "Kha" (No), and went away. I was thus spared the shame of a rickshaw ride.

We had no alternative now but to proceed to our destination on foot. The mob followed us. With every step we advanced, it grew larger and larger. The gathering was enormous when we reached West Street. A man of powerful build caught hold of Mr. Laughton and tore him away from me. He was not therefore in a position to come up with me. The crowd began to abuse me and showered upon me stones and whatever else they could lay their hands on. They threw down my turban. Meanwhile, a burly fellow came up to me, slapped me in the face and then kicked me. I was about to fall unconscious when I held on to the railings of a house near-by. For a while I took breath, and when the fainting was over proceeded on my way. At that time, I had almost given up any hope of reaching home alive. But I remember well that even then my heart did not arraign my assailants.

While I was thus slowly wending my way, the wife of the Superintendent of Police at Durban, Mrs. Alexander, was coming from the opposite direction. We knew each other well. She was a brave lady. Although the sky was cloudy and the sun about to set, she opened her sunshade for my protection and began to walk at my side. The Europeans would not insult a lady, especially the wife of the old, popular Superintendent of Police, nor would they hurt her. They must avoid injuring her while aiming blows at me. The injuries, therefore, which I received after she joined me, were not serious. Meanwhile the Superintendent of Police came to know of the attack upon me and sent a party of constables for my protection. The police surrounded me. The Police Station was on our way. When we reached there, I saw that the Superintendent of Police was waiting for us. He offered asylum in the police station, but I declined the offer with thanks and said, "I must reach my destination. I have faith in the fair play of the citizens of Durban and in the righteousness of my own cause. I am thankful to you for sending the police party for my protection. Mrs. Alexander too has contributed much to my safety."

I reached Rustomji's house without further trouble. It was nearly evening when I reached there. The medical officer of the *Courland*, who was present, began to examine my wounds. There were not many of them. One blind wound in particular was very painful. But I was not yet privileged to rest in peace. Thousands of Europeans gathered before Rustomji Sheth's house. After nightfall, hooligans also joined the crowd. The crowd sent word to Rustomji Sheth that if he did not hand me over to them, they would burn him and his house along with me. Rustomji Sheth was too good an Indian to be daunted. When Superintendent Alexander came to know how matters stood, he quietly joined the crowd with a number of detectives. He sent for a bench and stood upon it. Thus under the pretence of talking to the crowd, he took possession of the entrance of Rustomji's house so that none could break in and enter it. He had already posted detectives at proper places. Immediately on arrival, he had instructed a subordinate to disguse himself as an Indian trader by putting on Indian dress and painting his face, to see me and deliver to me the following message: "If you wish to save your friend, his guests and property, and your own family, I advise you to disguise yourself as an Indian constable, come out through Rustomji's go-down, steal through the crowd with my man and reach the Police Station. A carriage is awaiting you at the corner of the street. This is the only way in which I can save you and others. The crowd is so excited that I am not in a position to control it. If you are not prompt in following my directions, I am afraid the crowd will rase Rustomji's house to the ground and it is impossible for me to imagine how many lives will be lost and how much property destroyed." I gauged the situation at once and soon disgused myself as a constable and left Rustomji's house. The Police Officer and I reached the Police Station in safety. In the meantime Mr. Alexander was humouring the crowd by singing topical songs and talking to them. When he knew that I had reached the Police Station, he became serious and asked:

"What do you want?" he called. "We want Gandhi." "What will you do with him?" "We'll burn him."

"What harm has he done you."

"He has blackened our face in India and wants to flood Natal with coolies."

"What if he does not come out?" "We will then burn his house."

"His wife and children are also there. There are other men and women besides. Would you not be ashamed of burning women and children?" "The responsibility for that will rest with you. We don't wish to hurt anyone else, but we want you to hand over Gandhi."

The Superintendent gently smiled and informed the crowd that I had left Rustomji's house, passed through their midst, and reached another place already. The crowd shouted, "It's a lie, it's a lie!"

The Superintendent said, "If you will not believe your old Superintendent of Police, please appoint a committee of three or four men amongst you. Let others promise that they will not enter the house, and that if the committee fail to find Gandhi in the house, you will peacefully return to your homes. You got excited to-day, and did not obey the police. That reflects discredit on you, not on the police. The police therefore played a trick with you; it removed your prey from your midst and you have lost the game. You will certainly not blame the police for this. The police, whom you appointed, have simply done their duty."

The Superintendent addressed the crowd with such suavity and determination, that they gave him the promise he had asked for. A committee was appointed. It searched Rustomji's house through and through, and reported to the crowd that the Superintendent was right and had beaten them in the game. The crowd was disappointed, but they kept their word and dispersed without committing any mischief. This happened on January 13, 1897.

The same morning after the quarantine on the steamers

had been removed, the reporter of a Durban newspaper had seen me on the steamer. He had asked me everything. It was quite easy to dispose of the charges against me to his satisfaction. I showed to him in detail that I had not indulged in the least exaggeration. What I had done was only my duty. If I had failed to discharge it, I would be unworthy of the name of man. All this appeared in the newspapers the next day. Sensible people among the Europeans admitted their mistake. The newspapers expressed their sympathy with the standpoint of the Europeans in Natal, but at the same time fully defended my action. This enhanced my reputation as well as the prestige of the Indian community. It was proved that the Indians, poor as they were, were no cowards, and that the Indian traders were prepared to fight for their self-respect and for their country regardless of loss. Thus though the Indian community had to suffer hardship and though Dada Abdulla incurred big losses, the ultimate result, I believe, was entirely beneficial. The community had an opportunity of measuring their own strength, and in consequence their self-confidence increased. I had a most valuable experience, and whenever I think of that day, I feel that God was preparing me for the practice of Satyagraha. The events in Natal had their repercussion in England. Mr. Chamberlain, Secretary of State for the Colonies, cabled to the Government of Natal asking them to prosecute my assailants and to see that justice was done to me.

Mr. Escombe, who was Attorney General with the Government of Natal, called me. He told me about Mr. Chamberlain's cable. He expressed his regret for the injuries I had sustained, and his pleasure that the consequences of the assault were not more serious. He added, "I can assure you that I did not at all intend that you or any other member of your community should be injured. As I feared that you might possibly be hurt, I sent you word to say that you should land at night. You did not like my suggestion. I do not wish to blame you in the least that you accepted Mr. Laughton's advice. You were perfectly entitled to do what you thought fit. The Government of Natal fully accepts Mr. Chamberlain's demand. We desire that the offenders should be brought to book. Can you identify any of your assailants?"

I replied that I might perhaps be able to identify one or two of them, but had already made up my mind not to prosecute anyone. What information they had, they had obtained from their leaders, and it was too much to expect a crowd to judge whether it was correct or otherwise. If all that they heard about me was true, it was natural for them to be excited and do something wrong in a fit of indignation. Excited crowds had always tried to deal out justice in that manner. If anyone was to blame it was the Committee of Europeans. Reuter might have cabled any distorted account; but when leading Europeans knew about my coming to Natal, it was their duty and the duty of the Committee to question me about the suspicions that had been entertained with regard to my activities in India.

Mr. Escombe replied, "I quite understand what you say, and I appreciate it. I was not prepared to hear that you were not willing to prosecute your assailants. I would not have been displeased in the least had you prosecuted them. But when you have signified your determination not to prosecute, I do not hesitate to say not only that you have come to a right decision in the matter, but you will render further service to your community by your self-restraint. I must at the same time admit that your refusal to prosecute your assailants will save the Government of Natal from a most awkward position. If you so desire, the Government will see that your assailants are arrested, but it is scarcely necessary to tell you that it would irritate the Europeans and give rise to all manner of criticism, which no Government would relish. But if you have finally made up your mind not to prosecute, you should write to me a note signifying your intention to the effect. I cannot defend my Government merely by sending Mr. Chamberlain a summary of our conversation. I should cable to him a summary of your note. I am not, however, asking you to let me have the note just now. You had better consult your friends. Consult Mr. Laughton also. And if after such consultations you still adhere to your resolution not to prosecute, write to me. But your note should clearly state that you, on your own responsibility, refuse to prosecute your assailants. Then only can I make use of it."

I said: "I had no idea that you had sent for me in this connexion. I have not consulted anyone on the subject, nor do I wish to consult anyone now. When I decided to land and proceed with Mr. Laughton, I had made up my mind that I should not feel aggrieved in case I was injured. Prosecuting my assailants is therefore out of the question. This is a religious question with me." After this, I obtained a blank sheet of paper, wrote out the desired note, and handed it over to him.

CHAPTER IX

THE BOER WAR

WHEN THE BOER WAR BROKE OUT in 1899, the question as to what the Indians in South Africa should do, immediately presented itself for solution. Among the Boers, the entire male population joined the war. Lawyers gave up their practice, farmers their farms, traders their trade, and servants left their service. The British in South Africa did not join the war in anything like the same proportion as the Boers. However, a large number of civilians in Cape Colony, Natal and Rhodesia enrolled themselves as volunteers. Many distinguished English traders and lawyers followed suit. One of the charges laid against the Indians was that they went to South Africa only for money-grubbing and were merely a dead weight upon the British. Like worms, it was said, which settle inside wood and eat it hollow, so the Indians were in South Africa only to fatten themselves; they would not render them the slightest aid if the country was invaded or if their homes were raided. The British in such a case would have not only to defend themselves against the enemy but at the same time to protect the Indians. We Indians carefully considered this charge. We felt that this was a golden opportunity for us to prove that it was baseless. But on the other hand the following considerations were also urged by some:

"The British oppress us equally with the Boers. If we are subjected to hardships in the Transvaal, we are not very much better off in Natal or the Cape Colony. The difference, if any, is only one of degree. Again we are more or less a community of slaves; knowing as we do that a small nation like the Boers is fighting for its very existence, why should we be instrumental in their destruction? Finally, from a practical point of view, no one will take it upon himself to predict a defeat for the Boers. And if they win, they will never fail to wreak vengeance upon us."

There was a powerful party amongst us which strongly advanced the above argument. I could understand it and allowed it due weight. However, it did not commend itself to me, and I refuted it to myself and to the community as follows:

"Our existence in South Africa is only in our capacity as British subjects. In every memorial we have presented, we have asserted our rights as such. We have been proud of our British citizenship, or have given our rulers and the world to believe that we are so proud. Our rulers profess to safeguard our rights because we are British subjects, and what little rights we still retain, we retain because we are British subjects. It would be unbecoming to our dignity as a nation to look on with folded hands at a time when ruin stared the British in the face as well as ourselves, simply because they ill-treat us here. And such criminal inaction could only aggravate our difficulties. If we missed this opportunity, which had come to us unsought, of proving the falsity of a charge which we believed to be false, we should stand self-condemned, and it would be no matter for surprise if then the English treated us worse than before and sneered at us more than ever. The fault in such a case would lie entirely at our door. To say that the charges preferred against ourselves had no foundation in fact and were absolutely untenable, would only be to deceive ourselves. It is true, we might argue, that we are helots in the Empire, but so far we have tried to better our condition, continuing the while to remain in the Empire. That has been the policy of all our leaders in India and ours also. And if we desire to win our freedom and achieve our welfare as members of the British Empire, here is a golden opportunity for us to do so by helping the British in the war by all the means at our disposal. It must largely be conceded that justice is on the side of the Boers. But every single subject of a state must not hope to enforce his private opinion in all cases. The authorities may not always be right, but so long as the subjects own allegiance to a state, it is their clear duty generally to accommodate themselves, and to accord their support, to acts of the state.

"Again, if any class among the subjects considers that the action of a government is immoral from a religious standpoint, then, before they help or hinder it, they must endeavour fully and even at the risk of their lives to dissuade the government from pursuing such a course. We have done nothing of the kind. Such a moral crisis is not present before us, and no one says that we wish to hold aloof from this war for any such universal and comprehensive reason. Our ordinary duty as subjects, therefore, is not to enter into the merits of the war, but when war has actually broken out, to render such assistance as we possibly can. Finally, to suggest that in case the Boers won—and a Boer victory was well within the range of possibility—our last state would be worse than our first, and the Boers would exact frightful revenge, would be doing injustice to the chivalrous Boers as well as to ourselves. To waste the slightest thought upon such a contingency would only be a sign of our effeminacy and a reflection on our loyalty. Would an Englishman think for a moment what would happen to himself if the English lost the war? A man about to join a war cannot advance such an argument without forfeiting his manhood."

My arguments commended themselves to many. But now the practical question arose. Who would lend an ear to the weak voice of the Indians when there was raging this terrible whirlwind of war? What weight would this offer of help carry? None of us had ever wielded a weapon of war. Even the work performed by non-combatants in a war required training. None of us knew even how to march in step. It was no easy task to perform long marches with one's baggage on one's own shoulders. Again, the whites would treat us all as "coolies," insult us and look down upon us. How was all this to be borne? And if we volunteered for service, how could we induce the Government to accept our offer? Finally, we came to the conclusion that if we had the will, God would grant us the ability to serve, that we need not worry how we could do the work entrusted but should train ourselves for it as best we might, and that having once decided to serve, we should cease to think of discriminating between different kinds of work and serve, putting up even with insults if it came to that.

We encountered formidable difficulties in getting our offer favourably entertained. The story is interesting, but this is not the place to detail it. Suffice it to say that the leaders among us received training in nursing the wounded and the sick, obtained medical certificates of physical fitness and sent a formal letter to the Government. This letter and the eagerness we evinced to serve in whatever capacity the Government would accept us created a very good impression. The Government thanked us in reply but rejected our offer for the time. Meanwhile the Boers continued to advance like a great flood, and it was feared that they might reach Durban. There were heaps of wounded and dead everywhere. We were continually renewing our offer, and sanction was given at last for the formation of an Indian Ambulance Corps. We had expressed our willingness even to do sweepers' or scavengers' work in hospitals. No wonder, therefore, that the idea of an Ambulance Corps was perfectly welcome to us. We had suggested the desirability of permitting the indentured Indians too to join the rest. As the Government was then in need of as many men as they could get, they approached the employers of indentured labourers to allow their men to volunteer. Thus a large and splendid corps composed of nearly eleven hundred Indians left Durban for the front. At the time of our departure, we received the congratulations and the blessings of Mr. Escombe, whose name is already familiar to the reader and who was the head of the European volunteers in Natal.

All this was a perfect revelation to the English newspapers. No one expected that the Indians would take any part in the war. Doctor Booth, under whom we had placed ourselves for training in first aid, joined the corps in the capacity of Medical Superintendent. He was a pious clergyman, and though his work lay chiefly among the

Indian Christians, he freely mixed with Indians of all denominations. There was a European Ambulance Corps as well as the Indian, and both worked side by side in the same place.

We soon got work and that too harder than we had expected. To carry the wounded seven or eight miles was part of our ordinary routine. But sometimes we had to carry badly wounded soldiers and officers over much longer distances up to twenty-five miles. The march would commence at eight in the morning, medicines must be administered on the way, and we were required to reach the base-hospital at five. This was very hard work indeed. It was only once that we had to carry the wounded twenty-five miles in a single day. Again the British army met with reverse after reverse in the beginning of the war and large numbers were wounded. The officers therefore were compelled to give up their idea of not taking us within the firing line. But it must be stated that when such an emergency arose we were told that as the terms of our contract included immunity from such service, General Buller had no intention of forcing us to work under fire if we were not prepared to accept such risk, but if we undertook it voluntarily, it would be greatly appreciated. We were only too willing to enter the danger zone and had never liked to remain outside it. We therefore welcomed this opportunity. But none of us received a bullet wound or any other injury. Although our corps often came in contact with the members of the temporary Ambulance Corps composed of Europeans as well as with the European soldiers, none of us felt that Europeans treated us with contempt or even with discourtesy. The temporary corps was composed of South African Europeans who had taken part in the anti-Indian agitation before the war. But the knowledge that the Indians, forgetful of their wrongs, were out to help them in the hour of their need, had melted their hearts for the time being. Our work was mentioned by General Buller in his despatches. War medals too were conferred on the thirty seven leaders.

When General Buller's operations in connexion with the relief of Ladysmith were over, our corps was disbanded as well as the European. The war continued long after this. We were always prepared to rejoin, and it was stated in the order disbanding our corps that the Government would certainly utilise our services if operations on a large scale were again necessary.

I must place one noteworthy incident on record. Among those who were in Ladysmith when it was invested by the Boers, there were besides Englishmen a few stray Indian settlers. Some of these were traders, while the rest were indentured labourers, working on the railways or as servants to English gentlemen; one of these was Parbhu Singh. The officer in command at Ladysmith assigned various duties to every resident of the place. The most dangerous and most responsible work was assigned to Parbhu Singh, who was called a "coolie." On a hill near Ladysmith the Boers had stationed a field-gun whose operations destroyed many buildings and even occasioned some loss of life. An interval of a minute or two must pass before a shell which had been fired from the gun reached a distant objective. If the besieged got even such a short notice, they could take cover before the shell dropped in the town and thus save themselves. Parbhu Singh was to sit perched up in a tree, all the time that the gun was working, with his eyes fixed on the hill and would ring a bell the moment he observed a flash. On hearing the bell, the residents of Ladysmith instantly took cover and saved themselves from the deadly cannon ball whose approach was thus announced.

The officer in charge of Ladysmith, in eulogising the invaluable services rendered by Parbhu Singh, stated that he worked so zealously that not once had he failed to ring the bell. It need hardly be said that his own life was constantly in peril.

CHAPTER X

THE BLACK PLAGUE

IN JOHANNESBURG where I resided for some time, after the Boer war was ended, my legal practice continued to increase. At one time I had as many as four Indian clerks, about whom it is difficult to say whether they were not more like my sons than clerks. But even these were not enough for my work.

I was at my wits' end. Arrears were fast mounting up, so much so that it seemed impossible for me, however much I might try, to cope with professional and public work. I was quite willing to entertain a European clerk, but I was not sure of getting a white man or woman to serve a coloured man like me. But I decided to try. I approached a typewriter's agent whom I knew, and asked him to get me a stenographer if he could. There were some available and he promised to try to secure the services of one. He came across a Scotch girl, called Miss Dick, who had come then fresh from Scotland. She had no objection to earning an honest livelihood, wherever available, and she was in need. So the agent sent her on to me. She immediately prepossessed me.

"Don't you mind serving under an Indian?" I asked her. "Not at all," was her firm reply.

"What salary do you expect?"

"Would seventeen pounds ten a month be too much?"

"Not too much, if you will give me the work I want from you. When can you join?"

"This moment, if you please."

I was very glad and started dictating letters to her.

Before very long she became more a daughter or a sister to me than a mere stenotypist. Scarcely ever had I any reason to find fault with her work. She was often entrusted with the management of funds amounting to thousands of pounds, and she was in charge of account books. She won my complete confidence, but what was perhaps more, she confided to me her innermost thoughts and feelings. She sought my advice in the final choice of her husband, and I had the privilege to give her away in marriage. As soon as Miss Dick became Mrs. Macdonald, she had to leave me, but even after her marriage she did not fail to respond whenever under pressure I made a call upon her.

But a permanent stenotypist was now needed in her place, and I was fortunate in getting another girl. She was Miss Schlesin, introduced to me by Mr. Kallenbach. She is at present at the head of a girls' school in the Transvaal. She was about seventeen when she came to me. Some of her idiosyncrasies were at times too much for Mr. Kallenbach and me. She had come less to work as a stenotypist than to gain experience. Colour prejudice was foreign to her temperament. She seemed to mind neither age nor experience. She would not hesitate even to the point of insulting a man and telling to his face what she thought of him. Her impetuosity often landed me in difficulties, but her open and guileless temperament removed them as soon as they were created.

Her sacrifice was great. For a considerable period she did not draw more than six pounds, and refused ever to receive more than ten pounds a month. When I urged her to take more, she would give me a good scolding and say, "I am not here to draw a salary from you. I am here because I like to work with you and I like your ideals." Her courage was equal to her sacrifice. She is one of the few women I have been privileged to come across, with character clear as crystal and courage that would shame a warrior. She is a grown-up woman now. I do not quite know her mind as well as when she was with me, but my contact with this young lady will ever be for me a sacred recollection. I would therefore be false to truth if I kept back what I know about her. She knew neither night nor day in toiling for the cause. She ventured out on errands in the darkness of the night all by herself, and angrily scouted any suggestion of an escort. Thousands of stalwart Indians looked up to her for guidance. When during the Satyagraha days almost every one of the leaders was in jail, she led the movement single-handed. She had the management of thousands, a tremendous amount of correspondence, and the weekly paper, "Indian Opinion," on her hands, but she never wearied.

Gokhale knew every one of my co-workers. He was pleased with many of them, and would often give his estimates of them. He gave the first place to Miss Schlesin amongst all the Indian and European co-workers. "I have rarely met with the sacrifice, the purity and the fearlessness I have seen in Miss Schlesin," said he. "Amongst your co-workers, she takes the first place in my estimation."

About this time Sjt. Madanjit approached me with a proposal to start "Indian Opinion" and sought my advice. He had been already conducting a press, and I approved of his proposal. So the journal was launched in 1904, and Sjt. Mansukhlal Nazar became the first editor. But I had to bear the brunt of the whole work, as indeed for most of the time I had to be practically in charge of the journal. Not that Sjt. Mansukhlal could not carry it on. He had been doing quite an amount of journalism whilst in India, but he would never venture to write on intricate South African problems so long as I was there. He had the greatest confidence in my discernment, and so threw on me the responsibility of attending to the editorial columns.

After all these years I feel that the journal has served the community well. It was never intended to be a commercial concern. So long as it was under my control, the changes in the journal were indicative of changes in my life. "Indian Opinion," like "Young India" and "Navajivan"[1] to-day, was a mirror of part of my life. Week after week I poured out my soul in its columns, and expounded the principles and practice of Satyagraha. During ten years, that is until 1914, excepting the intervals of my enforced rest in prison, there was hardly a single issue without an article from me. I cannot recall a word in these articles set down without thought or deliberation, or a word of conscious exaggeration, or anything merely to please. Indeed the journal had become for me a training in self-restraint, and for friends a medium through which to keep in touch with my thoughts. The critic found very little therein to object to. In fact I know that the tone of "Indian Opinion" compelled the critic to put a curb on his own pen. Satyagraha would probably have been impossible without this weekly paper. For me it became a means for the study of human nature in all its shades. As I always aimed at establishing an intimate and clean bond between the editor and the readers, I was inundated with letters containing the outpourings of my correspond-

[1] *Navajivan* is Mr. Gandhi's Gujerati weekly in India.

ents' hearts. They were friendly, critical or bitter, according to the temper of the writer. It was a fine education for me to study and digest and answer all this correspondence. It was as though the community thought audibly through this correspondence with me. It made me understand thoroughly the responsibility of a journalist, and the hold I secured through it over the community made the future campaign workable, dignified and irresistible.

In the very first month of its existence, I had realised that the sole aim of journalism should be service. The newspaper press is a great power, but as unchained torrents of water submerge whole countrysides and devastate crops, even so an uncontrolled pen serves but to destroy. If the control is from without, it proves more poisonous than want to control. It can be profitable only when exercised from within.

Some of the classes that are rendering us the greatest social service, and whom we Hindus have chosen to regard as "untouchables," are relegated to remote quarters of a town or a village. Even so in Christian Europe the Jews were once its "untouchables," and the quarters that were assigned to them had the odious name "ghettoes." In a similar way we have become the untouchables of South Africa to-day.

The ancient Jews regarded themselves as the chosen people of God, to the exclusion of others, with the result that their descendants were visited with a strange and even unjust retribution. Almost in a similar way the Hindus have considered themselves Aryas or civilised, and a section of their own kith and kin as untouchables, with the result that a strange, if unjust, nemesis is being visited not only upon the Hindus in South Africa, but on the Musalmans and Parsis as well, inasmuch as these belong to the same country and have the same colour as they.

In South Africa we have acquired the odious name of "coolies." The word "coolie" in India means only a porter, but in South Africa it has a contemptuous connotation and means what a pariah or an untouchable means to us, and the quarters assigned to the "coolies" are known as "coolie locations." Johannesburg had one such location. The Indians were densely packed in it, and the area never increased with the increase in population. Beyond arranging to clean the latrines in a haphazard way, the Municipality did nothing to provide any other sanitary facilities, much less good roads or lights. It was hardly likely that it would safeguard its sanitation. The Indians living there were too ignorant of the rules of municipal sanitation to do without the supervision of the Municipality.

The criminal negligence of the Municipality and the ignorance of the Indian settlers thus conspired to render the location thoroughly insanitary. The Municipality, far from doing anything to improve this condition, used the insanitation caused by their own neglect as a lever for destroying the location, and for that purpose obtained from the local legislature authority to dispossess the settlers.

While the Indians were fretting over this state of things, there was a sudden outbreak of the black plague, called the pneumonic plague, more terrible and fatal than the bubonic. Fortunately it was not the Indian location but one of the gold mines in the vicinity of Johannesburg that was responsible for the outbreak. The workers in this mine were for the most part negroes for whose cleanliness their white employers were solely responsible. There were a few Indians also working in connexion with the mine, twenty-three of whom suddenly caught the infection, and they came back one evening to their quarters in the location with an acute attack of the plague. Sjt. Madanjit, who was then going about canvassing subscribers for "Indian Opinion," happened to be in the location at this moment. He was a remarkably fearless man. His heart wept to see these victims of the scourge, and he sent a pencil note to me to the following effect: "There has been a sudden outbreak of the black plague. You must come immediately and take prompt measures, otherwise we should be prepared for dire consequences. Please come immediately."

Sjt. Madanjit bravely broke open the lock of a vacant house, and put all the patients there. I cycled to the location, and wrote to the Town Clerk to inform him of the circumstances. Dr. William Godfrey who was practising in Johannesburg ran to the rescue as soon as he got the news, and became both nurse and doctor to the patients. But twenty-three patients were more than three of us could cope with. It is my faith based on experience that if one's heart is pure calamity brings in its train men and measures to fight it. I had at that time four Indians in my office,—Sjts. Kalyandas, Maneklal and two whose names I cannot recollect. Kalyandas had been entrusted to me by his father. I have rarely come across, in South Africa, anyone more obliging and willing to render implicit obedience than he was. He was fortunately unmarried then, and I therefore did not hesitate to impose on him duties involving risks, however great. Maneklal I had got hold of in Johannesburg. He too, so far as I can remember, was unmarried. So I decided to sacrifice all the four,—call them clerks, co-workers or sons. There was no need at all to consult Kalyandas. The others expressed their readiness as soon as they were asked. "Where you are, we will also go," was the short and sweet reply they gave.

It was a terrible night,—that night of vigil and nursing. I had nursed a number of patients before, but never one attacked by the black plague. Dr. Godfrey's pluck proved infectious. There was not much nursing required. To give them their doses of medicine, to attend to their wants, to keep them and their beds clean and tidy, and to cheer them up, was all that we had to do. The indefatigable zeal and fearlessness with which the youths worked delighted me beyond measure. One could understand the bravery of Dr. Godfrey and of an experienced man like Sjt. Madanjit. But oh for the spirit of these youths!

The Town Clerk expressed his gratefulness to me for having taken charge of the vacant house and the patients. He frankly confessed that the Town Council had no immediate means of coping with such an emergency but that they would render all the help in their power. Once awakened to a sense of its duty, the Municipality made no delay in taking prompt measures.

The next day they placed a vacant shed at my disposal, and suggested that the patients be removed there; but the Municipality did not undertake to clean the premises. The building was unkempt and unclean. We cleaned it up ourselves, raised a few beds and other necessities through the offices of charitable Indians, and improvised a temporary hospital. The Municipality lent the services of a nurse. Dr. Godfrey still remained in charge.

The nurse was a kindly lady and would fain have attended to the patients, but we rarely allowed her to touch the patients, lest she should catch the contagion.

Twenty died whilst we were still in the shed. Meanwhile the Municipality was busy taking other measures. There was a lazaretto for contagious diseases about seven miles from Johannesburg. The three surviving patients were removed to tents near the lazaretto, and arrangements were made to send fresh cases also there. We were thus relieved from our work. In the course of a few days we learnt that the good nurse had had an attack and immediately succumbed.

On the outbreak of the plague, I had addressed a strong letter to the press holding the Municipality responsible for the negligence after the location came into its possession and for the outbreak of the plague itself. This letter secured me Mr. Henry Polak, and was partly responsible for the friendship of the late Rev. Joseph Doke.

CHAPTER XI

"UNTO THIS LAST"

I HAVE SAID in the earlier chapter, that I used to have my meals at a vegetarian restaurant. Here I met Mr. Albert West. We used to meet here every evening and go out walking after dinner. Mr. West was a partner in a small printing press. He read my letter in the press about the outbreak of the plague, and not finding me in the restaurant felt uneasy.

My co-workers and I had reduced our diet since the outbreak, as I had long made it a rule to go on a light diet during epidemics. I had therefore given up my evening dinner these days. I knew the proprietor of the restaurant very well, and I had informed him that as I was engaged in nursing the plague patients I wanted to avoid the contacts of friends as much as possible and therefore I would finish lunch before the other guests arrived.

Not finding me in the restaurant for a day or two, Mr. West knocked at my door early one morning just as I was getting ready to go out for a walk. When I opened the door he said, "I did not find you in the restaurant and was really afraid lest something might have happened to you. So I decided to come and see you in the morning in order to make sure of finding you at home. Well, here I am, at your disposal. I am ready to help in nursing the patients. You know that I have no one depending upon me."

I expressed my gratefulness and answered without taking even a second to think: "I will not have you as a nurse.

If there are no more cases, we ought to be free in a day or two. There is one thing, however."

"Yes, what is it?"

"Could you take charge of the 'Indian Opinion' press at Durban?"

"You know that I have a press. Most probably I will go, but may I give my final reply in the evening? We shall talk it over during our evening walk."

I was delighted. We had the talk, and he agreed to go. Salary was no consideration with him, as money was not his motive. But a salary of ten pounds per month and a part of the profit was fixed up. The very next day Mr. West left for Durban by the evening mail. From that day until the time I left the shores of South Africa, he remained a partner of my joys and sorrows.

Mr. West belonged to a peasant family in Louth. He had an ordinary school education, but had learnt a good deal in the school of experience and by dint of self-help. I have always known him to be a pure, sober, God-fearing, humane Englishman.

Though my co-workers and I were relieved of the charge of patients, there were many things arising out of the plague still to be disposed of. I have dealt with the negligence of the Municipality about the location. But it was wide awake so far as the health of its white citizens was concerned. Now it poured out money like water for scotching the plague. In spite of the many sins of omission and commission against the Indians that I laid at the door of the Municipality, I could not help commending its solicitude for the white citizens and I rendered it as much help as I could in its laudable efforts. I have an impression that if I had withheld my co-operation, the task would have been more difficult for the Municipality, and it would not have hesitated to use armed force and to do its worst. But all that was averted. The Municipal authorities were pleased over the Indians' behaviour and much of the future work regarding plague measures was simplified. I used all the influence I could command with the Indians to make them submit to the requirements of the Municipality. It was far from easy for the Indians to go all that length, but I do not remember any one having resisted my advice.

The location was put under a strong guard, passage in and out being made impossible without permission. My co-workers and I had free permits of entry and exit. The object was to make all the people in the location vacate it and live under canvas for three weeks in an open plain about thirteen miles from Johannesburg and then to set fire to the location. The settling down under canvas with provisions and other necessaries was bound to take some time, and a guard became necessary during the interval. The people were in an awful fright, but my constant presence was a consolation to them.

The location was put to the flames at once after its evacuation. About this very time, and for the same reason, the Municipality had burnt down all its timber in the market, and incurred a loss of about ten thousand pounds. The reason for this drastic step was the discovery of some dead rats in the market. Thus the Municipality had to go in for heavy expenditure, but it successfully arrested the further progress of the plague, and the city breathed freely once more.

The plague enhanced my influence with the poorer Indians, and increased my business with my responsibility.

Some of the new contacts with Europeans became so close that they added considerably to my moral obligations.

I made the acquaintance of Mr. Henry Polak in the vegetarian restaurant, just like that of Mr. West. One evening a young man dining at a table away from me sent me his card expressing a desire to see me. I invited him to come to my table, which he did.

"I am sub-editor of the 'Critic'," said he. "When I read your letter to the press about the plague, I felt strongly moved to see you. I am glad to have this opportunity."

Mr. Polak's candour drew me to him. The same evening we got to know each other and we seemed to hold very closely similar views on the essential things. He liked the simple life. He had a wonderful faculty of translating into practice anything that appealed to his intellect. Some of the changes that he had made in his own life were as prompt as they were radical.

"Indian Opinion" was getting more and more expensive every day. The very first report from Mr. West was alarming. He wrote: "I do not expect from the concern the profit that you think there would be. I am afraid there may be even a loss. The books are not in order. There are heavy arrears to be recovered, but one can make no head or tail of them. Considerable overhauling will have to be done. But all this need not alarm you. I shall try to put things right as best I can. I remain on, whether there is profit or not."

Mr. West might have left when he discovered that there was no profit, and I could not have blamed him. In fact, he had a right to arraign me for having described the concern as profitable without proper proof. But he never even once uttered a word of complaint. I have, however, an impression that this discovery must have led Mr. West to regard me as credulous.

On receipt of Mr. West's letter I left for Natal. I had taken Mr. Polak into my fullest confidence. He came to see me off at the station, and left with me a book to read during the journey, which he said I was sure to like. It was Ruskin's "Unto this Last."

It was impossible to lay the book aside, once I had begun it. It gripped me. It was a twenty-four hours' journey from Johannesburg to Natal. The train reached Durban in the evening. I could not get sleep that night. I determined to change my life in the light of the book. I had not read a single book of Ruskin's before this. During the days of my education I had read practically nothing outside textbooks, and after I had launched into active life I had very little time left for reading. I cannot therefore claim much book knowledge. I believe I have not lost much because of this enforced restraint. On the contrary, the limited reading may be said to have enabled me fairly to digest what I did read. The one book that brought about an instantaneous and practical transformation in my life was "Unto this Last" and I translated it later into Gujarati.

My belief is that I discovered some of my deepest convictions reflected in this great book of Ruskin and that is why the book so captured me and made me transform my life. A poet is one who can call forth the good latent in the human breast. Poets do not influence all alike, for every one is not evolved in an equal measure.

This is how I understood Ruskin's teachings:

1. The good of the individual is contained in the good of all.

2. A lawyer's labour has the same value as the barber's, inasmuch as all have the same right of earning their livelihood from their labour.

3. A life of labour, i.e. of the tiller of the soil and handicraftsman, is the life worth living.

The first of these I knew. The second I had dimly realised. The third had never occurred to me. Ruskin made it as clear as possible for me that the second and the third were contained in the first. I awoke with the dawn, ready to reduce these principles to practice.

Then I talked the whole thing over with Mr. West, described to him the effect that Ruskin's book had produced on my mind, and proposed that "Indian Opinion" should be removed to a farm, on which every one should labour, drawing the same living wage, and attending to the press work in spare time. Mr. West approved of the proposal, and three pounds was laid down as monthly allowance, irrespective of colour or nationality.

But it was a question whether all of the ten workers in the press would agree to go and settle on a farm, and be satisfied with a bare maintenance. We therefore proposed that those who could not fit in with the scheme should continue to draw their salaries and gradually try to reach the goal of becoming members of the settlement.

Among the men working in the press was Chhaganlal Gandhi, one of my cousins. I had broached the proposal to him at the same time as to West. He had a wife and children, but he had from childhood chosen to be trained and work under me. He had full faith in me. So without any argument he agreed to the proposal, and has been with me ever since. There was the machinist, Govindswami, who also fell in with the proposal. The rest did not join the scheme, but agreed to go wherever I removed the press.

I do not think I took more than two days to fix up these things with the men. Thereafter I at once advertised for a piece of land situated near a railyway station in the vicinity of Durban. An offer came in respect of Phoenix. Mr. West and I went to inspect the estate, and within a week purchased twenty acres of land. It had a nice little spring and a few orange and mango trees. Adjoining it was an area of eighty acres which had many more fruit trees and a dilapidated cottage. We purchased this too, both costing a thousand pounds.

Mr. Parsee Rustomji was always my help in such enterprises. He liked the project. He placed at my disposal second-hand corrugated iron sheets of a big shed and other building material. Some Indian carpenters who had worked with me in the Boer War helped me in erecting a shed for the press.

I now tried to carry with me and to draw to Phoenix those relations and friends who had come with me from India to try their fortune and were engaged in some business or other. They had come in search of wealth and it was a difficult job to persuade them, but some agreed. Of these I can single out only Maganlal Gandhi's name here. The others went back to business. Maganlal Gandhi left his business for good to cast in his lot with me, and by his ability, sacrifice and devotion he stands foremost among my original co-workers in these ethical experiments, and as a self-taught handicraftsman his place is unique among them.

Thus the Phoenix Settlement was started in 1904, and

in spite of numerous odds "Indian Opinion" continues to be published at the Settlement.

It was no easy thing to issue the first number of the paper from Phoenix Settlement. If I had not taken two precautions, the first issue would have had to be dropped altogether. There was little inclination on my part to have an engine to work the press: I had thought that hand-power would be more in keeping with the atmosphere where agricultural work too was to be done by the hand. But as it had not appeared feasible, we had installed an oil-engine. I had however suggested to West to have something handy to fall back upon in case the engine failed. He had therefore a wheel which could be worked by the hand.

The first night was unforgettable. The pages of type were locked, but the engine refused to work. We had got out from Durban an engineer to put up the engine. He and West tried their hardest, but to no avail. Every one was anxious. West in despair at last came to me, with eyes wet, and said: "The engine will not work, and I am afraid we cannot issue the paper in time."

"If that is the case," I said, comforting him, "we cannot help it. But it is no use shedding tears over it. Let us do whatever else it is humanly possible to do. What about the hand wheel?"

"Where have we the men to work it? We are not enough to cope with it. It requires relays of four men each, and our own men are dead tired."

Building work in the Settlement had not yet been completed, and so the carpenters were still with us. They were sleeping on the press floor. I said, pointing to them, "But can't we make use of these carpenters? We may have a whole night of work. I think this device is still open to us."

"I dare not myself wake up the carpenters," said West, "and our men are really too tired."

"Well, that's for me to negotiate," said I.

So I woke up the carpenters and requested their co-operation. They needed no pressure. They said, "If we cannot be called upon in an emergency what use are we? You rest yourselves and we will work the wheel. For us it is easy work." Our own men were of course ready.

West was greatly delighted and started singing a hymn as we set to work. I partnered the carpenters, and all the rest joined turn by turn, and thus we went on until 7 a.m. There was still quite a lot to do. So I suggested to West that the engineer might be asked to get up and try again to start the engine, so that if he succeeded we might finish in time.

West woke him up, and he immediately went into the engine room. And—lo and behold!—the engine worked almost as soon as he started it. The whole press rang with peals of joy. "How could this be? How is it that all our labours last night were of no avail, and this morning it has been set going as though there was nothing wrong with it?" I enquired.

"It is difficult to say," said West. "Machines sometimes seem to behave as though they required rest like us."

It has been a perpetual regret with me that though I started the settlement at Phoenix I could stay there only for brief intervals. My original idea was gradually to retire from legal practice, settle at Phoenix, earn my livelihood by manual work there, and find the joy of service in the fulfilment of Phoenix. But it was not to be. I have found in my experience that man makes his plans to be often upset by God; but I have also seen that where the ultimate goal is the search for truth, no matter how one's plans are frustrated, the issue is never injurious and is often better than expected. The unexpected turn that Phoenix took and the unexpected happenings were certainly not injurious.

In order to enable every one of us to make a living on manual labour, we parcelled out the land round the press in pieces of three acres each. One of these fell to my lot. On all these plots, in spite of ourselves, we were obliged to build houses with corrugated iron. Our desire was to have mud huts thatched with straw, or small brick houses such as would be fitting for ordinary peasants, but it could not be. They would have been more expensive and would have meant more time, and every one was eager to settle down as soon as possible.

On my return to Johannesburg, I informed Polak of the important changes I had made. His joy knew no bounds to learn that the loan of his book had been so fruitful. "Is it not possible," he asked, "for me to take part in the new venture?" "Certainly," said I. "You may if you like to join the Settlement." "I am quite ready," he replied, "if you will admit me." And so he joined us.

His determination captured me. He gave a month's notice to his chief to be relieved from the "Critic," and reached Phoenix in due season. By his sociability he won the hearts of all and soon became a member of the family. Simplicity was so much in his nature that far from feeling the life at Phoenix in any way strange or hard, he took to it like a fish to water.

CHAPTER XII

THE ZULU REBELLION

NOT LONG AFTER THIS, the papers brought news of an outbreak of Zulu "rebellion" in Natal. I bore no grudge against the Zulus; they had harmed no Indian in South Africa and I had grave doubts about the "rebellion" itself. But I then believed that the British Empire existed for the welfare of the world. A genuine sense of loyalty prevented me from wishing ill to the Empire. The rightness or otherwise of the "rebellion" was therefore not likely to affect my decision. Natal had a Volunteers' Defence Force, and it was open to it to recruit more men. I read that this force had already been mobilised to quell the "rebellion." Considering myself a citizen of Natal and being intimately connected with it, I wrote to the Governor, expressing my readiness, if necessary, to form an Indian Ambulance Corps. He sent immediately an affirmative reply. I had not expected such prompt acceptance of my offer. Fortunately I had made all the necessary arrangements even before I wrote the letter. If my offer were accepted, I had decided to break up the Johannesburg home. Polak was to have a smaller house and Mrs. Gandhi was to go and settle at Phoenix. I had her full co-operation in this decision and I do not remember her having ever stood in my way in matters like this. As soon therefore as the reply came from the Governor, I went to Durban and appealed for men. A large contingent was not necessary. We were a party of twenty-four, of whom, besides me, four were Gujaratis.

The rest were ex-indentured men from South India excepting one who was a "free" Pathan.[1]

In order to give me a status and to facilitate work, as also in accordance with the existing convention, the Chief Medical Officer appointed me to the temporary rank of Sergeant Major and three men selected by me to be sergeants and one to be corporal. On reaching the scene of the "rebellion," I saw that there was nothing there to justify the name of "rebellion." There was no resistance that one could see. The reason why the disturbance was magnified into a rebellion was that a Zulu chief had advised non-payment of a new tax imposed on the Zulus, and had assegaied a sergeant who had gone to collect the tax. Whatever may be the case, my heart was with the Zulus; and I was greatly delighted on reaching the headquarters to be told that our main work was to be to nurse the wounded Zulus. The Medical Officer in charge welcomed us. He said the white people were not willing nurses for the wounded Zulus, that their wounds were festering, and that he was at his wits' end. He hailed our arrival as a godsend for those innocent people, and he equipped us with bandages, disinfectants, etc., and took us to the improvised hospital. The Zulus were delighted to see us. The white soldiers at first would peep through the railings that separated us from them and try to dissuade us from attending to the wounds. And as we would not heed them, they would be enraged and pour abuse on the Zulus. Gradually I came into closer touch with these soldiers and they ceased to interfere.

The wounded who were in our charge were not wounded in battle. A section of them had been taken prisoners as

[1] I. e. not under indenture.

suspects. The general had sentenced them to be flogged and the flogging had caused severe sores. These, through want of proper attention, were festering. The others were Zulu friendlies. Although these had badges given them to distinguish them from the "enemy," they had been shot at by the soldiers by mistake. Besides this work I had to compound and dispense prescriptions for the white soldiers. This was easy enough for me, as I had received a year's training in Dr. Booth's little hospital. This work brought me in close contact with many Europeans. We were attached to a swift moving column. It had orders to march wherever danger was reported. It was for the most part cavalry. As soon as our camp was moved, we had to follow on foot with our stretchers on our shoulders. Twice or thrice we had to march forty miles a day. But wherever we went, I am thankful that we had God's good work to do. We had to carry to the camp on our stretchers the Zulu friendlies inadvertently wounded and to attend upon them as nurses.

The Zulu "rebellion" was full of new experiences for me and gave me much food for thought. The Boer War had not brought home to me the horrors of war with anything like the vividness that the "rebellion" did. This was no war but a man hunt, not only in my opinion, but also in that of many Englishmen with whom I had occasion to talk. To hear every morning reports of the soldiers' rifles exploding like crackers in innocent hamlets, and to live in the midst of them was a trial. But I swallowed the bitter draught, especially when the work of my corps consisted only in nursing the wounded Zulus. I could see that but for us the Zulus would have been uncared for. This work, therefore, eased my conscience.

But there was much else to set one a-thinking. It was a sparsely populated part of the country. Few and far between in hills and dales were the scattered kraals of the simple and so-called "uncivilised" Zulus. Marching, with or without the wounded, through these solemn solitudes, I often fell into deep thought.

I pondered over Brahmacharya [2] and its implications, and my convictions took deeper root. I had not realised then how indispensable continence was for self-realisation, but I clearly saw that one aspiring to serve humanity with his whole soul could not do without it. It was borne in upon me that I would have more and more occasions of service of the kind I was rendering, and that I should find myself unequal to my task if I was engaged in the pleasures of family life and in the propagation and rearing of children. In a word, I could not live both after the flesh and the spirit. On the present occasion, for instance, I should not have been able to throw myself into the fray, had my wife been expecting a baby. Without the observance of Brahmacharya, service of the family would be inconsistent with service of the community. With it, on the other hand, both would be perfectly consistent. So thinking, I became rather impatient to take a final vow. The prospect of the vow brought a certain kind of exultation. Imagination also found free play and opened out interminable vistas of service.

On my arrival at Phoenix I broached with zest the subject of Brahmacharya to Chhaganlal, Maganlal, West and others. They liked the idea and accepted the necessity of taking the vow; but they also represented the difficulties of the task. Some of them set themselves bravely to

[2] Strict continence, or chastity.

observe Brahmacharya, and some, I know, succeeded. I too took the plunge,—the vow to observe Brahmacharya for life. I must confess that I had not then fully realised the magnitude and immensity of the task I had undertaken. The difficulties are even to-day staring me in the face. The importance of the vow is being more and more borne in upon me. Life, without Brahmacharya, appears to me to be insipid and animal-like. The brute by nature knows no self-restraint. Man is Man, because he is capable of self-restraint. What formerly appeared to me to be extravagant praise of Brahmacharya in our religious books seemed now, with increasing clearness every day, to be absolutely proper and founded in experience.

I saw that Brahmacharya, which is full of that wonderful potency, can by no means be an easy affair, and certainly not a mere matter of the body. Brahmacharya begins with bodily restraint, but it does not end there. Its perfection precludes even an impure thought. A true Brahmachari will not even dream of satisfying fleshly appetite, and until he is in that condition he has a great deal of ground to cover.

For me the observance of even bodily Brahmacharya has been full of difficulties. To-day I may say that I feel myself fairly safe; but I have yet to achieve complete mastery over thought which is so essential. Not that the will or effort is lacking, but it is yet a problem to me wherefrom undesirable thoughts spring their insidious invasions. I have no doubt that man possesses the key by which to lock out undesirable thoughts; but every one has to find it out for himself. Saints and seers have left their experiences for us; but they have given us no infallible and universal prescriptions. For perfection or freedom from error comes only out of grace and so seekers after God have left us sacred texts, such as "Ramanama," [3] hallowed by their own austerities and charged with their own purity. Without an unreserved surrender to His grace, complete mastery over thought is impossible. This is the teaching of every great book of religion, and I am realising the truth of it every moment of my striving after that perfect Brahmacharya.

Events were so shaping themselves in Johannesburg that this self-purification on my part was, as it were, a preliminary to Satyagraha.[4] I can now see that all the principal events of my life culminating in this vow were secretly preparing me for it. The principle, called Satyagraha, came into being before that name was invented. Indeed, when it was born, I myself could not say what it was. In Gujarati also we used the English phrase "passive resistance" to describe it. When in a meeting of Europeans I found that the term "passive resistance" was too narrowly construed; that it was supposed to be a weapon of the weak; that it could be characterised by hatred, and that it could finally manifest itself as violence, I had to demur to all these statements and explain the real nature of the Indian movement. It was clear that a new word must be coined by the Indians to denote their struggle.

But I could not for the life of me find out a new name, and therefore offered a nominal prize through "Indian Opinion" to the reader who made the best suggestion on the point. As a result Maganlal Gandhi coined the word "Sadagraha" (Sat—truth, Agraha—firmness) and won the prize. But in order to make it clearer I

[3] Recitation of the name of Rama.

[4] Mr. Gandhi's name for passive resistance.

changed the word to "Satyagraha" which has since become current in Gujarati as a designation for the struggle. The history of the Satyagraha struggle is for all practical purposes a history of my life in South Africa and especially of my experiments with Truth in that sub-continent.

Thrice in her life Mrs. Gandhi narrowly escaped death through serious illness. The cure was due to household remedies. At the time of the first of these occasions, Satyagraha was going on or was about to commence. She had frequent hæmorrhage. A medical friend advised a surgical operation, to which she agreed after some hesitation. She was extremely emaciated, and the doctor had to perform the operation without chloroform. It was successful but she had to suffer much pain. She, however, went through it with wonderful bravery. The doctor and his wife who nursed her were all attention. This was in Durban. The doctor gave me leave to go to Johannesburg and told me not to have any anxiety about the patient.

In a few days, however, I received a letter to the effect that Kasturbai was worse, too weak to sit up in bed, and had once become unconscious. The doctor knew that he might not, without my consent, give her wine or meat. So he telephoned to me at Johannesburg for permission to give her beef tea. I telephoned back saying I could not grant the permission, but that if she was in a condition to express her wish in the matter she might be consulted, and she was free to do as she liked. "But," said the doctor, "I refuse to consult the patient's wishes in the matter. You must come yourself. If you do not leave me free to prescribe whatever diet I like, I will not hold myself responsible for your wife's recovery."

I took the train for Durban the same day, and met the doctor, who quietly broke this news to me: "I had already given Mrs. Gandhi beef tea when I telephoned to you."

"Now, doctor, I call this a fraud," said I.

"There is no question" he replied, "of fraud in prescribing medicine or diet for a patient. In fact we doctors consider it a virtue to deceive our patients or their relatives, if thereby we can save human life."

I was deeply pained, but kept cool. The doctor was a good man and a personal friend. He and his wife had laid me under a debt of gratitude, but I was not prepared to put up with his medical morals.

"Doctor, tell me what you propose to do now. I would never allow my wife to be given meat or beef, even if it means her death, unless of course she desires to take it."

"You are welcome to your philosophy. I tell you that so long as you keep your wife under my treatment I should have the option to give her anything I like. If you don't like this, I must regretfully ask you to remove her. I can't see her die under my roof."

"Do you mean to say that I must remove her at once?"

"When did I ever ask you to remove her? I only want to be left entirely free. If you do so, my wife and I will do all that is possible for her, and you may go without the least anxiety on her score. But if you will not understand this simple thing, you compel me to ask you to remove your wife from my place."

I think one of my sons was with me. He entirely agreed with me, and said that Kasturbai should certainly not be given beef tea. I next spoke to my wife. She was really too weak to be consulted in this matter. But I thought it my painful duty to do so. I told her what had passed between the doctor and myself. She gave a resolute reply: "I will not take beef tea. It is a rare thing in this world to be born as a human being; and I would far rather die in your arms than pollute my body with such abominations."

I pleaded with her. I told her that she was not bound to follow me. I cited to her the instances of Hindu friends and acquaintances who had no scruples about taking meat or wine as medicine. But she was adamant. "No," said she, "pray remove me at once."

I was delighted. Not without some agitation, I decided to remove her. I informed the doctor of her resolve. "What a callous man you are!" he exclaimed. "You should have been ashamed to broach the matter to her in her present condition. I tell you your wife is not in a fit state to be removed. She cannot stand the least little hustling. I shouldn't be surprised if she died on the way. But if you must persist, you are free to do so. If you will not give her beef tea, I will not take the risk of keeping her under my roof for even a single day."

So we decided to leave the place at once. It was drizzling and the station was some distance. We had to take the train from Durban for Phoenix, whence our settlement was reached by a road of two miles and a half. I was undoubtedly taking a very great risk, but I trusted in God and proceeded with my task. I sent a messenger to Phoenix in advance, with a message to West to receive us at the station with a hammock, a bottle of hot milk and one of hot water, and six men to carry Mrs. Gandhi in the hammock. I got a rickshaw to enable me to take her by the next available train, put her into it in that dangerous condition, and marched away.

Kasturbai needed no cheering up. On the contrary, she comforted me, saying, "Nothing will happen to me. Don't worry."

She was mere skin and bone, having had no nourishment for days. The station platform was very long, and as the rickshaw could not be taken inside, we had to walk some distance before we could reach the train. So I carried her in my arms and put her into the train. From Phoenix we carried her in the hammock, and there she slowly picked up strength under hydropathic treatment.

Within two or three days of our arrival at Phoenix a Swami came to our place. He had heard of the resolute way in which we had rejected the doctor's advice and he had out of sympathy come to plead with us. My second and third sons, Manilal and Ramdas, were present when the Swami came. He held forth on the religious harmlessness of taking meat, citing authorities from Manu.[5] I did not like his carrying on this disputation in the presence of my wife, but I suffered him to do so out of courtesy. I knew the verses from Manu and did not need them for my conviction. Also I knew that there was a school which regarded these verses as apocryphal; but even if they were not, I held my views on vegetarianism independently of religious texts, and Kasturbai's faith was unshakable. The scriptural texts were a sealed book to her, but the traditional religion of her forefathers was enough for her. The children swore by their father's creed and so they made light of the Swami's discourse. But Kasturbai put an end to the dialogue at once. "Swamiji," she

[5] The earliest Hindu lawgiver.

said, "whatever you may say, I do not want to recover by means of beef tea. Pray don't worry me any more. You may discuss the thing with my husband and children if you like. But my mind has been made up."

I had read in some books on vegetarianism that salt was not a necessary article of diet for man, that on the contrary saltless diet was better for the health. From this I had deduced that a Brahmachari benefited by a saltless diet. I had read and realised that the weak bodied should avoid pulses. I was very fond of them. Now it happened that Kasturbai, who had a brief respite after that operation, had again begun getting hæmorrhage and the malady seemed to be obstinate. Hydropathic treatment by itself did not answer. Kasturbai had not much faith in my remedies though she did not resist them. She certainly did not ask for outside help. So when all my remedies had failed, I entreated her to give up salt and pulses. She would not agree, however much I pleaded with her, supporting myself with authorities. At last she challenged me saying that even I could not give up these articles if I was advised to do so. I was pained and delighted at the same time—delighted in that I got an opportunity to shower my love on her. I said to her: "You are mistaken. If I was ailing and the doctor advised me to give up these or any other articles, I should unhesitatingly do so. But there! Without any medical advice I give up salt and pulses for one year, whether you do so or not."

She was rudely shocked and exclaimed in deep sorrow: "Pray forgive me. Knowing you as I do, I ought not to have provoked you. I promise to abstain from these things; but for heaven's sake take back your vow. This is too hard on me!"

"It is very good for you," said I, "to give up these articles and I have not the slightest doubt that you will be all the better without them. As for me, I cannot retract a vow seriously taken, and it is sure to benefit me; for all restraint, whatever prompts it, is wholesome for man. You will therefore leave me alone. It will be a test for me, and a moral support to you in carrying out your resolve."

So she gave me up. "You are too obstinate. You will listen to none!" she said, and sought relief in tears.

I would like to count this incident as an instance of Satyagraha and as one of the sweetest recollections of my life.

After this Kasturbai began to pick up quickly. Whether this was the result of the saltless and pulseless diet or of the other consequent changes in it; whether it was the result of my strict vigilance in exacting observance of the other rules of life, or an effect of the mental exhilaration produced by the incident, I cannot say. But she rallied quickly, hæmorrhage completely stopped, and I added somewhat to my reputation as a quack.

As for me, I was all the better for the new denials. I never craved for the things I had left; the year sped away, and I found the senses to be more subdued than ever. The experiment stimulated the inclination for self-restraint, and I continued the abstention from the articles until long after I returned to India.

I have tried the experiment of a saltless and pulseless diet of many of my co-workers, and with good results in South Africa. Medically there may be two opinions as to its value, but morally I have no doubt that all self-denial is good for the soul. The diet of a man of self-restraint must be different from that of a man of pleasure, just as their ways of life are different. Aspirants after Brahmacharya often defeat their own end by adopting courses suited to a life of pleasure.

CHAPTER XIII

SPIRITUAL TRAINING

THE SPIRITUAL TRAINING of the boys was a much more difficult matter than their physical and mental training. I relied little on religious books for the training of the spirit. Of course I believed that every student should be acquainted with the elements of his own religion and have a general knowledge of his own scriptures and therefore I provided for such knowledge as best I could. But that, to my mind, was part of the intellectual training. Long before I undertook the education of the youngsters of the Tolstoy Farm[1] I had realised that the training of the spirit was a thing by itself. To develop the spirit is to build character and to gain a knowledge of God and to have self-realisation. And I held that this was an essential part of the training of the young, and that all other training without culture of the spirit was of no use, and might be even harmful.

How then was this spiritual training to be given? I made the children memorise and recite hymns, and I read to them from books on moral training. But that was far from satisfying me. As I came into closer contact with them I saw that it was not through books that one could impart training of the spirit. Just as physical training was to be imparted through physical exercise, and the intellectual through intellectual exercise, even so the training of the spirit was possible only through the exercise of the spirit. And this depended on the life and character of the teacher. It would be idle for me, if I were a liar, to teach

[1] See "Mahatma Gandhi's Ideas," pp. 206-214.

my boys to tell the truth. A coward of a teacher would never succeed in making his boys valiant, and a stranger to self-restraint could never teach his pupils the value of self-restraint. I saw therefore that I must be an eternal object lesson for the boys and girls living with me. They thus became my teachers, and I learnt that I must be good and live straight, if only for their sake. I may say that the increasing discipline and restraint I imposed on myself at the Tolstoy Farm was mostly due to those wards of mine.

One of them was wild, unruly, given to lying, and quarrelsome. On one occasion he broke out most violently. I was exasperated. I never punished my boys, but this time I was very angry. I tried to reason with him. But he was adamant, and even tried to overreach me. At last I picked up a ruler lying at hand and delivered a blow on his arm. I trembled as I struck him, and I daresay he noticed it. This was an entirely novel experience for them all. The boy cried out and begged to be forgiven. He cried not because the beating was painful to him; he could, if he had been so minded, have paid me back in the same coin, being a stoutly built youth of seventeen. But he realised my pain in being driven to this violent resource. Never again after this incident did he disobey me. But I still repent that violence. I am afraid I exhibited before him that day, not the spirit, but the brute in me.

I have always been opposed to corporal punishment. I remember only one occasion on which I physically punished one of my sons. I have therefore never until this day been able to decide whether I was right or wrong in using the ruler. Probably it was improper, for it was prompted by anger and a desire to punish. Had it been an expression only of my distress I should have considered it justified. But the motive in this case was mixed. This incident set me thinking and taught me a better method of correcting students. I do not know how that method would have availed on the occasion in question. The youngster soon forgot the incident and I do not think he ever showed great improvement. But the incident made me understand better the duty of a teacher towards his pupils. Cases of misconduct on the part of the boys often occurred after this, but I never resorted to corporal punishment. Thus in my endeavour to impart spiritual training to the boys and girls under me I came to understand better and better the power of the spirit.

It was at Tolstoy Farm that Mr. Kallenbach [2] drew my attention to a problem that had never before struck me. As I have already said, some of the boys at the Farm were bad and unruly. There were loafers, too, amongst them. With these my three boys came in daily contact, as also did other children of the same type as my own sons. This troubled Mr. Kallenbach, but his attention was centred on the impropriety of keeping my boys with those unruly youngsters.

One day he spoke out. "Your way," he said, "of mixing your own boys with the bad ones does not appeal to me. It can have only one result. They will become demoralised through this bad company."

I do not remember whether the question puzzled me at the moment, but I recollect what I said to him:

"How can I distinguish between my boys and the loafers? I am equally responsible for both. The youngsters have come because I invited them. To tell you the truth,

[2] See "Mahatma Gandhi's Ideas," pp. 206-214.

it is quite likely that they and their guardians believe that by having come here they have laid me under an obligation. That they have to put up with a good deal of inconvenience here, you and I know very well. But my duty is clear. I must have them here, and therefore my boys also must needs live with them. And surely you do not want me to teach my boys to feel from to-day that they are superior to other boys! To put that sense of superiority into their heads would be to lead them astray. This association with other boys will be a good discipline for them, and they will, of their own accord, learn to discriminate between good and evil. Why should we not believe that if there is really anything good in them, it is bound to react on their companions? However that may be, I cannot help keeping them here, and if that means some risk, we must run it."

Mr. Kallenbach shook his head, but the result, I think, cannot be said to have been bad. My sons were not any the worse for the experiment. In fact I can see that they gained something. If there was the slightest trace of superiority in them, it was destroyed; and they learnt to mix with all kinds of children. They were tested and disciplined. This and similar experiments have shown me that if good children are taught together with bad ones and thrown into their company, they will lose nothing, provided the experiment is conducted under the watchful care of their parents and guardians.

It does not necessarily follow that children wrapped up in cotton-wool are proof to all temptation or contamination. It is true, however, that when boys and girls of all kinds of upbringing are kept and taught together the parents and the teachers are put to the severest test. They have continually to be on their guard.

It became increasingly clear to me, day by day, how very difficult it was to bring up and educate boys and girls in the right way. If I was to be their real teacher and guardian, I must touch their hearts, I must share their joys and sorrows, I must help them to solve the problems that faced them, I must take along the right channel the surging aspirations of their youth. Once when I was in Johannesburg I received the tidings of the moral fall of two of the inmates of the Ashram. News of an apparent failure or reverse in the Satyagraha struggle would not shock me, but this news came upon me like a thunderbolt. The same day I took the train for Phoenix. Mr. Kallenbach insisted on accompanying me. He had noticed the state I was in. He would not brook the thought of my going alone, for he happened to be the bearer of the tidings which had so upset me. On the way my duty became clear to me. I felt that the guardian or the teacher was responsible, to some extent at least, for the lapse of his pupil. My responsibility in the matter in question became therefore clear to me as daylight. My wife had already warned me, but being of a trusting nature I had ignored her warning. I also felt that the parties to the guilt could be made to realise my distress, and the depth of their fall, only if I did some penance for it. So I imposed upon myself a fast for seven days and a vow of having only one meal for a period of four months and a half. Mr. Kallenbach tried to dissuade me, but in vain. He ultimately accepted the propriety of the penance, and insisted on joining me. I could not resist his transparent affection.

The decision meant a heavy load off my mind, and I

felt considerably relieved. The anger against the guilty parties subsided, and gave place to the purest pity for them. Thus considerably relieved, I reached Phoenix. I made further investigation and acquainted myself with some more details I needed to know. My penance pained everybody, but it cleared the atmosphere. Every one came to realise what a terrible thing it was to be sinful, and the bond that bound me to the boys and girls became stronger and truer. A circumstance arising out of this incident compelled me, a little while after, to go into a fast for fourteen days, the results of which exceeded even my expectations.

It is not my purpose to make out from these incidents that it is the duty of a teacher to resort to fasting whenever there is a delinquency on the part of his pupils. But I hold that some occasions do call for this drastic remedy. But it presupposes clearness of vision and spiritual fitness. Where there is no true love between the teacher and the pupil, where the pupil's delinquency has not touched the very being of the teacher, where the pupil has no respect for the teacher, fasting is out of place and may even be harmful. Though there is thus room for doubting the propriety of fasts in such cases, there is no question about the teacher's responsibility for the errors of his pupil.

The first penance did not prove difficult for any of us. I had no necessity of stopping any of my normal activities. And it may be recalled that during the whole of this period I was a strict fruitarian. The latter part of the second fast went fairly hard with me. I had not then completely understood the wonderful efficacy of Ramanama, and my capacity for suffering was to that extent less. I did not know too the technique of fasting, especially the necessity of drinking plenty of water however nauseating or distasteful it may be. And then the fact that the first fast had been an easy affair had made me rather careless as to the second. During the second fast I drank very little water, as it was distasteful and produced nausea. The throat became parched and weak and during the last days I could speak only in a very low voice. In spite of this, however, my work was carried on through dictation where writing was necessary. Regularly readings from the Ramayana and other sacred books were given to me and I had sufficient strength to discuss and advise in all urgent matters.

A variety of incidents in my life have conspired to bring me in close contact with people of many creeds and many communities, and my experience with all of them warrants the statement that I have known no distinction between relatives and strangers, countrymen and foreigners, white and coloured, Hindus and Indians of other faiths, whether Musalmans, Parsis, Christians or Jews. I may say that my heart has been incapable of making any such distinction. I cannot claim this as a special virtue, as it has been in my very nature, rather than a result of any effort on my part, whereas in the case of Ahimsa (non-violence), Brahmacharya (celibacy), and other cardinal virtues, I am fully conscious of a continuous striving for the cultivation of them.

When I was practising at the bar, my office clerks often stayed with me, and there were among them Hindus and Christians. I do not recollect having ever regarded them as anything but my kith and kin. I treated them as members of my family and had unpleasantnesses with my wife if ever she stood in my way of treating them as such. One of the clerks was a Christian, born of Panchama [3] parents.

The rooms of the house, which was built after the Western model, had no outlets. Each room had its slop pails and utensils. Rather than have these cleaned by a servant, either my wife or I attended to them. The clerks who made themselves completely at home would naturally clean their own vessels, but the Christian clerk was a newcomer, and it was our duty to attend to his bedroom. Mrs. Gandhi managed those of the other guests, but to clean those used by one who had been a Panchama seemed to her to be the limit, and we fell out. She could not bear them being cleaned by me, neither did she like doing so herself. Even to-day I can picture her chiding me with her eyes red with anger and pearl-drops streaming through them, as she was descending the stairs with the slop pail in her hand. But I was a cruelly kind husband at that time and regarded myself as her teacher, and so harassed her out of my blind love for her. Indeed, I was far from being satisfied by her merely carrying them. I would have her do it cheerfully. So I said, raising my voice, "I will not stand this nonsense in my house."

The words pierced her like an arrow. She shouted back: "Keep your house to yourself and let me go." I had forgotten myself, and the spring of compassion had dried up in me. I caught her by the hand, dragged the helpless woman to the gate, which was just opposite the outer stairs, and proceeded to open it to push her out. The tears were running down her cheeks in torrents, and she said: "Have you no sense of shame? Must you so far forget yourself? Where am I to go? I have no parents or relatives here to harbour me. Being your wife you think I must put up

[3] Untouchable.

with your cuffs and kicks? For Heaven's sake behave yourself, and shut the gate. Let us not be found making scenes like this!"

I put on a brave face, but was thoroughly ashamed, and shut the gate. If my wife could not leave me, neither could I leave her. We have had numerous bickerings, but the end has always been peace between us. My wife, with her matchless powers of endurance, has always been the victor.

To-day, I am in a position to narrate the incident with some detachment, as it belongs to a period out of which I have fortunately emerged. I am no longer a blind, infatuated husband and am no more my wife's teacher. Mrs. Gandhi can, if she will, be as unpleasant to me today as I used to be to her before. We are tried friends, the one no longer regarding the other as the object of passion. She has been a faithful nurse throughout my illnesses, serving without any thought of reward.

The incident in question occurred in 1898, when I had no conception of Brahmacharya. It was a time when I thought that the wife was the object of her husband's lust, born to do her husband's behest, rather than a helpmate and a comrade and a partner in the husband's joys and sorrows.

Let no one conclude from this narrative of a sacred recollection that we are by any means an ideal couple, or that there is a complete identity of ideals between us. Mrs. Gandhi herself does not perhaps know whether she has any ideals independently of me. It is likely that many of my doings have not her approval even to-day. We never discuss them; I see no good in discussing them. For she was educated neither by her parents, nor by me when I ought to have done so. But she is blessed with one great quality in a very considerable measure, a quality which most Hindu wives possess. And it is this: Willingly or unwillingly, consciously or unconsciously, she has considered herself blessed in following my footsteps, and has never stood in the way of my endeavour to lead a life of restraint. Though, therefore, there is a wide difference between us intellectually, I have always had the feeling that ours is a life of contentment, happiness and progress.

CHAPTER XIV

SATYAGRAHA IN NATAL

AN OCCASION AROSE for offering Satyagraha in Natal soon after Gokhale's departure.[1] He supposed that the three pounds poll tax would be taken off in a year and the necessary legislation would be introduced in the next ensuing session of the Union Parliament. Instead of this, General Smuts from his seat in the House of Assembly said that as the Europeans in Natal objected to the repeal of the tax, the Union Government were unable to pass legislation directing its removal, which however was not the case. The members from Natal by themselves could do nothing in a body upon which the four Colonies were represented. Again General Smuts ought to have brought forward the necessary bill in the Assembly on behalf of the Cabinet and then left the measure to its fate. But he did nothing of the kind, and provided us with the welcome opportunity of including this despicable impost as a cause of "war." There were two reasons for this. First, if in course of the struggle the Government made a promise and then went back upon it, the programme would naturally be extended so as to embrace such repudiation as well, and secondly, the breach of a promise, made to such a representative of India as Gokhale was, was not only a personal insult to him but also to the whole of India, and as such could not be taken lying down.

[1] Mr. Gokhale had visited South Africa in order to obtain the removal of an iniquitous tax of three pounds per head upon each Indian man and woman and adult child who came out of indenture. The tax was intended to drive them back under indenture, in which case it was remitted. Mr. Gokhale went away with the belief that this poll tax would be abolished.

It was impossible to pocket an insult offered to the mother country, and therefore we felt the Satyagrahis were bound to include the three pound tax in their programme, and when this tax thus fell within the scope of the struggle, the indentured Indians had an opportunity of participating in it. The reader must note that thus far this class had been kept out of the fray. This new orientation of our policy increased our burden of responsibility on the one hand, and on the other opened up a fresh field of recruitment for our "army."

Thus far Satyagraha had not been so much as talked of among the indentured labourers; still less had they been educated to take part in it. Being illiterate, they could not read "Indian Opinion" or other newspapers. Still I found that these poor folk were keen observers of the struggle and understood the movement, while some of them regretted their inability to join it. But when the Union ministers broke their pledged word, and the repeal of the three pound poll tax was also included in our programme, I was not at all aware as to which of them would participate in the struggle.

I wrote to Gokhale about the breach of pledge, and he was deeply pained to hear of it. I asked him not to be anxious and assured him that we would fight unto death and wring a repeal of the tax out of the unwilling hands of the Transvaal Government. The idea, however, of my returning to India in a year had to be abandoned, and it was impossible to say when I would be able to go. Gokhale was nothing if not a man of figures. He asked me to let him know the maximum and the minimum strength of our army of peace, along with the names of the fighters. As far as I can now remember, I sent sixty-five or sixty-six names as the highest and sixteen as the lowest number, and also informed Gokhale that I would not expect monetary assistance from India for such small numbers.

While preparations were still being made for resuming the struggle, a fresh grievance came into being, which afforded an opportunity even to women to take their part in the struggle. Some brave women had already offered to participate, and when Satyagrahis went to jail for hawking without a licence, their wives had expressed a desire to follow suit. But we did not then think it proper to send women to jail in a foreign land.

As if, unseen by anyone, God was preparing the ingredients for the Indians' victory and demonstrating still more clearly the injustice of the Europeans in South Africa, an event happened which none had expected.

Many married men came to South Africa from India, whilst some Indians contracted a marriage in South Africa itself. There is no law for the registration of ordinary marriages in India, and the religious ceremony suffices to confer validity upon them. The same custom ought to apply to Indians in South Africa as well, and although Indians had settled in South Africa for the last forty years the validity of marriages solemnised according to the rites of the various religions of India had never been called in question. But at this time there was a case in which Mr. Justice Searle of the Cape Supreme Court gave judgment on March 14, 1913, to the effect that all marriages were outside the pale of legal marriages in South Africa with the exception of such as were celebrated according to Christian rites and registered by the Registrar of Marriages.

This terrible judgment thus nullified in South Africa at a stroke of the pen all marriages celebrated according to the Hindu, Musalman and Zoroastrian rites. The many married Indian women in South Africa in terms of this judgment ceased to rank as the wives of their husbands and were degraded to the rank of concubines, while their progeny were deprived of their right to inherit the parents' property. This was an insufferable situation for women no less than men, and the Indians in South Africa were deeply agitated.

According to my usual practice I wrote to the Government, asking them whether they agreed to the Searle judgment and whether, if the judge was right in interpreting it, they would amend the law so as to recognise the validity of Indian marriages consecrated according to the religious customs of the parties and recognised as legal in India. The Government were not then in a mood to listen and could not see their way to comply with my request.

The Satyagraha Association held a meeting to consider whether they should appeal against the Searle judgment, and came to the conclusion that no appeal was possible on a question of this nature. If there was to be an appeal, it must be preferred by Government, or if they so desired, by the Indians provided that the Government openly sided with them through their Attorney General. To appeal when these conditions were not satisfied would be in a way tantamount to tolerating the invalidation of Indian marriages. Satyagraha would have to be resorted to, even if such an appeal was made and if it was rejected. In these circumstances therefore it seemed best not to prefer any appeal against this unspeakable insult.

A crisis now arrived, when there could not be any waiting for an auspicious day or hour. Patience was impossible in the face of this insult offered to our womanhood. We decided to offer stubborn Satyagraha irrespective of the number of fighters. Not only could the women now be not prevented from joining the struggle, but we decided even to invite them to come into line along with the men. We first invited the sisters who had lived on Tolstoy Farm. I found that they were only too glad to enter the struggle. I gave them an idea of the risks incidental to such participation. I explained to them that they would have to put up with restraints in the matter of food, dress and personal movements. I warned them that they might be given hard work in jail, made to wash clothes and even subjected to insult by the warders. But these sisters were all brave and feared none of these things. One of them was new to child-birth while six of them had young babies in arms. But one and all were eager to join and I simply could not come in their way. These sisters were with one exception all Tamilians. Here are their names:

Mrs. Thambi Naidoo, Mrs. N. Pillay, Mrs. K. Murugasa Pillay, Mrs. A. Perumal Naidoo, Mrs. P. K. Naidoo, Mrs. K. Chinnaswami Pillay, Mrs. N. S. Pillay, Mrs. R. A. Mudalingam, Mrs. Bhavani Dayal, Miss Minachi Pillay, Miss Baijum Murugasa Pillay.

It is easy to get into prison by committing a crime but it is difficult to get in in spite of one's innocence. As the criminal seeks to escape arrest, the police pursue and arrest him. But they lay their hands upon the innocent man who courts arrest of his own free will only when they cannot help it. The first attempts of these sisters were not crowned with success. They entered the Transvaal at Vereeniging without permits, but they were not arrested. They took to hawking without a licence, but still the police ignored them. It now became a problem with the women how they should get arrested. There were not many men ready to go to jail and those who were ready could not easily have their wish.

We now decided to take a step which we had reserved till the last, and which in the event fully answered our expectations. I had contemplated sacrificing all the settlers in Phoenix at a critical period. That was to be my final offering to the God of Truth. The settlers at Phoenix were mostly my close co-workers and relations. The idea was to send all of them to jail with the exception of a few who would be required for "Indian Opinion" and of children below sixteen. This was the maximum of sacrifice open to me in the circumstances. The sixteen stalwarts to whom I had referred in writing to Gokhale were among the pioneers of the Phoenix settlement. It was proposed that these friends should cross over into the Transvaal and as they crossed over, get arrested for entering the country without permits.

As it was an offence to enter the Transvaal from Natal without a permit it was equally an offence to enter Natal from the Transvaal. If the sisters were arrested upon entering Natal, well and good. But if they were not arrested, it was arranged that they should proceed to and post themselves at Newcastle, the great coal-mining centre in Natal, and advise the indentured Indian labourers there to go on strike. The mother tongue of the sisters was Tamil, and they could speak a little Hindustani besides. The majority of labourers on the coal mines hailed from the Madras Presidency and spoke Tamil or Telugu, though there were many from North India as well. If the labourers struck in response to the sisters' appeal, the Government was bound to arrest them along with the labourers, who would thereby probably be fired with still greater enthusiasm. This was the strategy I thought out and unfolded before the Transvaal sisters.

I went to Phoenix, and talked to the settlers about my plans. First of all I held a consultation with the sisters living there. I knew that the step of sending women to jail was fraught with serious risk. Most of the sisters in Phoenix spoke Gujarati. They had not had the training or experience of the Transvaal sisters. Moreover, most of them were related to me, and might think of going to jail only on account of my influence with them. If afterwards they flinched at the time of actual trial or could not stand the jail, they might be led to apologise, thus not only giving me a deep shock but also causing serious damage to the movement. I decided not to broach the subject to my wife, as she could not say "no" to any proposal I made, and if she said "yes," I would not know what value to attach to her assent; and I knew that in a serious matter like this the husband should leave the wife to take what step she liked on her own initiative, and should not be offended at all even if she did not take any step whatever. I talked to the other sisters who readily fell in with my proposal and expressed their readiness to go to jail. They assured me that they would complete their term in jail, come what might. My wife overheard my conversation with the sisters, and addressing me, said,

"I am sorry that you are not telling me about this. What defect is there in me which disqualifies me for jail?

I also wish to take the path to which you are inviting the others."

"You know I am the last person to cause you pain," I replied. "There is no question of my distrust in you. I would be only too glad if you went to jail, but it should not appear at all as if you went at my instance. In matters like this every one should act relying solely upon one's own strength and courage. If I asked you, you might be inclined to go just for the sake of complying with my request. And then if you began to tremble in the law court or were terrified by hardships in jail, I could not find fault with you, but how would it stand with me? How could I then harbour you or look the world in the face? It is fears like these which have prevented me from asking you too to court jail."

"You may have nothing to do with me," she said, "if being unable to stand jail I secure my release by an apology. If you can endure hardships and so can my boys, why cannot I? I am bound to join the struggle."

"Then I am bound to admit you to it," said I. "You know my conditions and you know my temperament. Even now reconsider the matter if you like, and if after mature thought you deliberately come to the conclusion not to join the movement, you are free to withdraw. And you must understand that there is nothing to be ashamed of in changing your decision even now."

"I have nothing to think about, I am fully determined," she said.

I suggested to the other settlers also that each should take his or her decision independently of all others. Again and again, and in a variety of ways I pressed this condition on their attention that none should fall away whether the struggle was short or long, whether the Phoenix settlement flourished or faded, and whether he or she kept good health or fell ill in jail. All were ready. The only member of the party from outside Phoenix was Rustomji Jivanji Ghorkhodu, from whom these conferences could not be concealed, and Kakaji, as he was affectionately called,[1] was not the man to lag behind on an occasion like the present. He had already been to jail, but he insisted upon paying it another visit. The "invading" party was composed of the following members:

Mrs. Kasturbai Gandhi, Mrs. Jayakunvar Manilal Doctor, Mrs. Kashi Chhaganlal Gandhi, Mrs. Santok Maganlal Gandhi, Parsi Rustomji Jivanji Ghorkhodu, Chhaganlal Khushalchand Gandhi, Ravjibhai Manibhai Patel, Maganbhai Haribhai Patel, Solomon Royeppen, Raju Govindu, Ramdas Mohandas Gandhi, Shivpujan Badari, V. Govindarajulu, Kuppuswami Moonlight Mudaliar, Gokuldas Hansraj, and Revashankar Ratansi Sodha.

These "invaders" were to go to jail for crossing the border and entering the Transvaal without permits. The reader who has seen the list of their names will have observed, that if some of them were disclosed beforehand, the police might not perhaps arrest the persons bearing them. Such in fact had been the case with me. I was arrested twice or thrice but after this the police ceased to meddle with me at the border. No one was informed of this party having started and the news was of course withheld from the papers. Moreover the party had been instructed not to give their names even to the police and to state that they would disclose their identity in court.

[1] "Kaka" literally means "Uncle."

The police were familiar with cases of this nature. After the Indians got into the habit of courting arrest, they would often not give their names just for the fun of the thing, and the police therefore did not notice anything strange about the behaviour of the Phoenix party, which was arrested accordingly. They were then tried and sentenced to three months' imprisonment with hard labour (September 23, 1913).

The sisters who had been disappointed in the Transvaal now entered Natal but were not arrested for entering the country without permits. They therefore proceeded to Newcastle and set about their work according to the plans previously settled. Their influence spread like wildfire. The pathetic story of the wrongs heaped up by the three pound tax touched the labourers to the quick, and they went on strike. I received the news by wire and was as much perplexed as I was pleased. What was I to do? I was not prepared for this marvellous awakening. I had neither men nor the money which would enable me to cope with the work before me. But I visualised my duty very clearly. I must go to Newcastle and do what I could. I left at once to go there.

The Government could not now any longer leave the brave Transvaal sisters free to pursue their activities. They too were sentenced to imprisonment for the same term—three months—and were kept in the same prison as the Phoenix party.

CHAPTER XV

THE PASSIVE RESISTERS

THESE EVENTS STIRRED UP the hearts of the Indians not only in South Africa but also in the motherland to their very depths. Sir Pherozeshah Mehta had been so far indifferent to our cause. In 1901 he had strongly advised me not to go to South Africa. He held that nothing could be done for Indian emigrants beyond the seas so long as India had not achieved her own freedom, and he was little impressed with the Satyagraha movement in its initial stages. But women in jail pleaded with him as nothing else could. As he himself put it, in his Bombay Town Hall speech, his blood boiled at the thought of those women lying in jails.

The women's bravery was beyond words. They were kept in Maritzburg jail, where they were considerably harassed. Their food was of the worst and they were given laundry work as their task. No food was permitted to be given them from outside till nearly the end of their term. One sister was under a religious vow to restrict herself to a particular diet. After great difficulty the jail authorities allowed her that diet, but the food supplied was unfit for human consumption. When the sister was released she was a mere skeleton and her life was saved only by a great effort. Another returned from jail with a fatal fever to which she succumbed within a few days of her release.

How can I ever forget Valliamma? She was a young girl of Johannesburg, only sixteen years of age, and she was confined to bed when I saw her. As she was a tall girl, her emaciated body was a terrible thing to behold.

"Valliamma," I asked, "do you repent of your having gone to jail?"

"Repent?" she said, "I am even now ready to go to jail again, if I am arrested."

"But what if it results in your death?" I pursued.

"I do not mind," she replied. "Who would not love to die for one's motherland?"

Within a few days after this conversation, Valliamma was no more with us in the flesh, but she left us the heritage of an immortal name. Condolence meetings were held at various places, and the Indians resolved to erect "Valliamma Hall," to commemorate the supreme sacrifice of this daughter of India. Unfortunately the resolution has not yet been translated in the action. Many difficulties have supervened. The community was torn by internal dissensions; the principal workers left one after another. But whether or not a Hall is built in stone or mortar, Valliamma's service is imperishable. She built her temple of service with her own hands. The name of Valliamma will live in the history of South African Satyagraha as long as India lives.

It was an absolutely pure sacrifice that was offered by these sisters, who were innocent of legal technicalities. Many of them had but little idea of country, their patriotism being based only upon faith. Some of them were illiterate and could not read papers. But they knew that a mortal blow was being aimed at the Indians' honour, and their going to jail was a cry of agony and prayer offered from the bottom of their hearts. It was in fact the purest of all sacrifices. Such heart prayer is always acceptable to God. Sacrifice is fruitful only to the extent that it is pure. God hungers after devotion in man. He is glad to accept the widow's mite offered with devotion, that is to say, without a selfish motive, and rewards it a hundredfold. The unsophisticated Sudama[1] offered a handful of rice, but the small offering put an end to many years' want and starvation. The imprisonment of many might have been fruitless but the devoted sacrifice of a single pure soul could never go in vain. None can tell whose sacrifice in South Africa was acceptable to God, and hence bore fruit. But we do know that Valliamma's sacrifice bore fruit and so did the sacrifice of the other sisters.

Souls without number spent themselves in the past, are spending themselves in the present and will spend themselves in the future in the service of country and humanity, and that is in the fitness of things, as no one knows who is pure. But Satyagrahis may rest assured, that even if there is only one among them who is pure as crystal, his sacrifice suffices to achieve the end in view. The world rests upon the bedrock of Satya or Truth. Asatya, meaning Untruth, also means "non-existent"; and Satya, or Truth, means "that which is." If untruth does not so much as exist, its victory is out of the question. And Truth being "that which is" can never be destroyed. This is the doctrine of Satyagraha in a nutshell.

The women's imprisonment worked like a charm upon the labourers on the mines near Newcastle who laid down their tools and entered the city in succeeding batches. As soon as I received the news, I left Phoenix for Newcastle.

These labourers have no houses of their own. The mine-

[1] Sudama in the Buddhist legend gave a handful of rice to the Buddha which was all that she had.

owners erect houses for them, set up lights upon their roads, and supply them with water, with the result that the labourers are reduced to a state of utter dependence. And as Tulasidas puts it, a dependent cannot hope for happiness even in a dream.

The strikers brought quite a host of complaints to me. Some said the mine-owners had stopped their lights or their water, while others stated that they had thrown the strikers' household chattels from their quarters. Saiyad Ibrahim, a Pathan, showed his back to me and said. "Look here, how severely they have thrashed me, I have let the rascals go for your sake, since such are your orders. I am a Pathan, and Pathans never take, but always give a beating."

"Well done, brother," I replied. "I look upon such conduct alone as pure bravery. We will win if we have people of your type."

I thus congratulated him, but thought to myself that the strike could not continue if many received the same treatment as the Pathan did. Leaving the question of flogging aside, there was not much room for complaint if the collieries cut off the lights, the water supply and other amenities enjoyed by the strikers. But whether or not complaint was justified, the strikers could not hold on in the circumstances, and I must find a way out of the difficulty; or else it was very much to be preferred that they should themselves own to be defeated and return to work at once rather than that they should resume work after a period of weary waiting. But defeatist counsel was not in my line. I therefore suggested that the only possible course was for the labourers to leave their masters' quarters, to fare forth in fact like pilgrims.

The labourers were not to be counted by tens but by hundreds. And their number might easily swell into thousands. How was I to house and feed this ever growing multitude? I would not appeal to India for monetary help. The river of gold which later flowed from the motherland had not yet started on its course. Indian traders were mortally afraid and not at all ready to help me publicly, as they had trading relations with the coal owners and other Europeans. Whenever I went to Newcastle, I used to stop with them. But this time, as I would place them in an awkward position, I resolved to put up at another place.

I had no means of housing them; the sky was the only roof over their heads. Luckily for us the weather was favourable, there being neither rain nor cold. But I was confident that the trader class would not fail to feed us. The traders of Newcastle supplied cooking pots and bags of rice. Other places also showered rice, dhal,[2] vegetables, condiments and other things upon us. The contributions exceeded my expectations. Not all were ready to go to jail; but all felt for the cause, and all were willing to bring their quota to the movement to the best of their ability. Those who could not give anything served as volunteer workers. Well-known and intelligent volunteers were required to look after these obscure and uneducated men, and they were forthcoming. They rendered priceless help, and many of them were also arrested. Thus every one did what he could and smoothed our path.

There was a huge concourse of men, which was continuously receiving accessions. It was a dangerous if not impossible task to keep them in one place and look after

[2] Dhal is a form of pulse or lentil.

them while they had no employment. They were generally ignorant of the laws of sanitation. Some of them had been to jail for criminal offenses such as murder, theft, or adultery. But I did not consider myself fit to sit in judgment over the morality of the strikers. It would have been silly of me to attempt at distinguishing between the sheep and the goats. My business was only to conduct the strike which could not be mixed up with any other reforming activity. I was indeed bound to see that the rules of morality were observed in the camp, but it was not for me to enquire into the antecedents of each striker.

I thought out a solution of my problem. I must take this "army" to the Transvaal and see them safely deposited in jail like the Phoenix party. The Transvaal border is thirty-six miles from Newcastle. The two border villages of Natal and the Transvaal are Charlestown and Volksrust respectively. Finally we decided to march on foot. I consulted the labourers who had their wives and children with them and some of whom therefore hesitated to agree to my proposal. But I had no alternative except to harden my heart, and declare that those were free to return to the mines. None of them would avail themselves of this liberty. We decided that those who were disabled in their limbs should be sent by rail, and all able-bodied persons announced their readiness to go to Charlestown on foot. The march was to be accomplished in two days. In the end every one was glad that the move was made. The Europeans in Newcastle anticipated an outbreak of plague and were anxious to take all manner of steps in order to prevent it.

I saw the mine-owners in Durban and observed that they were somewhat impressed by the strike; but I did not expect anything big to come out of the conference. The humility of a Satyagraha, however, knows no bounds. He does not let slip a single opportunity for settlement, and he does not mind if any one looks upon him as timid. The man who has faith and the strength which flows from faith, does not care if he is looked down upon by others. He relies solely upon his internal strength. He is therefore courteous to all, and thus cultivates and enlists world opinion in favour of his own cause. Therefore I welcomed the coal-owners' invitation; and when I met them I saw that the atmosphere was surcharged with the heat and passion of the moment. Instead of hearing me explain the situation, their representative proceeded to cross-examine me. I gave him suitable answers.

"It is in your power," I said, "to bring the strike to an end."

"We are not officials," was the reply.

"You can do a great deal," said I, "though you are not officials. You can fight the labourer's battle for them. If you ask the Government to take off the three-pound tax, I do not think they will refuse to repeal it. You can also educate European opinion on the question."

"But what has the three-pound tax to do with the strike? If the labourers have any grievance against the coal-owners, you should approach them for redress in due form."

"I do not see that the labourers have any other weapon except a strike in their hands. The three-pound tax has been imposed in the interests of the mine-owners who want the labourers to work for them but do not wish that they should work as free men. If therefore the labourers strike work in order to secure a repeal of the three-pound tax,

I do not see that it involved any impropriety or injustice to the mine-owners."

I cannot now remember the whole of the conversation. I saw that the mine-owners understood the weakness of their case, for they had already put themselves in communication with the Government.

During my journey to Durban and back I saw that the strike and the peaceful behaviour of the strikers had produced an excellent effect upon the railway guards and others. I travelled in third class as usual, but even there the guard and other officers would surround me, make diligent enquiries and wish me success. These officers were astonished to find that poor, illiterate and ignorant labourers made such a splendid display of endurance. Firmness and courage were qualities which are bound to leave their impress, even upon the opponent.

Then I returned to Newcastle. Labourers were still pouring in from all directions and I clearly explained the whole situation to the "army" saying that they were still free to return to work if they wished. I told them about the threats held out by the coal-owners, and pictured before them the risks of the future, and described the hardships of jail; and yet they would not flinch. They fearlessly replied that I should not be anxious about them as they were inured to hardships.

It was now only left for us to march. The labourers were informed one evening that they were to commence the march early next morning (October 28, 1913), and the rules to be observed on the march were read to them. It was no joke to control a multitude of five to six thousand men. I could not afford to give them anything on the road beyond the daily ration of one pound and half of bread and an ounce of sugar for each "soldier." If possible, I would try to get something more from the Indian traders on the way, but if I failed they must content themselves with bread and sugar. My experience of the Boer War and the Zulu "rebellion" stood me in good stead on the present occasion. None of the "invaders" was to keep with him any more clothes than necessary. None was to touch anyone's property on the way. They were to bear it patiently if any official or non-official European met them and abused them, or even flogged them. They were to allow themselves to be arrested. All these points were explained to the men, and I also announced the names of those who should successively lead the "army" in place of me, if I was arrested first. The men understood the instructions issued to them, and our caravan safely reached Charlestown where the traders rendered us great help. They gave us the use of their houses, and permitted us to make our cooking arrangements on the grounds of the mosque. The ration supplied on the march would be exhausted when camp was reached and therefore we were in need of cooking pots, which were cheerfully supplied by the traders. We had with us a plentiful store of rice, etc., to which also the traders contributed their share.

Charlestown was a small village with a population of hardly one thousand souls. Only women and children were lodged in houses. All the rest camped in the open. There are many sweet and some bitter reminiscences of our stay in Charlestown. The pleasant memories are connected with the sanitary department, and the District Health Officer, Dr. Briscoe, who, though alarmed at the phenomenal increase in the population, instead of adopting any stringent measures, met me, made some suggestions and offered to help me. Europeans are careful and we are careless about the purity of the water supply and the keeping of roads and sanitary conveniences clean. Dr. Briscoe asked me to see that no water was thrown on the roads and to prevent our men from dirtying the place or throwing refuse promiscuously. It was very difficult to have our people observe these rules. But the pilgrims and co-workers lightened my task. It has been my constant experience that much can be done if the servant actually serves and does not dictate to the people. If the servant puts in body labour himself, others will follow in his wake. And such was my experience in the present occasion. My co-workers and I never hesitated to do sweeping, scavenging and similar work, with the result that others also took it up enthusiastically. Kallenbach was already in Charlestown. And so was Miss Schlesin, whose industry, accuracy and honesty were beyond all praise. Of the Indians, the late P. K. Naidoo and Albert Christopher were with us and there were others besides who worked hard and rendered valuable help.

When I think of the patience and endurance of the men, I am overpowered by a sense of the greatness of God. Amongst the cooks I was the leader. Sometimes there was too much water in the dhal, and at other times it was insufficiently cooked. The vegetable and even the rice was sometimes ill-cooked. I have not seen many in the world who would cheerfully gulp down such food. On the other hand, I have observed in the South African jails that even those who pass as well educated men lose their temper, if they are given food somewhat less than sufficient, or ill-cooked, or even if they get it a little late.

Bai Fatma Mehtab of Durban could no longer be at

peace when the Tamilian sisters received sentences of imprisonment in Newcastle. She therefore left for Volksrust to court arrest along with her mother Hanifabai and a seven years' old son. Mother and daughter were arrested but the Government declined to arrest the boy. Fatma Bai was called upon to give her finger impressions at the charge office but she fearlessly refused to submit to the indignity. Eventually she and her mother were sent to prison for three months.

The labourers' strike was in full swing at this time. Men as well as women were on the move between the mining district and Charlestown. Of these, there were two women with their little ones, one of whom died of exposure on the march. The other fell down from the arms of its mother while she was crossing a spruit and was drowned. But the brave mothers refused to be dejected and continued their march. One of them said, "We must not pine for the dead who will not come back to us for all our pining. It is the living for whom we must work." I have often among the poor come across such instances of quiet heroism, sterling faith and saving knowledge.

The men and women in Charlestown held to their difficult post of duty in this stoical spirit. For it was no mission of peace that took us to that border village. If any one wanted peace, he had to search for it within. Outwardly the words "there is no peace here" were placarded everywhere, as it were. But it is in the midst of such storm that a devotee like Miranbai[3] takes the cup of poison to her lips with cheerful equanimity; that Socrates quietly embraces death in his dark and solitary cell and initiates his friends and us into the mysterious doctrine that he who seeks

[3] A saintly queen and devotee whose religious songs are cherished in India.

peace must look for it within himself. With such ineffable peace brooding over them Satyagrahis were living in their camp, careless of what the morrow would bring.

I wrote to the Government, that we did not propose to enter the Transvaal with a view to domicile, but as an effective protest against the minister's breach of pledge and as pure demonstration of our distress at the loss of our self-respect. The Government would be relieving us of all anxiety if they were good enough to arrest us where we were then, that is, in Charlestown. There was no secrecy about our movement. We would not like it if any of us secretly entered the Transvaal. But we could not hold ourselves responsible for the acts of any, because we had to deal with thousands of unknown men and could not command any other sanction but that of love. Finally, I assured the Government that if they repealed the three-pound tax, the strike would be called off and the indentured labourers would return to work; for we would not ask them to join the general struggle directed against the rest of our grievances.

The position then was quite uncertain, and there was no knowing when the Government would arrest us. But at a crisis like this we could not await the reply of the Government for a number of days. We therefore decided to leave Charlestown and enter the Transvaal at once, if the Government did not put us under arrest. If we were not arrested on the way, the "army of peace" was to march twenty-four miles a day for eight days together, with a view to reaching Tolstoy Farm, and to stop there till the struggle was over and in the meanwhile to maintain themselves by working the Farm. Mr. Kallenbach had made all the necessary arrangements. The idea was to construct mud huts with the help of the pilgrims themselves. The only difficulty was, that the rains were now about to set in, and everyone must have a shelter over his head while it rained. But Mr. Kallenbach was courageously confident of solving it somehow or other.

Volksrust is a town about double the size of Charlestown. A large European Bakery there willingly contracted to supply bread. The baker did not take advantage of our awkward plight to charge us higher than the market rates and supplied bread made of excellent flour. He sent it in time by rail, and the railway officials, also Europeans, not only honestly delivered it to us, but took good care of it in transit and gave us some special facilities. They knew that we harboured no enmity in our hearts, intended no harm to any living soul and sought redress only through self-suffering. The atmosphere around us was thus purified and continued to be pure. The feeling of love which is dormant, though present, in all mankind was roused into activity. Everyone realised that we are all brothers whether we are ourselves Christian, Jews, Hindus, Musalmans, or anything else.

As the night advanced, all noises ceased and I too was preparing to retire when I heard a tread. I saw a European coming, lantern in hand. I understood what it meant, but had no preparations to make.

"I have a warrant of arrest for you," said the officer. "I want to arrest you."

"Where will you take me?"

"To the adjoining railway station now, and to Volksrust when we get a train for it."

"I will go with you without informing any one; but I will leave some instructions with one co-worker."

CHAPTER XVI

IMPRISONMENT AND VICTORY

THEREUPON, I roused P. K. Naidoo who was sleeping near me. I informed him about my arrest and asked him not to awake the pilgrims before morning. At daybreak they must regularly resume the march. The march would commence before sunrise, and when it was time for them to halt and get their rations, he must break the news of my arrest. He might inform anyone who enquired about me in the interval, if the pilgrims were arrested. Otherwise they must continue the march according to the programme. Naidoo had no fears at all. I told him what was to be done in case he was arrested. Mr. Kallenbach was in Volksrust at the time. I went with the police officer, and we took the train for Volksrust, but the public prosecutor himself asked for a remand until the fourteenth, as he was not yet ready with the evidence. The case was postponed accordingly and I was released on bail of fifty pounds. Mr. Kallenbach had kept a car ready for me, and he took me at once to rejoin the "invaders." The special reporter of the "Transvaal Leader" wanted to go with us. We took him in the car, and he published at the time a vivid description of the case, the journey, and the meeting with the pilgrims, who received me with enthusiasm and were transported with joy on my return. We continued the march, but it could not suit the Government to leave me in state of freedom. I was therefore re-arrested at Standerton on the eighth. Standerton presented us with some tins of marmalade, and the distribution therefore took more time than usual.

I asked the pilgrims to continue their march, and then left with the Magistrate who had himself arrested me. As soon as I reached the court room, I found that some of my co-workers had also been arrested. There were five of them there, P. K. Naidoo, Biharilal Maharaj, Ramnarayan Sinha, Rahu Narasu, and Rahim Khan. The Government would not like that men should thus be attracted to jail, nor did they appreciate the fact that prisoners upon their release should carry my messages outside. They therefore decided to separate Kallenbach, Polak and me, send us away from Volksrust, and take me in particular to a place where no Indian could come to see me.

I was sent accordingly to the jail in Bloemfontein. In Bloemfontein itself there were not more than fifty Indians, all of them serving as waiters in hotels. I was the only Indian prisoner, the rest being Europeans and Negroes. I was not troubled at this isolation but hailed it as a blessing. There was no need now for me to keep my eyes or ears open; and I was glad that a novel experience was in store for me. Again I never had had time for study for years together, particularly since 1893, and the prospect of uninterrupted study for a year filled me with joy. In Bloemfontein jail I had as much solitude as I could wish. There were many discomforts, but they were all bearable. The medical officer of the jail became my friend. The jailer could think only of his own powers, while the doctor was anxious to maintain the prisoners in their rights. In these days I was purely a fruitarian. I lived upon a diet of bananas, tomatoes, raw groundnuts, limes and olive oil. It meant starvation for me if the supply of any one of these things was in bad quality. The doctor was therefore very careful in ordering them out, and he added almonds, walnuts and Brazil nuts to my diet. He inspected everything intended for me in person. There was not sufficient ventilation in the cell which was assigned to me. The doctor tried his best to have the cell doors kept open but in vain. The jailer threatened to resign if the doors were kept open. He was not a bad man, but he had been moving in a single rut from which he could not deviate.

Mr. Kallenbach was taken to Pretoria jail and Mr. Polak to Germiston jail. But the Government might have saved all this trouble. They were like Mrs. Partington trying to stem the rising tide of the ocean, broom in hand. The Indian labourers of Natal were wide awake, and no power on earth could hold them in check. The jeweller rubs gold on the touchstone. If he is not still satisfied as to its purity, he puts it into the fire and hammers it so that the dross if any is removed and only pure gold remains. The Indians in South Africa passed through a similar test. They were hammered and passed through fire and had the hall-mark attached to them only when they emerged unscathed through all the stages of examination. The pilgrims were taken on special trains not for a picnic but for baptism through fire. On the way the Government did not care to arrange even to feed them; and when they reached Natal they were prosecuted and sent to jail straightaway. We expected and even desired as much. But the Government would have to incur additional expenditure and would appear to have played into the Indians' hands if they kept thousands of labourers in prison. And the coal mines would close down in the interval. If such a state of things lasted for any length of time, the Government would be compelled to repeal the three-pound tax. They therefore struck out a new plan. Surrounding them with wire netting, the Government proclaimed the mine compounds as outstations to the Dundee and Newcastle jails and appointed the mine-owners' European staff as warders. In this way they forced the labourers underground against their will and mines began to work at once. There is this difference between the status of a servant and that of a slave, that if a servant leaves his post, only a civil suit can be filed against him, whereas the slave who leaves his master can be brought back to work by main force. The labourers therefore were now reduced to slavery pure and simple.

But that was enough. The labourers were brave men, and they flatly declined to work on the mines, with the result that they were brutally whipped. The insolent men dressed in a brief authority over them kicked and abused them and heaped upon them other wrongs which have never been placed on record. But the poor labourers patiently put up with all their tribulations.

Cablegrams regarding these outrages were sent to India addressed to Gokhale who would enquire in his turn if he did not even for a day receive a fully detailed message. Gokhale broadcast the news from his sickbed, as he was seriously ill at the time. In spite of his illness, however, he insisted upon attending to the South African business himself and was at it at night no less than by day. Eventually all India was deeply stirred, and the South African question became the burning topic of the day.

It was then that Lord Hardinge in Madras made his famous speech which created a stir in South Africa as well as in England. The Viceroy may not publicly criticise other members of the Empire, but Lord Hardinge not only passed severe criticism upon the Union Government, but he also whole-heartedly defended the action of the Satyagrahis and supported their civil disobedience of unjust and invidious legislation. The conduct of Lord Hardinge came in for some adverse comment in England, but even then he did not repent, but on the other hand asserted the perfect propriety of the step he had been driven to adopt. Lord Hardinge's firmness created a good impression all around.

Let us leave for the moment these brave but unhappy labourers confined to their mines, and consider the situation in other parts of Natal. The mines were situated in the northwest of Natal, but the largest number of Indian labourers was to be found employed on the north and south coasts. I was fairly intimate with the labourers on the north coast, many of whom served with me in the Boer War. I had not met the labourers on the south coast at such close quarters, and I had but few co-workers in those parts. But the news of the strike and the arrests spread everywhere at lightning speed, and thousands of labourers unexpectedly and spontaneously came out on the south as well as on the north coast. Some of them sold their household chattels from an impression that it would be a long drawn out struggle, and they could not expect to be fed by others. When I went to jail, I had warned my co-workers against allowing any more labourers to go on strike. I hoped that a victory could be achieved only with the help of the miners. If all the labourers—there were about sixty thousand of them in all—were called out it would be difficult to maintain them. We had not the means of taking so many on the march; we had neither the men to control them, nor the money to feed them.

Moreover, with such a large body of men it would be impossible to prevent a breach of the peace. But when the floodgates were opened, there is no checking the universal deluge. The labourers everywhere struck work of their own accord, and volunteers also posted themselves in the various places to look after them.

Government now adopted a policy of blood and iron. They prevented the labourers from striking by sheer force. Mounted military policemen chased the strikers and brought them back to their work. The slightest disturbance on the part of the labourers was answered by rifle fire. A body of strikers resisted the attempt to take them back to work. Some of them even threw stones. Fire was opened upon them, wounding many and killing some. But the labourers refused to be cowed down. The volunteers prevented a strike near Verulam with great difficulty. But all the labourers did not return to work. Some hid themselves for fear and did not go back.

One incident deserves to be placed on record. Many labourers came out in Verulam and would not return in spite of all the efforts of the authorities. General Lukin was present on the scene with his soldiers and was about to order his men to open fire. Brave Sorabji, son of the late Parsi Rustomji, then hardly eighteen years of age, had reached here from Durban. He seized the reins of the General's horse and exclaimed, "You must not order firing. I undertake to induce my people peacefully to return to work." General Lukin was charmed with the young man's courage and gave him time to try his method of love. Sorabji reasoned with the labourers who came round and returned to their work. Thus a number of murders was prevented by the presence of mind, valour and loving-kindness of one young man.

It became somewhat risky to live in Phoenix, and yet even children there accomplished dangerous tasks with courage. West was arrested in the meanwhile, though as a matter of fact there was no reason for arresting him. Our understanding was that West and Maganlal Gandhi should not only not try to be arrested, but on the other hand should, as far as possible, avoid any occasion for arrest. West had not therefore allowed any ground to arise for the Government to arrest him. But the Government could scarcely be expected to consult the convenience of the Satyagrahis, nor did they need to wait for some occasion to arise for arresting any one whose freedom jarred upon their nerves. The authorities' very desire to take such a step amply sufficed as a reason for adopting it.

As soon as the news of the arrest of West was cabled to Gokhale, he initiated the policy of sending out able men from India. When a meeting was held in Lahore in support of the Satyagrahis of South Africa, C. F. Andrews gave away in their interest all the money in his possession, and ever since then Gokhale had had his eye upon him. No sooner, therefore, did he hear about West's arrest, than he enquired of Andrews by wire if he was ready to proceed to South Africa at once. Andrews soon replied in the affirmative. His beloved friend Pearson also got ready to go the same moment, and the two friends left India for South Africa by the first available steamer.

But the struggle was now about to close. The Union Government had not the power to keep thousands of innocent men in jail. The Viceroy would not tolerate it, and all the world was waiting to see what General Smuts would do. The Union Government now did what all governments similarly situated do. No enquiry was really needed. The wrong perpetrated was well known on all hands, and every one realised that it must be redressed. General Smuts too saw that there had been injustice, which called for remedy; but he was in the same predicament as a snake which has made the mouthful of a rat which it can neither gulp down nor cast out. He had given the Europeans in South Africa to understand that he would not repeal the three-pound tax nor carry out any other reform. And now he felt compelled to abolish the tax as well as to undertake other remedial legislation. States amenable to public opinion get out of such awkward positions by appointing a Commission which conducts only a nominal inquiry, as its recommendations are a foregone conclusion. It is a general practice that the recommendations of such a Commission should be accepted by the State, and therefore under the guise of carrying out the recommendations, governments give the justice they have first refused. General Smuts appointed a Commission of three members, with which the Indians pledged themselves to have nothing to do so long as certain demands of theirs were not granted by the government. One of these demands was that the Satyagrahi prisoners should be released, and another that the Indians should be represented on the Commission by at least one member. To a certain extent, the first demand was accepted by the commission itself which recommended to the Government "with a view to enabling the enquiry to be made as thorough as possible" that Mr. Kallenbach, Mr. Polak and I should be released unconditionally. The Government accepted this recommendation and released all three of us after an imprisonment of hardly six weeks. West, who had been arrested, was also released, as the Government had nothing against him.

All these events transpired before the arrival of Andrews and Pearson, whom I was thus able to welcome as they landed at Durban. They were agreeably surprised to see me, as they knew nothing of the events which happened during their voyage. This was my first meeting with these noble Englishmen.

All three of us were disappointed upon our release. We knew nothing of the events outside. The news of the Commission came to us as a surprise, but we saw that we could not co-operate with it in any shape or form. We felt that the Indians should be certainly allowed to nominate at least one representative on it. We three, therefore, upon reaching Durban, addressed a letter to General Smuts on 21st December, 1913, to this effect:

"We welcome the appointment of the Commission, but we strongly object to the inclusion on it of Messrs. Esselen and Wylie. We have nothing against them personally. They are well-known and able citizens. But as both of them have often expressed their dislike for Indians, there is likelihood of their doing injustice without being conscious of it. Man cannot change his temperament all at once. It is against the laws of nature to suppose that these gentlemen will suddenly become different from what they are. However, we do not ask for their removal from the Commission. We only suggest that some impartial men be appointed in addition to them, and in this connexion we would mention Sir James Rose Innes and the Hon. Mr. W. P. Schreiner, both of them men well known for their sense of justice. Secondly, we request that all the

Satyagrahi prisoners should be released. If this is not done, it would be difficult for us to remain outside jail. There is no reason now for keeping the Satyagrahis in jail any longer. Thirdly, if we tender evidence before the Commission, we should be allowed to go to the mines and factories where the indentured labourers are at work. If these requests are not complied with, we are sorry that we shall have to explore fresh avenues for going to jail."

When Gokhale heard that a fresh march was under contemplation, he sent a long cablegram, saying that such a step on our part would land Lord Hardinge and himself in an awkward position and strongly advising us to give up the march, and assist the commission by tendering evidence before it.

We were on the horns of a dilemma. The Indians were pledged to a boycott of the Commission if its personnel was not enlarged to their satisfaction. Lord Hardinge might be displeased, Gokhale might be pained, but how could we go back upon our pledged word? Andrews suggested to us the consideration of Gokhale's delicate health and the shock which our decision was calculated to impart to him. But in fact these considerations were never absent from my mind. The leaders held a conference and finally reached the decision that the boycott must stand at any cost if more members were not co-opted to the commission. We therefore sent a long cablegram to Gokhale. Andrews too concurred with the message which was to the following effect:

"We realise how you are pained, and would like to follow your advice at considerable sacrifice. Lord Hardinge has rendered priceless aid, which we would continue to receive to the end. But we are anxious that you should understand our position. It is a question of thousands of men having given a pledge to which no exception can be taken. Our entire struggle has been built upon a foundation of pledges. Many of us would have fallen back today had it not been for the compelling force of our pledges. All moral bonds would be relaxed at once if thousands of men once proved false to their plighted word. The pledge was taken after full and mature deliberation, and there is nothing immoral about it. The community has no unquestionable right to pledge itself to boycott. We wish that even you should advise that a pledge of this nature should not be broken but be observed inviolate by all, come what might. Please show this cable to Lord Hardinge. We wish you might not be placed in a false position. We have commenced this struggle with God as our witness and His help as our sole support."

This cable, when it reached Gokhale, had a bad effect upon his health, but he continued to help us with unabated or even greater zeal than before. He wired to Lord Hardinge on the matter. Not only did he refuse to throw us overboard, but on the contrary he defended our own standpoint. Lord Hardinge too remained unmoved in our support.

I went to Pretoria with Andrews. Just at this time there was a great strike of the European employés of the Union railways, which made the position of the Government extremely delicate. I was invited to commence the Indian march at such a fortunate juncture, and thus assist the railway strikers, and win on our own terms. But, in answer to this, I declared that the Indians could not thus assist the railway strikers, as they were not out to harass the Government, their struggle being entirely different and differently conceived. Even if we undertook the march, we would begin it at some other time when the railway struggle had ended. This decision of ours created a deep impression, and was cabled to England by Reuter. Lord Ampthill cabled his congratulations from England. English friends in South Africa too appreciated our decision. One of the secretaries of General Smuts jocularly said: "I do not like your people, and do not care to assist them at all. But what am I to do? You help us in our days of need. How can we lay hands upon you? I often wish you took to violence like the English strikers, and then we would know at once how to dispose of you. But you will not injure even the enemy. You desire victory by self-suffering alone and never transgress your self-imposed limits of courtesy and chivalry. And that is what reduces us to sheer helplessness." General Smuts also gave expression to similar sentiments.

This was not the first incident of chivalrous consideration of others being shown by the Satyagrahis. When the Indian labourers on the north coast went on strike the planters at Mount Edgecombe would have been put to great losses if all the cane that had been cut was not brought to the mill and crushed. Twelve hundred Indians therefore returned to work, and joined their compatriots only when it was finished. Again when the Indian employés of the Durban Municipality struck work, those who were engaged in the sanitary services of the borough or as attendants upon the patients in hospitals were sent back, and they willingly returned to their duties. If the sanitary services were dislocated, and if there was no one to attend upon the patients in the hospitals, there might be an outbreak of disease in the city and the sick would be deprived of medical aid, and no Satyagrahi would wish for such consequences to ensue. Employés of this description were therefore exempted from the strike. In every step that he takes, the Satyagrahi is bound to consider the position of his opponent. I could see that the numerous cases of such chivalry left their invisible yet potent impress everywhere, enhanced the prestige of the Indians, and prepared a suitable atmosphere for a settlement.

The atmosphere was thus becoming favourable for a settlement. Sir Benjamin Robertson, who had been sent by Lord Hardinge in a special steamer, was to arrive about the same time that Andrews and I went to Pretoria. But we did not wait for him and set out, as we had to reach Pretoria on the day fixed by General Smuts. There was no reason indeed to await his arrival, as the final result could only be commensurate with our strength.

Andrews and I reached Pretoria. But I alone was to interview General Smuts. The General was pre-occupied with the railway strike, which was so serious in nature that the Union Government had declared martial law. The European workmen not only demanded their wages, but aimed at seizing the reins of government in their own hands. My first interview with the General was very short but I saw that General Smuts did not ride the same high horse as he did before, when the great march began. At that time the General would not so much as talk to me. The threat of Satyagraha was the same then as it was now. Yet he had declined to enter into negotiations. But now he was ready to confer with me.

We thus reached a provisional agreement, and Satyagraha was suspended for the last time. Many English friends were glad of this, and promised their assistance in the final settlement. It was rather difficult to get the Indians to endorse this agreement. Some reminded me of the fiasco in 1908, and said, "General Smuts once played us false, and yet what a pity that you have not learnt the necessary lesson of declining to trust him? This man will betray you once again, and you will again propose to revive Satyagraha. But who will then listen to you? Is it possible that men should every now and then go to jail, and be ready to face failure each time with a man who pledges his word and then breaks it?"

I knew that such arguments would be brought forward, and was not therefore surprised when they were made. No matter how often a Satyagrahi is betrayed, he will repose his trust in the adversary so long as there are not cogent grounds for distrust. Pain to a Satyagrahi is as pleasure. He will not therefore be misled by the mere fear of suffering into groundless distrust. On the other hand, relying as he does upon his own strength, he will not mind being betrayed by the adversary. He will continue to trust in spite of frequent betrayals, and will believe that he thereby strengthens the forces of truth and brings victory nearer. Meetings were therefore held in various places, and I was able at last to pursuade the Indians to approve of the terms of the agreement. The Indians came now to a better understanding of the spirit of Satyagraha. Andrews was the mediator and the witness in the present agreement. If I had obstinately refused to accept the agreement, it would have become a count of indictment against the Indians, and the victory which was achieved in the next six months would have been beset with various obstacles. The author of the Sanskrit saying, "Forgiveness is an ornament to the brave," drew upon his rich experience of Satyagrahis never giving any one the least opportunity of finding fault with them. Distrust is a sign of weakness and Satyagraha implies the banishment of all weakness and therefore of distrust, which is clearly out of place when the adversary is not to be destroyed but to be won over.

When the struggle was finally over Gokhale was in England. He had sent word to me to meet him there. So in July, 1914, Kallenbach, Kasturbai and I sailed for Southampton.

In Madeira we heard that the Great War might break out at any moment. As we entered the English Channel we received the news of its actual outbreak, and we were stopped for some time. It was a difficult business to tow the boat through the submarine mines which had been laid throughout the Channel, and it took about two days to reach Southampton.

The War was declared on the fourth of August. We reached London on the sixth.

On arrival in England I learned that Gokhale had been stranded in Paris, where he had gone for reasons of health, and as communication between Paris and London had been cut off, there was no knowing when he would return. I did not want to go home without having seen him, but no one could say definitely when he would arrive.

What then was I to do in the meanwhile? What was my duty as regards the War? Sorabji Adajania, my comrade in jail and a Satyagrahi, was then reading for the Bar in London. As one of the best Satyagrahis he had been sent to England to qualify himself as a barrister, so that on return to South Africa, he might take my place.[1] With him and through him, I had conferences with Dr. Jivraj Mehta and others who were prosecuting their studies in England. In consultation with them, a meeting of the Indian residents in Great Britain and Ireland was called. I placed my views before them.

I felt that Indians residing in England ought to take their share in the War. English students had volunteered to serve in the Army, and Indians might do no less. A number of objections were taken to this line of argument. There was, it was contended, a world of difference between the Indians and the English. We were slaves and they were masters. How could a slave co-operate with the master in the hour of the latter's need? Was it not the duty of the slave, seeking to be free, to make the master's need his opportunity? This argument failed to appeal to me then. I knew the difference of status between an Indian and an Englishman, but I did not believe that we had been quite reduced to slavery. I felt then that it was more of the fault of individual British officials than of the British system, and that we could convert them by love. If we would improve our status through the help and co-operation of the British, it was our duty to win their help by standing by them in their hour of need. Though the system was faulty, it did not seem to me to be intolerable, as it does to-day. But if having lost my faith in the system, I refuse to co-operate with the British Government to-day, how could those friends then do so, having lost their faith not only in the system but in the officials as well?

The opposing friends felt that that was the hour for

[1] Mr. Sorabji met an early death soon after this time, and the Satyagraha cause in South Africa then suffered an irreparable loss.

making a bold declaration of the Indian demands and for improving the Indians' status. I thought that England's need should not be turned into our opportunity, and that it was more becoming and farsighted not to press our demands while the War lasted. I therefore adhered to the advice and invited those who would to enlist as volunteers. There was a good response, practically all the provinces and all the religions being represented among the volunteers.

I wrote a letter to Lord Crewe, acquainting him with these facts, and expressing our readiness to be trained for ambulance work, if that should be considered as a condition precedent to the acceptance of our offer. Lord Crewe accepted the offer after some hesitation, and thanked us for having tendered our services to the Empire at that critical hour.

London in those days was a sight worth seeing. There was no panic, but all were busy helping to the best of their ability. Able-bodied adults began training as combatants, but what were the old, the infirm and the women to do? There was enough work for them, if they wanted. So they employed themselves in cutting and making clothes and dressings for the wounded.

[Owing to a serious attack of pleurisy Mahatma Gandhi was obliged to return to a warmer climate. He left England for India in December, 1914. C. F. A.]

CHAPTER XVII

HOME AT LAST

BEFORE I REACHED INDIA the party which had started from Phoenix had already arrived. According to our original plan I was to have preceded them, but my preoccupation in England with the War had upset all our calculations, and when I saw that I had to be detained in England indefinitely I was faced with the question of finding a place for accommodating the Phoenix party. I wanted them all to stay together in India, if possible, and to live the life they had led at Phoenix. I did not know of any Ashram where I could recommend them to go, and therefore I cabled to them to meet Andrews and do as he advised.

So they were first put in the Gurukul, Kangri,[1] where Mahatma Munshiram treated them like his own children. After this they were put in the Shantiniketan Ashram where the Poet Rabindranath Tagore and his people showered the same love upon them. The experiences they gathered at both these places served them and me in good stead.

The poet, Mahatma Munshiram, and Sushil Rudra, as I used to say laughingly to Andrews, composed his trinity. When in South Africa he was never tired of speaking of them, and of many sweet memories of South Africa, Andrews' talks, day in and day out, of this great trinity, are amongst the sweetest and most vivid. Andrews therefore put the Phoenix party in touch also with Sushil

[1] The Gurukul is a school belonging to the reforming Hindu Society called the Arya Samaj. Mahatma Munshiram was its Principal who became afterwards a Sanyari and was called Swami Shraddhanand.

Rudra. Principal Rudra had no Ashram, but he had a home which he placed completely at the disposal of the Phoenix family. Within a day of their arrival he and his people made them feel so thoroughly at home that they did not seem to miss Phoenix at all. It was only when I landed in Bombay that I learnt that the Phoenix party was at Shantiniketan. I was therefore impatient to meet them as soon as I could after my meeting with Gokhale.

The moment I reached Bombay Gokhale sent me word that the Governor was desirous of seeing me and that it might be proper for me to respond before I left for Poona. Accordingly I called on His Excellency. After the usual enquiries, he said:

"I ask one thing of you. I would like you to come and see me whenever you propose to take any steps concerning Government."

I replied: "I can very easily give the promise, inasmuch as it is my rule as a Satyagrahi to understand the viewpoint of the party I propose to deal with, and to try to agree with him as far as may be possible. I strictly observed the rule in South Africa and I mean to do the same here."

Lord Willingdon thanked me and said: "You may come to me whenever you like, and you will see that my Government does not wilfully do anything wrong."

To which I replied: "It is that faith which sustains me."

After this I went to Poona. It is impossible for me to set down all the reminiscences of this precious time. Gokhale and the members of the Servants of India Society overwhelmed me with affection. He had summoned them to meet me and I had a frank talk with them on every sort of subject. Gokhale was very keen that I should join the

Society and so was I. But the members felt that since there was a great difference between my ideals and methods of work and theirs, it might not be proper for me to join the Society. Gokhale believed that in spite of my insistence on my principles I was equally ready and able to tolerate theirs.

"But," he said, "they have not yet understood your readiness to compromise and are tenacious of their own principles. I am hoping that they will accept you; but if they don't, you will not for a moment think that they are lacking in respect or love for you. They are hesitating to take any risk, lest their high regard for you should be jeopardized. But whether you are formally admitted as a member or not, I am going to look upon you as one."

I informed Gokhale of my intentions. Whether I was admitted as a member or not, I wanted to have an Ashram where I could settle down with my Phoenix family, preferably somewhere in Gujarat, since I thought I was best fitted to serve the country through serving Gujarat. Gokhale liked the idea. He said: "You should certainly do so. Whatever may be the results of your talks you must look to me for the expenses of the Ashram which I shall regard as my own."

My heart overflowed with joy. It was a pleasure to feel free from the responsibility of raising funds and to realise that I should not be obliged to set about the work alone, but should be able to count on a sure guide whenever I was in difficulty.

So Dr. Dev was summoned and told to open an account for me in the Society's books and to give me whatever I might require for the Ashram and for public expenses.

After this I proceeded to Shantiniketan. The teachers

and students overwhelmed me with affection. The reception was a beautiful combination of simplicity, art and love.

The Phoenix family had been assigned separate quarters at Shantiniketan. Maganlal Gandhi was at their head and he had made it his business to see that all the rules of the Phoenix Ashram should be scrupulously observed. I saw that by dint of his love, knowledge and perseverance he had made his fragrance felt in the whole of Shantiniketan.

Andrews was there, and also Pearson. Amongst the Bengali teachers we came in fairly close contact with were Jagadananda Roy, Nepal Chandra Roy, Santosh Mozumdar, Khitimohan Sen, Nagen Ganguly, Sarad Babu, and Kalimohan Ghose. As is my wont, I quickly mixed with the teachers and students, and engaged them in a discussion on self-help. To the teachers I suggested that if they and the boys dispensed with the services of paid cooks and cooked their food themselves, it would enable the teachers to control the kitchen from the point of view of the boys' physical and moral health, and it would afford to the students an object-lesson in self-help. One or two of them were inclined to shake their heads. Some of them strongly approved of the proposal. The boys welcomed it, if only because of their instinctive taste for novelty. So we launched the experiment. When I invited the poet to express his opinion; he said that he did not mind it, provided the teachers were favourable. To the boys he said, "The experiment contains the key to Swaraj."

Pearson began to wear away his body in making the experiment a success. He threw himself into it with zest. A batch was formed to cut vegetables, another to clean the grain. Others undertook to see to the sanitary cleaning of the kitchen and its surroundings. It was a delight to me to see them working spade in hand. But it was too much to expect the boys with their teachers to take this work of physical labour like fish to water. There used to be daily discussions.

Some began early to show fatigue. But Pearson was not the man to be tired. One would always find him with his smiling face doing something or other in or about the kitchen. He had taken upon himself the cleaning of the bigger utensils. A party of students played on their "sitar" [2] before this cleaning party in order to beguile the tedium of the operation. All alike took the thing up with zest and Shantiniketan became a busy hive.

I had intended to stay at Shantiniketan for some time, but fate had willed it otherwise. I had hardly been there a week when I received from Poona a telegram about Gokhale's death. Shantiniketan was immersed in grief. All the members came over to me to express their condolences. A special meeting was called in the Ashram temple to mourn the national loss. It was a solemn function. The same day I left for Poona with my wife and Maganlal. All the rest stayed at Shantiniketan.

Andrews accompanied me up to Burdwan. "Do you think," he asked me, "that a time will come for Satyagraha in India? And if so, have you an idea when it will come?"

"It is difficult to say," said I. "For one year I am to do nothing. For Gokhale took from me a promise that I would travel in India to gain experience and express no opinion on public questions until I have finished the period

[2] A stringed musical instrument.

of probation. Even after the year is over, I shall be in no hurry to speak, and pronounce opinions. And so I do not suppose there will be any occasion for Satyagraha for five years or so."

On arrival in Poona, we found ourselves, after the performance of the funeral ceremonies, discussing the future of the Society and the question as to whether I should join it or not. This question of membership proved a very delicate matter for me to handle. While Gokhale was there I did not have to seek admission as a member. I had simply to obey his wish, a position I loved to be in. Launching on the stormy sea of Indian public life I was in need of a sure pilot. I had had one in Gokhale and had felt secure in his keeping. Now that he was gone, I was thrown on my own resources, and I felt that it was my duty to seek admission.

Most of the members of the Society were in Poona at this juncture. I set about pleading with them and tried to dispel their fears about me. But I saw that they were divided. One section favoured my admission, the other was strongly against it. I knew that neither yielded to the other in its affection for me, but possibly their loyalty to the Society was greater, at any rate not less than their love for me. All our discussions were therefore free from bitterness and strictly confined to matters of principle. The section that was opposed to me held that they and I were as the poles asunder in various vital matters, and they felt that my membership was likely to imperil the very objects for which the Society was founded. This naturally was more than they could bear. We dispersed after prolonged discussions, the final decision being postponed to a later date.

As I returned home I was considerably agitated. Was it right for me to be admitted by a majority vote? Would it be consonant with my loyalty to Gokhale? I saw clearly that when there was such a sharp division amongst the members of the Society over admitting me, by far the best course for me was to withdraw my application. Therein I thought lay my loyalty to the Society and to Gokhale. The decision came to me in a flash, and immediately I wrote to Mr. Shastri asking him not to have the adjourned meeting at all. Those who had opposed my application fully appreciated the decision. It saved them from an awkward position and bound us in closer bonds of friendship. The withdrawal of my application made me truly a member of the Society. Experience now tells me that it was well that I did not formally become a member and that the opposition of those who had been against me was justified. Experience has shown too that our views on matters of principle were widely divergent. But the recognition of the differences has meant no estrangement or bitterness between us. We have remained like brothers and the Society's Poona home has always been for me a place of pilgrimage.

It is true that I did not officially become a member of the Society, but I have ever been a member in spirit. Spiritual relationship is far more precious than the physical. Physical relationship divorced from the spiritual is like body without soul.

This year, 1915, was the year of the Kumbha fair,[3] which is held at Hardwar once every twelve years. I was by no means eager to attend the fair, but I was anxious

[3] The Kumbha Mela, or Fair, is a special occasion when Hindu pilgrims come to bathe together in the Sacred River Ganges.

to meet Mahatma Munshiram who was in his Gurukul. Gokhale's Society had sent a big volunteer corps for service at the Kumbha Mela. Pandit Hridayanath Kunzru was its leader and Dr. Dev was the medical officer. I was invited to send the Phoenix party to assist them, and so Maganlal Gandhi had already preceded me.

The journey to Hardwar was particularly trying. Sometimes the compartments had no lights. From Saharanpur we were huddled into carriages for heavy goods or cattle. These had no roofs, and what with the blazing midday sun overhead and the scorching iron floor beneath, we were all but roasted. The pangs of thirst caused by even such a journey as this could not persuade orthodox Hindus to take water, if it was "Musalmani." They waited until they could get the "Hindu" water. These very Hindus, let it be noted, do not so much as hesitate or enquire, when during illness the doctor administers them wine, or prescribes beef tea, or a Musalman or Christian compounder gives them water!

Dr. Dev had dug some pits to be used as latrines. He had to depend on paid scavengers for looking after these. Here was work for the Phoenix party. Dr. Dev gladly accepted our offer. The offer was naturally made by me, but it was Maganlal Gandhi who had to execute it. My business was mostly to keep sitting in the tent holding religious discussions with numerous pilgrims who called on me. This left me not a minute which I could call my own. Thus it was in Hardwar that I realised what a deep impression the struggle in South Africa had made throughout the whole of India.

But this was no enviable position to be in. I felt as though I was between the devil and the deep sea. Where no one recognised me, I had to put up with the hardships that fall to the lot of the millions in this land, such as third class railway travelling. But where I was surrounded by people who had heard of me I was the victim of the craze for "darshan."[4] Which of the two conditions was more pitiable, I have often been at a loss to determine.

The day of the Kumbha fair was now upon us. I had not gone to Hardwar with the sentiments of a pilgrim. I have never thought of frequenting places of pilgrimage in search of piety. But the two million men that were reported to be there could not all be hypocrites, or mere sightseers. I had no doubt that countless people amongst them had gone there to earn merit, and for self-purification. It is difficult, if not impossible, to say to what extent this kind of faith uplifts the soul. I therefore passed the whole night immersed in deep thought. There were those pious souls in the midst of the hypocrisy that surrounded them. They would be free of guilt before their Maker. If the visit to Hardwar was in itself a sin, I must publicly protest against it, and leave Hardwar on the day of Kumbha. If the pilgrimage to Hardwar and to the Kumbha fair was not sinful, I must impose some act of self-denial on myself in atonement for the iniquity prevailing there and thus purify myself.

This was quite natural for me. My life is based on disciplinary resolutions. I thought of the unnecessary trouble I had caused to my hosts in India hitherto who had so lavishly entertained me. I therefore decided to limit the articles of my diet and to have my final meal before sunset. I was convinced that if I did not impose these restrictions on myself, I should put my future hosts to

[4] Darshan implies the look or sight of a god or holy person.

considerable inconvenience and should engage them in serving me rather than engage myself in service. So I pledged myself never whilst in India to take more than five articles in twenty-four hours, and never to eat after dark. I gave the fullest thought to the difficulties I might have to face. But I wanted to leave no loophole. I rehearsed to myself what would happen during an illness, if I counted medicine among the five articles, and made no exception in favour of special articles of diet. I finally decided that there should be no exception on any account whatsoever. For fifteen years, I have been under these vows. They have subjected me to a severe test, but I am able to testify that they have also served as my shield. They have added a few years to my life and saved me from many an illness.

It was a positive relief to reach the Gurukul and meet Mahatma Munshiram with his giant frame. At once I felt the wonderful contrast between the peace of the Gurukul and the din and noise of Hardwar. The Mahatma overwhelmed me with affection. The Brahmacharis were all attention. It was here that I was first introduced to Acharya [6] Ramadevji and I could immediately see what a force and a power he must be. We had different viewpoints in several matters, nevertheless our acquaintance soon ripened into friendship. I had long discussions with Acharya Ramadevji and other professors about the necessity of introducing industrial training into the Gurukul. When the time came for going away it was a wrench to leave the place. I went on to Hrishikesh.

Many sannyasis called on me when I arrived. One of

[6] Acharya means the "Principal of a religious house or College." It is a title of honour.

them was particularly attracted towards me. The Phoenix party was there and their presence drew from the Swami many questions. We had discussions about religion and he realised that I felt deeply about matters of religion. He saw me bareheaded and without an upper garment returning from my bath in the Ganges. He was pained to miss the shikha (tuft of hair) on my head and the sacred thread on me and said:

"It pains me to see you, a believing Hindu, going without the sacred thread and the shikha. These are the two external symbols of Hinduism and every Hindu ought to wear them."

There is a history attached to this. When I was an urchin of ten, I envied the Brahman lads sporting bunches of keys tied to their sacred threads and I wished I could do likewise. The practice of wearing the sacred thread was not then common among the Vaishya families in Kathiawar. But a movement had just been started for making it obligatory for the first three castes. As a result several members of the Gandhi clan adopted the sacred thread. A Brahman invested us with the thread and although I had no occasion to possess a bunch of keys, I got one and began to sport it. Later, when the thread gave way, I do not remember whether I missed it very much. But I know that I did not go in for a fresh one. As I grew up several well-meaning attempts were made both in India and South Africa to re-invest me with the sacred thread, but with little success. If the Shudras may not wear it, I argued, what right have the other castes to do so?

On the eve of my going to England I got rid of the shikha, lest when I was bareheaded it should expose me to ridicule and make me look as I then thought a barbarian in the eyes of the Englishmen. In fact, this cowardly feeling carried me so far, that in South Africa I got my cousin, Chhaganlal Gandhi, who was religiously wearing the shikha, to do away with it. I feared that it might come in the way of his public work and so even at the risk of paining him I made him get rid of it. I therefore made a clean breast of the whole matter to the Swami and said:

"I will not wear the sacred thread, for I see no necessity for it, when countless Hindus can go without it and yet remain Hindus. Moreover, the sacred thread should be a symbol of spiritual regeneration, presupposing a deliberate attempt on the part of the wearer at a higher and purer life. I doubt whether in the present state of Hinduism and of India, Hindus can substantiate the right to wear a symbol charged with such a meaning. That right can come only after Hinduism has purged itself of untouchability, has removed all distinctions of superiority and inferiority, and shed a host of other evils and shams that have become rampant in it. My mind, therefore, rebels against the idea of wearing the sacred thread. But I am sure your suggestion about the shikha is worth considering."

The Swami did not appreciate my position with regard to the sacred thread. The very reasons that seemed to me to point to not wearing it appeared to him to tell the other way. Even to-day my position remains about the same as it was at Hrishikesh. So long as there are different religions, every one of them may need some outward distinctive symbol. But when the symbol is made into a fetish and an instrument of proving the superiority of one's own religion over that of others, then it is fit only to be discarded.

As for the shikha, cowardice having been the reason for discarding it, after consultation with friends I decided to let it grow again.

When I happened to pass through Ahmedabad many of my friends pressed me to settle down there and they volunteered to find the expenses of the Ashram, as well as a house for us to live in. I had a predilection for Ahmedabad. Being a Gujarati, I thought I should be able to render the greatest service to the country through the Gujarati language. And then as Ahmedabad was an ancient centre of handloom weaving, it was likely to be the most favourable field for the revival of the cottage industry of handspinning. There was also the hope that the city, being the capital of Gujarat, monetary help from its wealthy citizens would be more available here than elsewhere. The question of untouchability was naturally among the subjects discussed with the Ahmedabad friends. I made it clear to them that I should take the first opportunity of admitting an untouchable candidate to the Ashram if he was otherwise worthy.

This is how the Ashram was started. All had their meals in a common kitchen, and strove to live as one family. We had only begun a few months when we were put to a test such as I had scarcely expected. I received a letter from Amritlal Thakkar to this effect: "A humble and honest untouchable family is desirous of joining your Ashram. Will you accept them?"

I was perturbed. I had never expected that an untouchable family would so soon be seeking admission. I shared the letter at once with my companions and they welcomed it. So I wrote to Amritlal Thakkar expressing our willingness to accept the family, provided all the members were ready to abide by the rules of the Ashram. The family consisted of Dudabhai, his wife Danibehn, and their daughter Lakshmi, then a mere toddling babe. Dudabhai had been a teacher in Bombay. They all agreed to abide by the rules and were accepted. But their admission created a flutter amongst the friends who had been helping us. The very first difficulty was found with regard to the use of the well, which was partly controlled by the owner of the bungalow. The man in charge of the water-lift objected that drops of water from our bucket would pollute him. So he took to swearing at us and molesting Dudabhai. I told every one to put up with the abuse and continue drawing water. When he saw that we did not return his abuse, the man became ashamed and ceased to bother us. All monetary help, however, was stopped. With the stopping of monetary help came rumours of a proposed social boycott. We were prepared for all this. I had told my companions that if we were boycotted and denied the usual facilities, we would not leave Ahmedabad. We would rather go and stay in the untouchables' quarter and live on whatever we could get by manual labour.

Matters came to such a pass that Maganlal Gandhi one day gave me this warning: "We are out of funds, and there is nothing for the next month."

I quietly replied: "Then we shall go to the untouchables' quarter."

This was not the first time I had been faced with such a trial. On all such occasions, God has sent help at the last moment. Shortly after Maganlal had given me warning of our monetary plight, one of the children came and said that a Sheth was waiting in a car outside and that he wanted to see me. I went out to him. "I want to give the Ashram some help. Will you accept it?" he asked.

"Most certainly," said I. "And I confess I am at the present moment at the end of my resources."

"I shall come to-morrow at this time," he said. "Will you be here?"

"Yes," said I. And he left. Next day, exactly at the appointed hour, the car drew up near our quarters and the horn was blown. The children came with the news. The Sheth did not come in. I went out to see him. He placed in my hands currency notes of the value of thirteen thousand rupees and drove away. I had never expected this help; and what a novel way of rendering it! The gentleman had never before visited the Ashram. So far as I can remember I had met him only once. No visit, no enquiries, but simply rendering help and going away! This was a unique experience for me. The help deferred the exodus to the untouchables' quarter. We now felt quite safe for a year.

Just as there was a storm outside, so was there a storm in the Ashram itself. Though in South Africa untouchable friends used to come to my place and live and feed with me, my wife and other women did not seem quite to relish their admission into the Ashram. My eyes and ears easily detected their indifference, if not their dislike, towards Danibehn. The monetary difficulty had caused me no anxiety, but this internal storm was more than I could bear. Danibehn was an ordinary woman. Dudabhai was a man with slight education but of good understanding. I liked his patience. Sometimes he did flare up, but on the whole I was well impressed with his forbearance.

I pleaded with him to swallow minor insults. He not only agreed but prevailed upon his wife to do likewise.

The admission of this family proved a valuable lesson to the Ashram. In the very beginning we proclaimed to the world that the Ashram would not countenance untouchability. Those who wanted to help the Ashram were thus put on their guard and the work in this direction was considerably simplified. The fact that it is mostly the real orthodox Hindus who have met the daily growing expenses of the Ashram is perhaps a clear indication that untouchability is shaken to its foundation. There are indeed many other proofs of this, but the fact that good Hindus do not scruple to help an Ashram where we go the length of dining with the untouchables is no small proof.

Now a question that had engaged my attention in South Africa came before me in India also. Indentured labourers were those who had emigrated from India to labour under an indenture for five years. Under the Smuts-Gandhi Settlement of 1914 the three-pound tax in respect of the indentured emigrants to Natal had been abolished; but the general emigration from India still needed treatment.

In March, 1916, Pandit Madan Mohan Malaviyaji moved a resolution in the Imperial Legislative Council for the abolition of the indenture system. In accepting the motion Lord Hardinge announced that he had "obtained from His Majesty's Government the promise of the abolition in due course" of the system. I felt, however, that India could not be satisfied with so very vague an assurance, but ought to agitate for immediate abolition. India had tolerated the system through sheer negligence and the time had come when people could successfully agitate for this redress. I met some of the leaders, wrote in the press, and saw that public opinion was solidly in favour of immediate abolition. Might this be a fit subject for Satyagraha? I had no doubt that it was. In the meantime, the Viceroy had made no secret of the meaning of "the eventual abolition" which as he said was abolition "within such reasonable time as will allow of alternative arrangements being introduced."

So in February, 1917, Pandit Malaviyaji asked for leave to introduce a bill for the immediate abolition of the system. Lord Chelmsford refused permission. It was time for me to tour the country for an All-India agitation.

Before I started the agitation I thought it proper to wait upon the Viceroy. So I applied for an interview. He immediately granted it. Mr. Maffey, now Sir John Maffey, was his private secretary. I came in close contact with him and had a satisfactory talk with Lord Chelmsford, who without being definite promised to be helpful. I began my tour from Bombay. Mr. Jehangir Petit undertook to convene the meeting under the auspices of the Imperial Citizenship Association. The discussion was concerned with the fixing of the period within which the Government was to be asked to abolish the system. There were three proposals, (1) abolition "by the thirty-first of May"; (2) for abolition "as soon as possible"; (3) "immediate abolition." I was for a definite date, as we could then decide what to do if the Government failed to accede to our request within the time limit. Sir Lallubhai Samaldas was for "immediate" abolition. He said "immediate" indicated a shorter period than the thirty-first of May. I explained that the people would not understand the word "immediate." If we wanted to get them to do something, they must have a more definite word. Every one would interpret "immediate" in his own way—Government one way, the people another way. There was no question of misunderstanding "the thirty-first of May" and if nothing was done by that date we could proceed further. We adopted May thirty-first as the latest date by which the abolition should be announced. A resolution to that effect was passed at the public meetings and meetings through India resolved accordingly.

Mrs. Jaiji Petit put all her energies into the organization of a ladies' deputation to the Viceroy. Amongst the ladies from Bombay who formed the deputation I remember the names of Lady Tata and the late Dilshad Begam. The deputation had a great effect. The Viceroy gave an encouraging reply.

After this I visited Karachi, Calcutta, and various other places. There were fine meetings everywhere and there was unbounded enthusiasm. I had not expected anything like it when the agitation was launched.

In those days I used to travel alone and had therefore wonderful experiences. The C.I.D. men[6] were always after me. But as I had nothing to conceal they did not molest me, nor did I cause them any trouble. Fortunately I had not then received the stamp of "Mahatma" though the shout of that name was quite common where people knew me. On one occasion the detectives disturbed me at several stations, asked me for my ticket and took down the number. Of course I readily replied to all the questions that they asked. My fellow passengers had taken me to be a "sadhu" or a "fakir." When they saw that I was being molested at every station they were exasperated and swore

[6] Criminal Investigation Department.

at the detectives. "Why are you worrying the poor sadhu for nothing?" they protested. "Don't show these scoundrels your ticket," they said, addressing me. I said to them gently: "It is no trouble to show them my ticket. They are doing their duty." The passengers were not satisfied; they evinced more and more sympathy, and strongly objected to this sort of ill-treatment of innocent men.

But the detectives were no trouble at all. The real hardship was the third class travelling. My bitterest experience was from Lahore to Delhi. I was going to Calcutta from Karachi, via Lahore, where I had to change trains. It was impossible to find a place in the train. It was full, and those who could get in did so by sheer force, often sneaking through windows if the doors were locked. I had to reach Calcutta on the date fixed for the meeting, and if I missed this train I could not arrive in time. I had almost given up hope of getting in. No one was willing to accept me, when a porter discovering my plight came to me and said, "Give me twelve annas and I'll get you a seat." "Yes," said I, "you shall have twelve annas if you do procure me a seat." The young man went from carriage to carriage entreating passengers, but no one heeded him. As the train was about to start some passengers said, "There is no room here, but you can shove him in if you like. He will have to stand." "Well?" asked the young porter. I readily agreed and he shoved me in bodily through the window. Thus I got in and the porter earned his twelve annas.

The night was a trial. The other passengers were sitting somehow. I stood two hours, holding the chain of the upper bunk. Meanwhile some of the passengers kept worrying me incessantly. "Why will you not sit down?" they asked. I tried to reason with them saying there was no room, but they could not tolerate my standing though they were lying full length on the upper bunks. They did not tire of worrying me, neither did I tire of gently replying to them. This at last mollified them. Some of them asked me my name and when I gave it they felt ashamed. They apologised and made room for me. Patience was thus rewarded. I was dead tired and my head was reeling. God sent help just when it was most needed.

In that way I somehow reached Delhi and thence Calcutta. The Maharaja of Cassimbazaar, the president of the Calcutta meeting, was my host. Just as in Karachi, here also there was unbounded enthusiasm. The meeting was attended by several Englishmen.

Before the thirty-first of May the Government announced that indentured emigration from India was stopped.

It was in 1894 that I drafted the first petition protesting against the system and I had then hoped that this "semi-slavery," as Sir W. W. Hunter used to call the system, would some day be brought to an end. Now the work was completed. There were many who aided in the agitation, which was started in 1894, but I cannot help saying that potential Satyagraha hastened the end.

CHAPTER XVIII

CHAMPARAN

CHAMPARAN IS THE LAND of King Janaka.[1] Just as it abounds in mango groves, so used it to be full of indigo plantations until the year 1917. The Champaran tenant was bound by law to plant three out of every twenty parts of his land with indigo for his landlord. This system was known as the tinkathia [2] system, as three kathas out of twenty (which make one acre) had to be planted with indigo.

I must confess that I did not then know even the name, much less the geographical position of Champaran, and I had hardly any notion of indigo plantations. I had seen packets of indigo, but little dreamed that it was grown and manufactured in Champaran at great hardship to thousands of cultivators. Rajkumar Shukla was one of this class who had been under this harrow of oppression, and he was filled with a passion to wash away the stain of indigo for the thousands who were suffering as he had suffered. He caught hold of me at Lucknow, where I had gone for the Congress of 1916. "Vakil Babu will tell you about our distress," he said, and urged me to go to Champaran. "Vakil Babu" [3] was none other than Vrajakishore Prasad who became my esteemed co-worker in Champaran, and who is now the soul of public work in Bihar. Rajkumar Shukla brought him to my tent. He was

[1] A king in Hindu legend who combined the virtues of a king and a saint. Champaran is in North Bihar, at the foot of the Himalayas.
[2] "Tin" means "three."
[3] Vakil means barrister. Babu is an honorific title. I have ventured to omit its constant repetition later on in this chapter.

dressed in black alpaca and failed then to make an impression on me. I took it that he must be some vakil exploiting the simple raiyats.[4] Having heard from him something of Champaran, I replied as was my wont: "I can give no opinion without seeing the condition with my own eyes. You will please move the resolution in the Congress, but leave me free for the present." Rajkumar Shukla of course wanted some help from the Congress. Vrajakishore Prasad moved the resolution expressing sympathy for the people of Champaran and it was unanimously passed. He wanted me personally to visit Champaran and witness the miseries of the raiyats there. I told him that I would include Champaran in my tour and give it a day or two. "One day will be enough," said he, "and you will see things with your own eyes." From Lucknow I went to Cawnpore. Rajkumar Shukla followed me there. "Champaran is very near here. Please give a day," he insisted. "Pray excuse me this time," said I. "But I promise that I will come later." I returned to the Ashram at Sabarmati. The ubiquitous Rajkumar was there too. "Pray fix the day now," said he. "Well," said I, "I have to be in Calcutta on such and such a date; come and meet me then, and take me from there." I did not know where I was to go, what to do, what things to see. Before I reached Calcutta, Rajkumar Shukla had gone and established himself there. Thus this ignorant, unsophisticated, but resolute agriculturist captured me. So early in 1917, we left Calcutta for Champaran, looking just like fellow rustics. I did not even know the train. He took me to it and we travelled together, reaching Patna in the morning.

This was my first visit to Patna. I had no friend with

[4] Raiyat means "peasant."

whom I could think of putting up. My original idea was that Rajkumar Shukla must have some influence in Patna. But I had come to know him a little more on the journey, and on reaching Patna I had no illusions left. He was perfectly innocent of everything. The vakils that he had taken to be his friends were really nothing of the sort. Poor Rajkumar was more or less as a menial to them. Between such clients and their vakils, there is a gulf as wide as the Ganges in flood. Rajkumar Shukla took me to Rajendra Prasad's[5] place in Patna. He had gone to Puri or some other place. There was a servant at the bungalow who paid us no attention. I had with me something to eat but I wanted dates also, which my companion procured for me from the bazaar. There was strict untouchability in Bihar. I might not draw water at the well while the servants were using it, lest drops of water from my bucket might pollute them, the servants not knowing to what caste I belonged. All this was far from surprising, for I was inured to such things. These entertaining experiences enhanced my regard for Rajkumar Shukla, if they also enabled me to know him better. I saw now that he could not guide me and that I must take the reins in my own hands.

I knew Maulana Mazharul Haq in London when he was studying for the bar, and when I met him at the Bombay Congress in 1915,—the year in which he was President of the Muslim League,—he had renewed the acquaintance and extended me an invitation to stay with him whenever I happened to go to Patna. I bethought myself of this invitation and sent him a note indicating

[5] Rajendra Prasad became one of Mahatma Gandhi's most devoted followers and remains so up to to-day.

the purpose of my visit. He immediately came in his car and pressed me to accept his hospitality. I thanked him and requested him to guide me to my destination by the first available train. He suggested that I should first go to Muzaffarpur. There was a train for that place the same evening, and he sent me off by it.

Principal Kripalani was then in Muzaffarpur. I had known of him ever since my visit to Hyderabad. Dr. Choithram had told me of his great sacrifice, of his simple life, and of the Ashram that Dr. Choithram was running out of funds provided by Professor Kripalani. He used to be a professor in the Government College, Muzaffarpur, and had just resigned the post when I went there. I had sent a telegram informing him of my arrival, and he met me at the station with a crowd of students, though the train reached there at midnight. He had no rooms of his own, and was staying with Professor Malkani who therefore virtually became my host. It was an extraordinary thing in those days for a Government professor to harbour a man like me.

Professor Kripalani spoke to me about the desperate condition of Bihar, particularly of the Tirhut division, and gave me an idea of the difficulty of my task. He had established very close contact with the Biharis and had already spoken to them about the mission that took me to Bihar.

Vrajakishore now arrived from Darbhanga and Rajendra Prasad from Puri. Vrajakishore impressed me this time with his humility, simplicity, goodness and extraordinary faith, so characteristic of the Biharis, and my heart was joyous over it.

Soon I felt myself becoming bound to him and his circle of friends in lifelong friendship. He soon acquainted me with all the facts and explained to me from his own legal experience how the raiyats were treated.

After he had finished I said to him: "Where the raiyats are so crushed and fear-stricken, law courts are useless. The real relief for them is to be free from fear. Clearly we cannot rest until we have driven the tinkathia system out of Bihar. Though I thought that I should be able to leave here in two days, I now realise that the work might take even two years, and I am prepared to give even that time, if necessary." Vrajakishore was exceptionally cool-headed. "We shall render all the help we can," he said quietly, "but pray tell us what kind of help you will need." And thus we sat talking until midnight. "I shall have little use for your legal knowledge," I said to them, "but shall want clerical assistance and help in interpretation. It may be necessary to face imprisonment; but much as I would love you to run that risk you will go only so far as you feel yourselves capable of going. Even turning yourselves into clerks and giving up your profession for an indefinite period is no small thing. I find it difficult to understand the local dialect of Hindi. I shall want you to interpret. We cannot afford to pay for any work. It should all be done for love and out of a spirit of service."

Vrajakishore understood this immediately, and he now cross-examined me and his companions by turns. He tried to ascertain the implications of all that I had said,—how long their service would be required, how many of them would be needed, whether they might serve by turns, and so on. Then he asked the vakils the capacity of their sacrifice.

Ultimately they gave me this assurance: "Such and

such a number of us will do whatever you may ask. Some of us will be with you for so much time as you may require. The idea of accommodating ourselves to imprisonment is a novel thing for us. We will try to assimilate it."

My object was to enquire into the condition of the Champaran agriculturists and understand their grievances against the indigo planters. For this purpose it was necessary that I should meet thousands of the raiyats. But I deemed it essential, before starting on my enquiry, to know the planters' side of the case and also see the Commissioner of the Division. The Secretary of the Planters' Association told me plainly that I was an outsider and had no business to come between the planters and their tenants, but if there was any representation to make, I might submit it in writing. In reply I told him politely that I did not regard myself as an outsider, and that I had every right to enquire into the condition of the tenants if they desired me to do so.

The Commissioner, on whom I called, proceeded to bully me and advised me forthwith to leave Tirhut. I acquainted my co-workers with all this, and told them that there was a likelihood of the Government stopping me from proceeding further and that I might have to go to jail earlier than I had expected; if so, it would be better that the arrest should take place in Motihari and if possible in Bettiah. It was advisable, therefore, that I should go there as early as possible. Champaran is a district of the Tirhut division and Motihari is its headquarters. Rajkumar Shukla's place was in the vicinity of Bettiah and the tenants in its neighbourhood were the poorest in the district. Rajkumar Shukla wanted me to see them and I was equally anxious to do so.

So I started with my co-workers for Motihari the same day. We heard that about five miles away a tenant had been ill-treated. It was decided that we should go to see him the next morning, and we accordingly set off for the place on an elephant's back. Elephant riding, by the way, is about as common in Champaran as a bullock-cart in Gujarat. We had scarcely gone half-way when a messenger from the Police Superintendent overtook us and said that the latter had sent his compliments. I saw what he meant and got into the hired carriage which the messenger had brought. He then served on me a notice to leave Champaran, and drove me to my place. On his asking me to acknowledge service of notice, I wrote to the effect that I did not propose to comply with it or leave Champaran till my enquiry was finished. Thereupon, I received a summons to take my trial the next day for disobeying the Government order. That whole night I kept awake writing letters and giving necessary instructions to Brajakishore Prasad. The news of the notice and the summons spread like wildfire and I was told that Motihari that day witnessed unprecedented scenes. Gorakh Babu's house and the court house overflowed. Fortunately I had finished all my work during the night and so was able to cope with the crowds. My companions proved the greatest help. They occupied themselves with regulating the crowds; for the latter followed me wherever I went. A sort of friendliness sprang up between the officials and myself. I might have legally resisted the notices served on me. Instead, I accepted them all, and my conduct towards the officials was correct. They thus saw that I did not want to offend them personally, and that I wanted to offer civil resistance to their orders. They were thus put at ease, and instead of harassing us they gladly availed themselves of our co-operation in regulating the crowds. But it was an ocular demonstration to them of the fact that their authority was shaken. The people had for the moment lost all fear of punishment, and yielded obedience to the power of love which their new friend exercised.

It should be remembered that no one knew me in Champaran. The peasants were all ignorant. Champaran, being far up north of the Ganges, and right at the foot of the Himalayas in close proximity to Nepal, was cut off from the rest of India. The Congress was practically unknown in these parts.

In consultation with my co-workers I had decided that nothing should be done in the name of the Congress. What we wanted was work and not name; substance and not shadow. The name of the Congress was disliked by the Government and their controllers, the planters. To them the Congress was a byword for lawyers' wrangles. No emissaries had been sent from the Congress to prepare the ground for our arrival. Rajkumar Shukla himself was incapable of reaching the thousands of peasants. Thus no political work had yet been done amongst them. The world outside Champaran was not known to them. And yet the crowds received me as though we had been age-long friends. It is no exaggeration to say that in this meeting with the raiyats I was face to face with God, Ahimsa and Truth. When I come to examine my title to this realisation, I find nothing but my love for the people. And this, in turn, is nothing but an expression of an unshakeable faith in Ahimsa.

That day in Champaran was an unforgettable event in

my life, and a red-letter day for the peasants and for me. According to the law I was to be on my trial, but truly speaking Government was to be on its trial. The Government pleader, the Magistrate, and other officials were on tenterhooks. They were at a loss to know what to do. The Government pleader was pressing the Magistrate to postpone the case. But I interfered and requested the Magistrate not to postpone the case as I wanted to plead guilty to having disobeyed the order to leave Champaran, and read a brief statement as follows:

"With the permission of the Court I would like to make a brief statement showing why I have taken the very serious step of seemingly disobeying the order passed under Sec. 144 of Cr. P. C. In my humble opinion it is a question of difference of opinion between the Local Administration and myself. I have entered the country with motives of rendering humanitarian and national service. I have done so in response to a pressing invitation to come and help the raiyats, who urge they are not being fairly treated by the indigo planters. I could not render any help without studying the problem. I have, therefore, come to study it with the assistance, if possible, of the Administration and the planters. I have no other motive and cannot believe that my coming can in any way disturb public peace and cause loss of life. I claim to have considerable experience in such matters. The Administration, however, have thought differently. I fully appreciate their difficulty and I admit too that they can only proceed upon information they received. As a law-abiding citizen my first instinct would be to obey the order served upon me. But I could not do so without doing violence to my sense of duty towards those for whom I have come. I feel that I could just now serve them only by remaining in their midst. I could not, therefore, voluntarily retire. Amid this conflict of duty I could only throw the responsibility of removing me from them on the Administration. I am fully conscious of the fact that a person holding, in the public life of India, a position such as I do, has to be most careful in setting an example. It is my firm belief that in the complex constitution under which we are living, the only safe and honourable course for a self-respecting man is, in the circumstances such as face me, to do what I have decided to do, that is, to submit without protest to the penalty of disobedience.

"I venture to make this statement not in any way in extenuation of the penalty to be awarded against me, but to show that I have disregarded the order served upon me not for want of respect for lawful authority, but in obedience to the higher law of our being, the voice of conscience."

There was now no occasion to postpone the hearing; but as both the Magistrate and the Government pleader had been taken by surprise, the Magistrate postponed judgment. Meanwhile I had wired full details to the Viceroy, to Patna friends, as also to Pandit Madan Mohan Malaviya [6] and others.

Before I could appear before the Court to receive the sentence the Magistrate sent a written message that His Excellency the Lieutenant Governor [7] had ordered the case against me to be withdrawn, and the Collector wrote to me saying that I was at liberty to conduct the proposed

[6] The distinguished Brahman leader of orthodox Hinduism.
[7] Sir Edward Gait.

enquiry and that I might count on whatever help I needed from the officials. None of us was prepared for this prompt and happy issue.

I called on the Collector, Mr. Heycock. He seemed to be a good man, anxious to do justice. He told me that I might ask for whatever papers I desired to see and that I was at liberty to see him whenever I liked. The country thus had its first direct object lesson in Civil Disobedience. The affair was freely discussed both locally and in the press, and my enquiry got unexpected publicity.

It was necessary for my enquiry that the Government should remain neutral. But the enquiry did not need support from press reporters or leading articles in the press. Indeed the situation in Champaran was so delicate and difficult that over-energetic criticism or highly coloured reports might easily damage the cause which I was seeking to espouse. So I wrote to the editors of the principal papers requesting them not to trouble to send any reporters, as I should send them whatever might be necessary for publication and keep them informed. The Government attitude countenancing my presence had displeased the Champaran planters, and I knew that even the officials, though they could say nothing openly, could hardly have liked it. Incorrect or misleading reports therefore were likely to incense them all the more; and their ire, instead of descending on me, would be sure to descend on the poor fear-stricken raiyats, and seriously hinder my search for the truth about the case. In spite of these precautions, the planters engineered against me a poisonous agitation. All sorts of falsehoods appeared in the press about my co-workers and myself. But my extreme cautiousness and my insistence on truth even to the minutest detail turned the edge of their sword. The planters left no stone unturned in maligning Brajakishore, but the more they maligned him, the more he rose in the estimation of the people.

In such a delicate situation as this, I did not think it proper to invite any leaders from other provinces. Pandit Malaviyaji had sent me an assurance that whenever I wanted him, I had only to send him word, but I did not trouble him. Thus the struggle was prevented from assuming a political aspect. But I sent to the leaders and the principal papers occasionally reports not for publication but merely for their information. I had seen that even where the end might be political, but where the cause was non-political, one damaged it by giving it a political aspect, and helped it by keeping it within its non-political limit. The Champaran struggle was a proof of the fact that disinterested service of the people in any sphere ultimately helps the country politically.

To give a full account of the Champaran enquiry would be to narrate the history of the villager himself, which is out of the question. The Champaran enquiry was a bold experiment with Truth and Ahimsa. It revealed their sovereign power to set right human wrongs. The enquiry could not be conducted in Gorakh Babu's house, without practically asking him to vacate it. And the people of Motihari had not yet shed their fear to the extent of renting a house to us. However Brajakishore tactfully secured a vacant bungalow with considerable open space about it, and we now removed there.

It was not quite possible to carry on the work without financial resources. It had not been the practice hitherto to appeal to the public for money for work of this kind.

Brajakishore and his friends were mainly vakils, who either contributed funds themselves or found it from friends whenever there was an occasion. I had made up my mind not to accept anything from the Champaran raiyats. I was equally determined not to appeal to the country at large for funds to conduct this enquiry. For that was likely to give it a political aspect. Friends from Bombay offered fifteen thousand [8] rupees, but I declined the offer with thanks, and decided to get as much as was possible from well-to-do Biharis living outside Champaran, and if more was needed to approach my friend Dr. P. J. Mehta of Rangoon. Dr. Mehta readily agreed to send me whatever might be needed. We were thus free from all anxiety on this score. We were not likely to require large funds, as we were bent on exercising the greatest economy in consonance with the poverty of Champaran. Indeed it was found in the end that we did not need any large amount. I have an impression that we expended in all not more than three thousand rupees, and as far as I remember we saved a few hundred rupees from what we had collected.

The curious way in which my companions lived in the early days was a constant theme of raillery at their expense. Each of the vakils had a servant and a cook, and therefore a separate kitchen, and they often had their dinner as late as midnight. Though they paid their own expenses, their irregularity worried me; but as we had become close friends there was no possibility of a misunderstanding between us and they received my ridicule of them in good part. Ultimately it was agreed that the servants should be dispensed with, that all the kitchens

[8] One thousand pounds sterling, or five thousand dollars.

should be amalgamated, and that regular hours should be observed. As all were not vegetarians and as two kitchens would have been expensive, a common vegetarian kitchen was decided upon. It was also felt necessary to insist on simple meals.

These arrangements considerably reduced the expenses and saved us a lot of time and energy when both of these were badly needed. Crowds of peasants came to make their statements and they were followed by an army of companions who filled the compound and garden to overflowing. The efforts of my companions to save me from "darshan" [9] seekers proved effective. At least five or six volunteers were required to take down statements, and even then some people had to go away in the evening without being able to make them. All these statements were not essential, many of them being repetitions, but the people could not be satisfied otherwise, and I appreciated their feelings in the matter. Those who took them down had to observe certain rules. Each peasant had to be closely cross-examined, and whoever failed to satisfy the test was rejected. This entailed a lot of extra time, but most of the statements were thus rendered incontrovertible. An officer from the C.I.D.[10] would always be present when these statements were recorded. We might have prevented him, but we had decided from the very beginning not only not to mind the presence of C.I.D. officers but to treat them with courtesy and to give them information. This was far from doing us any harm. On the contrary the very fact that the statements were taken

[9] "Darshan" here implied obtaining the sight of a saint. Mahatma Gandhi greatly dislikes the practice when applied to himself, but with simple illiterate people it is difficult to avoid it.

[10] Criminal Investigation Department.

down in the presence of the C.I.D. officers made the peasants more fearless. Whilst on the one hand excessive fear of them was driven out of the peasants' minds, on the other hand their presence exercised a natural restraint on exaggeration. It was the business of C.I.D. friends to entrap people, and so the peasants had necessarily to be cautious.

As I did not want to irritate the planters, but to win them over by gentleness, I made a point of writing to and meeting such of them against whom allegations of a serious nature were made. I met the Planters' Association as well, placed the peasants' grievances before them and acquainted myself with their point of view. Some of the planters hated me, some were indifferent, whilst a few treated me with courtesy. Brajakishore and Rajendra Prasad were a matchless pair. Their devotion made it impossible for me to take a single step without their help. Their disciples, or their companions, were always with us. All these were Biharis. Their principal work was to take down the raiyats' statements.

Professor Kripalani could not but cast in his lot with us. Though a Sindhi he was more Bihari than a born Bihari. I have seen few workers more capable of merging themselves in the province of their adoption. He made it impossible for anyone to feel that he belonged to a different province. He was my gatekeeper in chief. For the time being he made it the end and aim of his life to save me from "darshan" seekers. He warded off people, calling to his aid now his unfailing humour, now his non-violent threats. At nightfall he would take up his occupation of a teacher, and regale his companions with his historical studies and observations, and quicken any timid visitor into bravery.

Maulana Mazharul Haq had registered his name on the standing list of helpers whom I might count upon whenever necessary, and he made a point of looking in once or twice a month. The pomp and splendour in which he then lived was in sharp contrast to his simple life of to-day. The way in which he associated with us made us feel that he was one of us, though his fashionable dress gave to a stranger a different impression.[11]

[11] Before his death in 1929 he retired completely from the world living the life of a religious ascetic.

CHAPTER XIX

KHAIRA

AS I GAINED MORE EXPERIENCE of Bihar, I became convinced that work of a permanent nature was impossible without proper village education. The raiyats' ignorance was pathetic. They either allowed their children to roam about, or made them toil on indigo plantations from morning to night for a couple of coppers a day. In those days a male labourer's wage did not exceed ten pice[1]; a female's did not exceed six, and a child's three. He who succeeded in earning four annas [2] a day was considered most fortunate. In consultation with my companions I decided to open primary schools in six villages. One of our conditions with the villagers was that they should provide the teachers with board and lodging while we would see to the other expenses. The village folk had hardly any cash in their hands, but they could well afford to provide goods. Indeed, they had already expressed their readiness to contribute grain and other raw materials. Whence to get the teachers was a great problem. It was difficult to find those locally who would work for a bare allowance or without remuneration. My idea was never to entrust children to commonplace teachers. Their literary qualification was not so essential as their moral fibre.

So I issued a public appeal for voluntary teachers. It received a ready response. Sjt. Gangadharrao Deshpande sent Babasaheb Soman and Pundarik. Mrs. Avantikabai Gokhale came from Bombay and Mrs. Anandibai

[1] Five cents.
[2] Eight cents.

Vaishampayan from Poona. I sent to the Ashram for Chhotalal, Surendranath and my son Devdas. About this time Mahadev Desai[3] and Narahari Parikh with their wives cast in their lot with me. My wife was also summoned for the work from Sabarmati. This was a fairly strong contingent. Shrimati Avantikabai and Shrimati Anandibai were educated enough, but Mrs. Durga Desai and Mrs. Manibehn Parikh had nothing more than a bare knowledge of Gujarati, and Kasturbai not even that. How were these ladies to instruct the children in Hindi? I explained to them that they were expected to teach the children not grammar so much as cleanliness and good manners. Even as regards letters there was not so great a difference between Gujarati, Hindi and Marathi as they imagined; and in the primary classes, at any rate, the teaching of the rudiments of the alphabet and numerals was not a difficult matter. The result was that the classes taken by these ladies were found to be most successful. The experience inspired them with confidence and interest in their work. Avantikabai's became a model school. She threw herself heart and soul into her work. She brought her exceptional gifts to bear on it. Through these ladies we could to some extent reach the village women.

But I did not want to stop at providing for primary education. The villages were unsanitary, the lanes full of filth, the wells surrounded by mud and stink and the court-yards unbearably untidy. The elder people badly needed education in cleanliness. They were all suffering from various skin diseases. So it was decided to do as much sanitary work as possible, and to penetrate every

[3] He has become during all these years the most devoted Secretary and friend of Mahatma Gandhi. The translation of this Autobiography from Gujarati into English is due mainly to him.

department of their lives. Doctors were needed for this work. I requested the Servants of India Society to lend us the services of Dr. Dev. We had been great friends, and he readily offered his services for six months. The teachers had all to work under him. All of them had express instructions not to concern themselves with grievances against planters or with politics. People who had any complaints to make were to be referred to me. No one was to venture beyond his beat. The friends carried out these instructions with wonderful fidelity. I do not remember a single occasion of breach of discipline. As far as was possible we placed each school in charge of one man and one woman. These volunteers had to look after medical relief and sanitation. The womenfolk had to be approached through women.

Medical relief was a very simple affair. Castor oil, quinine, and sulphur ointment were the only drugs provided to the volunteers. If the patient showed a furred tongue or complained of constipation castor oil was administered; in case of fever quinine was given after an opening dose of castor oil, and the sulphur ointment was applied in case of boils and itches after thoroughly washing the affected parts. No patient was permitted to take home any medicine. Whenever there was some complication Dr. Dev was consulted. Dr. Dev used to visit each centre on certain fixed days in the week.

Quite a number of people availed themselves of this simple relief. This plan of work will not seem strange when it is remembered that the prevailing ailments were few and amenable to simple treatment, by no means requiring expert help. As for the people the arrangement answered excellently.

Sanitation was a difficult affair. The people were not prepared to do anything themselves. Even the field labourers were not ready to do their own scavenging. But Dr. Dev was not a man easily to lose heart. He and the volunteers concentrated their energies on making a village ideally clean. They swept the roads and the court yards, cleaned out the wells, filled up the pools near-by, and lovingly persuaded the villagers to raise volunteers from amongst themselves. In some villages they shamed people into taking up the work, and in others the people were so enthusiastic that they even prepared roads to enable my car to go from place to place. These sweet experiences were not unmixed with bitter ones of people's apathy. I remember some villagers having frankly expressed their dislike for this work.

It may not be out of place here to narrate an experience that I have described before now in many meetings. Bhitiharva was a small village in which was one of our schools. I happened to visit a smaller village in its vicinity and found some of the women dressed very dirtily. So I told Mrs. Gandhi to ask them why they did not wash their clothes. She spoke to them. One of the women took her into her hut and said: "Look now, there is no box or cupboard here containing other clothes. The sari [4] I am wearing is the only one I have. How am I to wash it? Tell Mahatmaji to get me another sari and I shall then promise to bathe and put on clean clothes every day."

This cottage was not an exception, but a type to be found in many Indian villages. In countless cottages in India people live without any furniture, and without any change of clothes, merely with a rag to cover their shame.

[4] The woman's dress.

One more experience I will note. In Champaran there is no lack of bamboo and grass. The school hut they had put up at Bhitiharva was made of these materials. Some one,—possibly some of the neighbouring planter's men,—set fire to it one night. It was not thought advisable to build another hut of bamboo and grass. The school was in charge of Sjt. Soman and Mrs. Gandhi. Sjt. Soman decided to build a permanent house, and, thanks to his infectious labour, many co-operated with him, and so a brick house was soon made ready. There was no fear now of this building being burnt down. Thus the volunteers with their schools, sanitation work, and medical relief gained the confidence and respect of the village folk and were able to bring good influence to bear upon them. But I must confess with great regret that my hope of putting this constructive work on a permanent footing was not fulfilled. The volunteers had come for temporary periods, I could not secure any more from outside, and permanent honorary workers from Bihar were not available. As soon as my work in Champaran was finished, work outside which had been preparing in the meantime drew me away. Nevertheless, the few months' work in Champaran took such deep root that its influence is to be observed there even to-day.

While social service work of the kind I have described was being carried out, the recording of the raiyats' grievances was also progressing apace. Thousands of such statements were taken and they could not but have their effect. The ever-growing number of raiyats coming to make their statements increased the planters' wrath and they moved heaven and earth to counteract my enquiry.

One day I received a letter from the Bihar Government to the effect that my enquiry had been sufficiently prolonged. The letter was couched in polite language but its meaning was obvious.

I wrote in reply that the enquiry was bound to be prolonged and unless and until it resulted in bringing relief to the people I had no intention of leaving Bihar. I pointed out that it was open to Government to terminate my enquiry by accepting the raiyats' grievances as genuine and redressing them, or by recognising that the raiyats had made out a case for an official enquiry.

Sir Edward Gait, the Lieutenant Governor, asked me to see him, expressed his willingness to appoint an enquiry and invited me to be a member of the Committee. I ascertained the names of the other members and after consultation with my co-workers agreed to serve on the Committee, on condition that I should be free to confer with my co-workers, that the Government should recognise that I did not cease to be the raiyats' advocate, and that, in case the result of the enquiry failed to give me satisfaction, I should be free to guide and advise the raiyats as to what line of action they should take.

Sir Edward Gait accepted this condition and announced the enquiry. Sir Frank Sly was appointed Chairman of the Committee. The Committee found in favour of the raiyats, and recommended that the planters should refund a portion of the exactions made by the planters which the Committee had found to be unlawful and that the tinkathia system should be abolished by law.

Sir Edward Gait had a large share in getting the Committee to make a unanimous report and also in getting the Agrarian Bill passed in accordance with the Committee's recommendations. Had he not adopted a firm attitude, and had he not brought all his tact to bear on the subject, the report would not have been unanimous and the Agrarian Act would not have been passed. The planters wielded extraordinary power. They offered strenuous opposition to the bill in spite of the report, but Sir Edward Gait remained firm up to the last and fully carried out the recommendations of the Committee.

The tinkathia system which had been in existence for about a century was thus abolished, and with it the "Planters' Raj" came to an end in Champaran. The raiyats who had all along remained crushed now somewhat came to their own, and the superstition that the stain of indigo could never be washed out was exploded. It was my great desire to continue the constructive work for some years, to establish more schools and to penetrate the villages more effectively. The ground had been prepared, but it did not please God, as often before, to allow my plans to be fulfilled.

After the Champaran struggle was over a condition approaching famine had arisen in the Khaira District owing to a widespread failure of crops. The farmers were considering the question of asking for the suspension of the revenue assessment for the year. Sjt. Amritlal Thakkar had already reported on the situation, and had personally discussed the question with the Commissioner, before I gave any definite advice to the cultivators. Sjts. Mohanlal Pandya and Shankarlal Parikh had also thrown themselves into the fight and had set up an agitation in Bombay Legislative Council through Sjt. Vithalbhai Patel and the late Sir Gokuldas Kahandas Parekh. More than one deputation had waited upon the Governor in that connexion. I was at this time President of the Gujarat

Sabha. The Sabha sent petitions and telegrams to the Government and even patiently swallowed the insults and threats of the Commissioner. The conduct of the officials on this occasion was so ridiculous and undignified as now to appear almost incredible.

The cultivators' demand was as clear as daylight and so moderate as to make out a strong case for its acceptance. Under the Land Revenue Rules, if the crop was four annas [5] or under, the cultivators could claim a full suspension of the revenue assessment for the year. According to the official figures the crop was said to be over four annas. The contention of the cultivators, on the other hand, was that it was less than four annas. But the Government was in no mood to listen. At last all petitioning and prayer having failed, after taking counsel with co-workers, I advised the farmers to resort to Satyagraha.

Besides the volunteers my principal comrades in this struggle were Sjts. Vallabhbhai Patel, Shankarlal Banker, Shrimati Anasuyaben, Sjts. Indulal Yajnik and Mahadev Desai and others. Vallabhbhai in joining the struggle had to suspend a splendid and growing practice at the bar, which for all practical purposes he was never able to resume. We fixed up our headquarters at the Nadiad Anathashram, no other place being available which would have been large enough to accommodate all of us. The following pledge was signed by the Satyagrahis:

"Knowing that the crops of our villages are less than four annas, we requested the Government to suspend the collection of revenue assessment till the ensuing year, but the Government has not acceded to our prayer. There-

[5] A rupee is sixteen annas. A four anna crop implies twenty-five per cent of a full harvest.

fore, we, the undersigned, hereby solemnly declare that we shall not, of our own accord, pay to the Government the full or the remaining revenue for the year. We shall let the Government take whatever legal steps it may think fit, and gladly suffer the consequences of our non-payment. We shall rather let our lands be forfeited than that by voluntary payment we should allow our case to be considered false or should compromise our self-respect. Should the Government, however, agree to suspend collection of the second instalment of the assessment throughout the District, such amongst us as are in a position to pay will pay up the whole or the balance of the revenue that may be due. The reason why those who are able to pay still withhold payment is that if they pay up, the poorer ryots may in a panic sell their chattels or incur debts to pay their dues, and thereby bring suffering upon themselves. In these circumstances we feel that for the sake of the poor, it is the duty even of those who can afford to pay to withhold payment of their assessment."

The campaign came to an unexpected end. It was clear that the people were exhausted and I hesitated to let the unbending be driven to utter ruin. I was casting about for some graceful way of terminating the struggle which would be acceptable to a Satyagrahi. Such a one appeared quite unexpectedly. News came to me that if well-to-do farmers paid up, the poorer ones would be granted suspension. I enquired of the Collector, who alone could give an undertaking in respect of the whole district, whether the Mamlatdar's undertaking was true for the whole district. He replied that orders declaring suspension in terms of the Mamlatdar's letter had been already issued. I was not aware of it, but if it was a fact, the people's pledge had been fulfilled. The pledge, it will be remembered, had the same thing for its object and so we expressed ourselves satisfied with the orders.

However the end was far from making me feel happy, inasmuch as it lacked the grace with which the termination of every Satyagraha campaign ought to be accomplished. The Collector carried on as though he had done nothing by way of a settlement. The poor were to be granted suspension, but hardly any got the benefit of it. It was the people's right to determine who was poor, but they could not exercise it. I was sad that they had not the strength to exercise the right. Although therefore the termination was celebrated as a triumph of Satyagraha, I could not be enthusiastic over it as it lacked the essentials of a complete triumph. The end of a Satyagraha campaign can only be described as worthy, when it leaves the Satyagrahis stronger and more spirited than they were in the beginning.

Champaran being in a far away corner of India, and the press having been kept away, it did not attract visitors from outside. Not so with the Khaira campaign. The Gujaratis were deeply interested in the fight which was for them a novel experiment. They were ready to pour forth their riches for the success of the cause. It was not easy for them to see that Satyagraha could not be conducted simply by means of money. Money is a thing which it needs least. In spite of my remonstrance, the Bombay merchants sent us more money than necessary, so that we had some balance left at the end of the campaign.

At the same time the Satyagrahi volunteers had to learn the new lesson of simplicity. I cannot say that they imbibed it fully, but they considerably changed their ways of life.

For the farmers too the fight was quite a new thing. We had, therefore, to go about from village to village explaining the principles of Satyagraha. The main thing was to rid the agriculturists of their fear by making them realise that the officers were not the masters, but the servants of the people, inasmuch as they received their salaries from the taxpayer. And then it seemed well nigh impossible to make them realise the duty of combining civility with fearlessness. Once they had shed the fear of the officials, how could they be stopped from returning their insults? And yet if they resorted to incivility it would spoil their Satyagraha, like a drop of arsenic in milk. I realised later that they had less fully learnt the lesson of civility than I had expected. Experience has taught me that civility is the most difficult part of Satyagraha. Civility does not here mean the mere outward gentleness of speech cultivated for the occasion but an inborn gentleness and desire to do the opponent good. These should show themselves in every act of a Satyagrahi.

In the initial stages though the people exhibited much courage the Government did not seem to be inclined to take strong action. But as the people seemed not to waver in their firmness, the Government began coercion. The attachment officers sold people's cattle and seized whatever moveables they could lay hands on. Penalty notices were served, and in some cases standing crops were attached. This unnerved the peasants, some of whom paid their dues while others desired to place safe moveables in the way of the officials so that they might attach them to realise the dues. On the other hand some were prepared to fight to the bitter end.

Whilst these things were going on, one of Sjt. Shankarlal Parikh's tenants paid up the assessment in respect of his land. This created a sensation. Sjt. Shankarlal Parikh immediately made amends for his tenant's mistake by giving away for charitable purposes the land for which the assessment had been paid. He thus saved his honour and set a good example to others.

With a view to steeling the hearts of those who were frightened, I advised the people, under the leadership of Sjt. Mohanlal Pandya, to remove a crop of onion from a field which had been in my opinion wrongly attached. I suggested that the attachment of standing crops, though it might be in accordance with law, was morally wrong, and was nothing short of looting, and that therefore it was the people's duty to remove the onion in spite of the order of attachment. This was a good opportunity for the people to learn a lesson in courting fines or imprisonment. For Sjt. Mohanlal Pandya it was a thing after his heart. He did not like the campaign to end without some one undergoing suffering for something done consistently with the principles of Satyagraha. So he volunteered to remove the onion crop from the field, and in this seven or eight friends joined him.

It was impossible for the Government to leave them free. The arrest of Sjt. Mohanlal and his companions added to the people's enthusiasm. When the fear of jail disappears, repression puts heart into the people. Crowds of them besieged the court-house on the day of the hearing. Pandya and his companions were convicted and sentenced to a brief term of imprisonment. I was of opinion that the conviction was wrong, because the act of removing the onion could not come under the definition of "theft" in the Penal Code. But no appeal was filed as the policy was to avoid the law courts.

A procession escorted the "convicts" to jail, and on that day Sjt. Mohanlal Pandya earned from the people the honoured title of "dungli chor" (onion thief) which he enjoys to this day.

CHAPTER XX

THE WAR CONFERENCE

THE DEADLY WAR IN EUROPE was still going on. A crisis had arrived, and the Viceroy had invited various leaders to a War Conference in Delhi. I had also been invited to attend. Cordial relations existed at this time between Lord Chelmsford, the Viceroy, and myself. In response to the invitation I went to Delhi. I had, however, objections to taking part in the Conference, the principal one being the exclusion from it of leaders like the Ali Brothers. They were then in jail. I had met them only once or twice, though I had heard much about them. Every one had spoken highly of their services and their courage. I had not then come in close touch with Hakim Ajmal Khan Sahib, but Principal Rudra and Andrews had told me a great deal in his praise. I had met Mr. Shuaib Qureshi and Mr. Khwaja at the Muslim League in Calcutta, and had also come in contact with Dr. Ansari and Dr. Abdur Rahman. I was seeking the friendship of good Musalmans, and was eager to understand the Musalman mind through contact with their purest and most patriotic representatives. Therefore, I never needed any pressure to go with them wherever they took me in order to get into intimate touch with them.

I had realised early enough in South Africa that there was no genuine friendship between the Hindus and the Musalmans and I never missed a single opportunity to remove obstacles in the way of unity. It was not in my nature to placate any one by adulation, or at the cost of self-respect; but my South African experiences had convinced me that it would be on the question of Hindu Muslim unity that my Ahimsa doctrine would be put to its severest test. The conviction is still there. Every moment of my life I realise that God is putting me on my trial. Having such strong convictions on the question when I returned from South Africa, I prized the contact with the Ali Brothers. But before closer touch could be established they were interned as prisoners. Maulana Mohamed Ali used to write long letters to me from Betul and Chhindwara whenever his jailers allowed him to do so. I applied for permission to visit the Brothers but to no purpose. It was after the internment that I was invited by Muslim friends to attend the session of the Muslim League at Calcutta. Being requested to speak, I addressed them on the duty of the Muslims to secure the Ali Brothers' release.

Next I opened correspondence with the Government for the release of the Brothers. In that connexion I studied the Brothers' views and activities about the Khilafat. I had discussion with my Musalman friends and felt that if I would become a true friend of the Muslims I must render all possible help in securing the release of the Brothers and a just settlement of the Khilafat question. It was not for me to enter into the absolute merits of the case, provided there was nothing immoral in their demands. In matters of religion, beliefs differ and each one's is supreme for himself. If all had the same belief about all matters of religion there would be only one religion in the world. I found that the Muslim demand about the Khilafat was not only not against any ethical principle, but that the British Prime Minister had admitted the justice of the Muslim demand. I felt therefore bound to render what help I could in securing a due fulfilment of the Prime Minister's pledge.

Friends and other critics have criticised my attitude regarding the Khilafat question. In spite of the criticism I have found no reason to revise it or to regret my co-operation with the Muslims. I should adopt the same attitude should a similar occasion arise again. When therefore I went to Delhi, I had fully intended to submit the Muslim case to the Viceroy. The Khilafat question had not then assumed the shape it did subsequently.

But on my reaching Delhi, another difficulty in the way of my attending the Conference arose. Andrews raised a question about the morality of my participation in the War Conference at that special juncture. He told me of the recent controversy in the British press regarding secret treaties between England and Italy. How could I participate in the Conference, asked Andrews, if England had entered into secret treaties of a predatory character with another European power? I knew nothing of these treaties, but Andrews' word was quite enough for me. Therefore I addressed a letter to Lord Chelmsford explaining my hesitation to take part in the War Conference owing to the secret treaties. He invited me to discuss the question. I had a prolonged discussion with him and his Private Secretary, Mr. Maffey. As a result, I agreed to take part in the Conference.

The Viceroy's argument was in effect as follows: "Surely you do not believe that the Viceroy knows everything done by the British Cabinet. I do not claim that the British Government is infallible. But if you agree that the Empire has been on the whole a power for good; if you believe that India has on the whole benefited by the

British connexion, would you not admit that it is the duty of every Indian citizen to help the Empire in the hour of its need? I too have read what the British papers say about the secret treaties. I can assure you that I know nothing beyond what the papers say, and you know the false reports that these papers frequently start. Can you, acting on a mere newspaper report, refuse to help the Empire at such a critical juncture? You may raise whatever moral issues you like and challenge us as much as you please after the conclusion of the War, not to-day."

The argument was not new, but it appealed to me as new because of the manner in which and the hour at which it was presented, and I agreed to attend the Conference. As regards the Muslim demands I was to address a letter to the Viceroy. So I attended the Conference. The Viceroy was very keen on my supporting the resolution about recruiting. I asked for permission to speak in Hindustani. The Viceroy acceded to my request, but suggested that I should speak also in English. I had no speech to make. I spoke but one sentence to this effect: "With a full sense of my responsibility, I beg to support the resolution." Many congratulated me on my having spoken in Hindustani. That was, they said, the first instance within living memory of any one's having spoken in Hindustani at such a meeting. The congratulations and the discovery that I was the first to speak in Hindustani at a Viceregal meeting hurt my national pride. I felt like shrinking into myself. What a tragedy that the language of the country should be tabooed in meetings held in that country, for work relating to the country, and that a speech there in Hindustani by a stray individual like myself should be a matter for congratulation! Incidents like these are reminders of the low state to which we have been reduced.

The one sentence that I uttered at the Conference had for me considerable significance. It was impossible for me to forget either the Conference or the resolution I supported. There was one undertaking that I had to fulfil while yet in Delhi. I had to write a letter to the Viceroy. This was no easy thing for me. I felt it my duty both in the interests of the Government and of the people to explain therein how and why I attended the Conference and to state clearly what the people expected from the Government. In the letter I expressed my regret for the exclusion from the Conference of leaders like Lokamanya Tilak and the Ali Brothers, and stated the people's minimum political demand as also the demands of the Muslims on account of the situation created by the War. I asked for permission to publish the letter and the Viceroy gladly gave it.

The letter had to be sent to Simla where the Viceroy had gone immediately after the Conference. It had for me considerable importance and sending it by post would have meant delay. I wanted to save time and yet I was not inclined to send it by any messenger I came across. I wanted some pure man to carry it and hand it personally at the Viceregal Lodge. Andrews and Principal Rudra suggested the name of good Mr. Ireland of the Cambridge Mission. He agreed to carry the letter, if he could read it and found it to be such as could appeal to him as good. I had no objection, as the letter was by no means private. He read it, liked it, and expressed his willingness to carry out the mission. I offered him second class fare, but he declined it, saying he was accustomed to travelling by the "intermediate" class. This he did, though it was a night's journey. His simplicity and his straight and plain spoken manner captivated me. The letter thus delivered at the hands of a pure minded man had the desired result. It eased my mind and cleared my way.

The other part of my obligation consisted in raising recruits. Where could I make a beginning except in Khaira? And whom could I invite to be the first recruits except my own co-workers? So as soon as I reached Nadiad I had a conference with Sjt. Vallabhbhai Patel and other friends. Some of them could not easily take to the proposal. Those who liked the proposal had misgivings about its success. There was no love lost between the Government and the classes to whom I wanted to make my appeal. The bitter experience they had of the Government officials was still fresh in their memory. And yet they were in favour of starting work. But as soon as I set about the task my eyes were opened. My optimism received a rude shock. Whereas during the campaigns against the land revenue the people readily offered their carts free of charge and two volunteers came forth when one was needed, it was difficult now to get a cart, even on hire, to say nothing of volunteers. But we would not be dismayed. We decided to dispense with the use of carts and to do our journeys on foot. At this rate we had to trudge about twenty miles a day. If carts were not forthcoming, it was idle to expect people to feed us. It was hardly proper to ask for food. So it was decided that every volunteer must carry his food in his satchel. No bedding or sheet was necessary, as it was summer.

We had meetings wherever we went. People did attend, but hardly more than one or two would offer themselves as recruits. "You are a votary of Ahimsa, how can you ask us to take up arms?" "What good has Government done for India to deserve our co-operation?" These and similar questions used to be put to us. However our steady work began to tell. Quite a number of names were registered, and we hoped that we should be able to have a regular supply as soon as the first batch was sent. I had already begun to confer with the Commissioner as to where the recruits were to be accommodated.

The Commissioners in every division were holding conferences on the Delhi model. One such was held in Gujarat. My co-workers and I were invited to it. We attended it, but I felt that there was even less place for me at such a meeting than at Delhi itself. In this atmosphere of servile submission I felt ill at ease. I spoke somewhat at length but could say nothing to please the officials and had certainly one or two hard things to say.

I used to issue leaflets asking people to enlist as recruits. One of the arguments I had used was distasteful to the Commissioner: "Among the many misdeeds," I wrote, "of the British rule in India, history will look upon the Act depriving a whole nation of arms as the blackest. If we want the Arms Act to be repealed, if we want to learn the use of Arms, here is a golden opportunity. If the middle classes render voluntary help to Government in the hour of its trial, distrust will disappear and the ban on possessing arms will be withdrawn."

During this recruiting campaign I very nearly ruined my constitution. In those days my food consisted principally of groundnut butter and lemons. I knew that the butter could be easily overeaten to the detriment of one's health and yet I allowed myself to overeat it. This gave me a slight attack of dysentery. I did not take serious notice of this and went that evening to the Ashram, as was my wont every now and then. In those days I scarcely took any medicine. If I skipped a meal I felt certain of getting well; and indeed I felt fairly free from trouble as I omitted the morning meal next day. However, I knew that to be entirely free I must prolong my fast, and if I must eat anything at all it should be nothing but fruit juices. There was some festival that day, and although I had told my wife that I should have nothing for my midday meal, she tempted me and I succumbed. As I was under a vow of taking no milk or milk products, she had specially prepared for me a sweet wheaten porridge with oil added to it. There was a bowlful of *mung* besides. Since I was fond of these things I readily took them, hoping that without coming to grief I should eat just enough to please my wife and satisfy my palate. But the Devil had been only waiting for an opportunity. Instead of eating very little I had my fill of the meal. This was enough invitation to the angel of death. Within an hour, the dysentery appeared in acute form. The same evening I had to be back to Nadiad and walked with very great difficulty to the Sabarmati station, a distance of only ten furlongs. Sjt. Vallabhbhai, who joined me at Ahmedabad, saw that I was unwell but I did not allow him to guess how unbearable the pain was.

We reached Nadiad at about ten o'clock. The Hindu Anath Ashram where we had our headquarters was only half a mile from the station; but it was as good as ten for me. Somehow I managed to reach the place but the griping pain had been on the increase. All my friends surrounded me and were deeply concerned. They were full of love and attention but they could not relieve my pain.

And my obstinacy added to their helplessness. I refused all medical aid and would not take medicine, but preferred to suffer the penalty for my folly. So they looked on in helpless dismay. I must have passed thirty to forty motions in twenty four hours. I fasted, not taking even fruit juices in the beginning. The appetite had all gone. I had thought all along that I had an iron frame, but now found that my body had become a lump of clay. It had lost all power of resistance. Dr. Kanuga came and pleaded with me to take medicine, but I declined. He offered to give me an injection, but I declined that also. My ignorance about injections was in those days quite ridiculous; for I believed that an injection must be some kind of animal serum. Later I discovered that the injection that the doctor suggested was a vegetable substance, but the discovery was too late to be of use. The motions still continued leaving me completely exhausted. The exhaustion brought on a delirious fever. My friends got more nervous and called in more doctors. But what could they do with a patient who would not listen to them?

Sheth Ambalal[1] with his good wife came down to Nadiad, conferred with my co-workers and removed me with the greatest care to his bungalow in Ahmedabad. It was impossible for anyone to receive more loving and selfless service than I had the privilege of having during this illness. But a sort of low fever persisted wearing away my body from day to day. I felt that the illness was bound to be prolonged and possibly fatal. Surrounded as I was with all the love and attention that could be showered on me under Sheth Ambalal's roof, I began to get restless

[1] Mr. Ambalal Sarabhai is a mill owner and philanthropist of Ahmedabad. He and his family have been devoted friends of Mahatma Gandhi.

and urged him to remove me to the Ashram. He had to yield to my importunity.

Whilst I was thus tossing on the bed of pain in the Ashram, Sjt. Vallabhbhai brought the news that Germany had been completely defeated and that the Commissioner had sent word that recruiting was no longer necessary. The news that I had no more to worry myself about recruiting came as a very great comfort to me. I had now been trying hydropathy which gave some relief, but it was a hard job to build up the body. The many medical advisers overwhelmed me with advice; but I could not persuade myself to take anything. Two or three suggested meat broth as a way out of the milk vow and cited authorities from the Ayurveda in support of their advice. One of them strongly recommended eggs. But for all of them I had but one answer, "No." For me the question of diet was not one to be determined on the authority of the Shastras. It was one interwoven with my course of life which is guided by principles no longer depending upon outside authority. I had no desire to live at the cost of them. How could I relinquish a principle in respect of myself, when I had enforced it relentlessly in respect of my wife, children and friends? This first long illness in my life thus afforded me a unique opportunity to examine my principles and to test them. One night I gave myself up to despair. I felt that I was at death's door. I sent word to Anasuyaben.[2] She ran down to the Ashram. Vallabhbhai came up with Dr. Kanuga who felt my pulse and said, "Your pulse is quite good. I see absolutely no danger. This is a nervous breakdown due to extreme weakness."

[2] The sister of Sheth Ambalal Sarabhai who is a devoted follower of Mahatma Gandhi and the President of the Labour Movement in Ahmedabad.

But I was far from being reassured. I passed the night without sleep. The morning broke without death coming. But I could not get rid of the feeling that the end was near, and so I began to devote all my waking hours to listening to the Gita being read to me by the inmates of the Ashram. I was incapable of reading and was hardly inclined to talk. The slightest talk meant a strain on the brain. All interest in living had ceased. As I have never cared to live merely for the sake of living, it was an agony to live thus helplessly on, doing nothing, receiving the service of friends and co-workers and watching the body slowly wearing away.

Whilst I lay thus, ever expectant of death, Dr. Tadwalker came one day with a strange person from Maharashtra. He is not known to fame, but the moment I saw him I found that he was a crank like myself. He had come to try his treatment on me. He had almost finished his course of studies in the Grant Medical College at Bombay without taking the degree. Later I came to know that he was a member of the Brahmo Samaj. Sjt. Kelkar, for that is his name, is a man of an independent and obstinate temperament. He swears by the ice treatment which he wanted to try on me. We gave him the name of "Ice Doctor." He is quite confident that he has discovered certain things which have escaped qualified doctors. It is a pity both for him and me that he has not been able to infect me with his faith in his system. I believe in his system up to a certain point, but I am afraid he has been hasty in arriving at certain conclusions. But whatever may be the merits of his discoveries I allowed him to experiment on my body. I did not mind his external treatment. It consisted in the application of ice all over the body.

Though I am unable to endorse the effect that he claims his treatment had on me, it certainly infused in me a new hope, and the mind naturally reacted on the body. I began to have an appetite and to take a gentle walk for five to ten minutes. He now suggested a reform in my diet. "I assure you," he said, "that you will have more energy if you take raw eggs. Eggs are as harmless as milk. They certainly cannot come under the category of meat. And do you know that all eggs are not fertilised? There are sterilised eggs on the market." I was not however prepared to take even the sterilised eggs. But the improvement was enough to interest me in public activities.

I had hardly begun to feel my way towards recovery when I happened casually to read in the papers the Rowlatt Committee's Report [8] that had just been published. Its recommendations startled me. I mentioned my apprehensions to Vallabhbhai who used to come to see me almost daily. "Something must be done," said I to him. "But what can we do in the circumstances?" he asked in reply. "If even a handful of men," I replied, "can be found to sign the pledge of resistance and the proposed measure is passed into law in defiance of it, then we ought to offer Satyagraha at once. If I were not laid up like this, I should give battle against it all alone and expect others to follow suit. But in my present helpless condition I feel myself to be altogether unequal to the task."

As a result of this talk it was decided to call a small meeting of such persons as were in touch with me. The recommendations of the Rowlatt Committee seemed to

[8] The Rowlatt Committee was called upon to report whether emergency legislation were needed to cope with the revolutionary movement in Bengal where terrorist actions had been taken to intimidate witnesses. The Report recommended very drastic proceedings involving imprisonment without open trial.

me to be altogether unwarranted by the evidence published in its Report and were such as, I felt, no self-respecting people could submit to.

The proposed Conference was at last held at the Ashram. Hardly a score of persons had been invited to it. The Satyagraha pledge was drafted at this meeting and as I recollect was signed by every one present. Shankarlal Banker took up the agitation in right earnest, and for the first time I got an idea of his wonderful capacity for organisation and sustained work. As all hope of any of the existing institutions adopting a novel weapon like Satyagraha seemed to me to be vain, a separate body called the Satyagraha Sabha was established at my instance. Its principal members were drawn from Bombay, where its headquarters were fixed. The intending covenanters began to sign the Satyagraha pledge in large numbers; bulletins were issued and popular meetings began to be held everywhere recalling all the familiar features of the Khaira campaign. But from the very beginning it seemed clear to me that the Sabha was not likely to live long. I could see that already my emphasis on Truth and Ahimsa had begun to be disliked by some of its members. Still, in its early stages our new activity proceeded at full blast and the movement gathered head rapidly.

As the work progressed, my desire to live grew with it, and I became impatient to get well once again; and being advised by the doctors that I would recuperate quicker by a change to Matheran,[4] thither I went. But the water at Matheran, being very hard, made my stay there very difficult. Before the week was over I had to flee from Matheran. Shankarlal Banker now constituted himself the

[4] A hill station not far from Bombay.

guardian of my health and pressed me to consult Dr. Dalal. Dr. Dalal was called accordingly. His capacity for taking instantaneous decisions captured me. He wanted to perform an operation at once. I readily consented. He saw no difficulty in performing the operation in my own room and it was so performed the next day with complete success. But that did not satisfy him. "I cannot rebuild your body," he said, "unless you take milk. If in addition you took iron and arsenic injections, I guarantee fully to renovate your constitution."

"You can give me the injections," I replied, "but milk is a different question; I have a vow against it."

"What exactly is the nature of your vow?" the doctor inquired.

I told him the whole history and the reasons behind my vow. My wife was standing near my bed listening.

"But surely," she interposed, "you cannot have any objection to goat's milk."

The doctor also took up the strain. "If you will take goat's milk," he urged, "it will be enough for me."

Then I succumbed. My intense eagerness to take up the Satyagraha fight had created in me a strong desire to live. So I contented myself with adhering to the letter of my vow and sacrificed its spirit. For although I had only the milk of the cow and of the buffalo in mind when I took the vow, by natural implication it covered the milk of all animals. Nor could it be right for me to use milk at all so long as I held that milk was not the natural diet of man. Yet knowing all this I agreed to take goat's milk. The will to live proved stronger than the devotion to Truth, and for once the votary of Truth compromised his sacred ideal by his eagerness to take up the Satyagraha fight. The memory of this action even now rankles in my breast and fills me with remorse and I am constantly thinking how to give up goat's milk. But I cannot yet free myself from that subject of my temptations, the desire to serve which still holds me. These experiments in dietetics are dear to me as a part of my researches in Ahimsa. They give me recreation and joy. But my use of goat's milk to-day troubles me, not from the view-point of dietetic Ahimsa, but from that of Truth, as a breach of a pledge. It seems to me that I understand the ideal of Truth better than that of Ahimsa; and my experience tells me that if I let go my hold of Truth I shall never be able to solve the riddle of Ahimsa. The ideal of Truth requires that vows taken should be fulfilled in the letter as well as in the spirit. In the present case I killed the spirit—the soul of my vow—by adhering to its outer form only, and that is what galls me. But in spite of this clear knowledge I cannot see my way straight before me. In other words, I have not the courage to follow the straight course. Both at bottom mean one and the same thing; for doubt is invariably the result of weakness of faith. Therefore, "Lord, give me faith," is my prayer day and night.

CHAPTER XXI

THE ROWLATT ACT

THUS, WHILE ON THE ONE HAND the agitation against the Rowlatt Committee's Report gathered intensity, on the other hand the Government grew all the more determined to give effect to its recommendations. The Rowlatt Bill was published. I have attended the proceedings of India's Legislative Chamber only once in my life and that was on the occasion of the debate on this Bill. Sastriji delivered an impassioned speech in which he uttered a solemn note of warning to the Government. The Viceroy seemed to be listening spell-bound, his eyes rivetted on Sastriji as the latter poured forth the hot stream of his eloquence. For the moment, it seemed to me as if the Viceroy could not but be deeply moved by it, it was so true and full of feeling; but you can wake a man only if he is really asleep; if he is merely pretending effort will produce no effect upon him. That was precisely the Government's position. It was anxious only to go through the farce of legal formality. Its decision had already been made. Sastriji's [1] solemn warning was therefore entirely lost upon it. In these circumstances, my voice could only be a cry in the wilderness. I earnestly pleaded with the Viceroy and addressed him private letters, as also public letters in the course of which I clearly told him that the Government's action left me no other course except to resort to Satyagraha. But it was all in vain.

[1] The Rt. Hon. V. Srinivasa Sastri was a member of the Viceroy's Council at the time.

The Bill had not yet been gazetted as an Act. I was in a very weak condition, but I decided to take the risk of a long journey when I received an invitation from Madras. I could not at that time sufficiently raise my voice to speak at meetings. My entire frame would shake and heavy throbs would start on an attempt to speak standing for any length of time. Thanks to my South African work, I felt I had some sort of special right over the Tamils and Telugus, and the good people of the South have never belied my belief. The invitation had come over the signature of the late Sjt. Kasturi Ranga Iyengar; but the man behind the invitation, as I subsequently learnt on my way to Madras, was Rajagopalachari. This might be said to be my first acquaintance with him; at any rate this was the first time that we came to know each other personally. He had only recently left Salem to settle down for legal practice in Madras, at the pressing invitation of friends like the late Sjt. Kasturi Ranga Iyengar. It was with him that we had put up in Madras.

We daily discussed together plans of the coming fight, but besides the holding of public meetings I could not then think of any other programme. I was at a loss to discover how to offer civil disobedience against the Rowlatt Bill if it was finally passed into law. One could disobey it only if the Government gave the opportunity. Failing that, could we civilly disobey other laws? And if so, where was the line to be drawn? These and a host of similar questions formed the theme of these discussions of ours. While these cogitations were still going on, news was received that the Rowlatt Bill had been published as an Act. That night I fell asleep while thinking over the question. Towards the small hours of the morning I woke up somewhat earlier than usual. I was still in that twilight condition between sleep and consciousness, when suddenly the idea broke upon me—it was as if in a dream. Early in the morning I related the whole story to Rajagopalachari.

"The idea came to me last night in a dream," I said, "that we should call upon the country to observe a general hartal.[2] Satyagraha is a process of self-purification, and ours is a sacred fight, and it seems to me to be in the fitness of things that it should be commenced with an act of self-purification. Let all the people of India therefore suspend their business on that day and observe the day as one of fasting and prayer. The Musalmans may not fast for more than one day; so the duration of the fast should be twenty-four hours. It is very difficult to say whether all the provinces will respond to this appeal of ours or not, but I feel fairly sure of Bombay, Madras, Bihar and Sindh. I think we should have every reason to feel satisfied even if all these places observe the hartal fittingly."

Rajagopalachari was at once attracted by my suggestion. Other friends too welcomed it when it was communicated to them later. I drafted a brief appeal. The date of the hartal was first fixed on March 30, but was subsequently changed to April 6. The people thus had only a short notice of it. As the work had to be started at once there was hardly any time to give a longer notice. But who knows how it all came about? The whole of India from one end to the other, towns as well as villages, observed a complete hartal on that day. It was a most wonderful scene.

[2] A closing of all shops and places of business as a sign of mourning.

After a short tour in South India I reached Bombay, I think, on the fourth of April, having received a wire from Sjt. Shankarlal Banker asking me to be present there for the sixth of April.

But in the meanwhile Delhi had already observed the hartal on the thirtieth of March. The word of Swami Shraddhanand [3] and Hakim Ajmal Khan was law there. The wire about the postponement of the hartal till the sixth of April had reached there too late. Delhi had never witnessed a hartal like that before. The Hindus and Musalmans seemed united like one man. Swami Shraddhanand was invited to deliver a speech in the Jumma Masjid [4] which he did. All this was more than the authorities could bear. The police checked the hartal procession as it was proceeding towards the railway station, and opened fire, causing a number of casualties and the reign of repression commenced in Delhi. Swami Shraddhanand urgently summoned me to Delhi. I wired back saying I would start for Delhi immediately after April 6.

The story of happenings in Delhi was repeated with variations in Lahore and Amritsar. From Amritsar, Drs. Satyapal and Kitchlu had sent me pressing invitation to go there. I was altogether unacquainted with them at that time, but I communicated to them my intention to visit Amritsar after Delhi.

On the morning of April the sixth the citizens of Bombay flocked in their thousands to the Chowpati beach for a bath in the sea after which they moved on in a proces-

[3] Swami Shraddhanand was the leader of the Arya Samaj, a reforming sect of Hinduism.

[4] The Great Mosque at Delhi. This was the first occasion when a Hindu had been asked to speak in this Mosque.

sion to Thakurdwar. The procession included a fair sprinkling of women and children, while the Musalmans joined it in their numbers. From Thakurdwar some of us were taken by the Musalman friends to a mosque near-by, where Mrs. Naidu and myself were made to deliver speeches.[5] Sjt. Vithaldas Jerajani proposed that we should then and there administer the Swadeshi and Hindu-Muslim unity pledges to the people; but I resisted the proposal on the ground that pledges should not be administered in a hurry and that we should be satisfied with what was already being done by the people. A pledge once taken must not be broken afterwards; therefore it was necessary that the Swadeshi pledge should be clearly understood and the grave responsibility entailed in Hindu-Muslim unity fully realised by all concerned. In the end, I suggested that those who wanted to take the pledges should again assemble on the following morning for the purpose.

Needless to say, the hartal in Bombay was a complete success. Full preparation had been made for starting civil disobedience. Two or three things had been discussed in this connexion. It was decided that civil disobedience might be offered in respect of such laws only as easily lent themselves to being disobeyed by the masses. The salt tax was extremely unpopular and a powerful movement had been for some time past going on to secure its repeal. I therefore suggested that the people might prepare salt from sea-water in their own houses in disregard of the salt laws. My other suggestion was about the sale of proscribed literature. Two of my books, "Hind

[5] Mr. Gandhi and Mrs. Sarojini Naidu were both Hindus. Therefore this was quite an exceptional occurrence, representing Hindu-Muslim unity.

Swaraj" and "Sarvodaya"[6] which had been already proscribed came handy for this purpose. To print and sell them openly seemed to be the easiest way of offering civil disobedience. Copies of the books were therefore printed and it was arranged to sell them at the end of the monster meeting that was to be held that evening after the breaking of the fast.

On the evening of April the sixth an army of volunteers issued forth with this prohibited literature to sell it among the people. Both Shrimati Sarojini Naidu and I went out in cars. All the copies were soon sold out. The proceeds of the sale were to be utilised for furthering the civil disobedience campaign. Both of these books were priced at four annas per copy, but I hardly remember anybody having purchased them from me at their face value. Quite a large number of people poured out all the cash that was in their pockets. Five and ten rupee notes flew out to cover the price of a single copy, while in one case I remember having sold a copy for fifty rupees! It was duly explained to the people, that they were liable to be arrested and imprisoned for purchasing the proscribed literature. But for the moment they had shed all fear of going to jail.

It was subsequently learnt that the Government had conveniently taken the view that the actual books that had been proscribed by it had not in fact been sold, and that what we had sold was a reprint. This was held by the Government to be a new edition of the books that had been proscribed and to sell them thus did not con-

[6] "Hind Swaraj" means "Indian Home Rule," "Sarvodaya" was a Gujarati translation of Ruskin's "Unto this Last."

stitute an offence under the law. This news caused general disappointment.

The next morning, another meeting was held for the administration of the pledges with regard to Swadeshi and Hindu-Muslim unity. Only a handful of persons came. I distinctly remember some of the sisters who were present on that occasion. Men who attended were also very few. I had already drafted the pledge and brought it with me. I thoroughly explained its meaning to those present before I administered it to them. The paucity of the attendance neither pained nor surprised me; for I have noticed this characteristic difference in the popular attitude—partiality for exciting work together with dislike for quiet constructive effort. The difference has persisted to this day.

On the night of April the seventh I started for Delhi and Amritsar. On reaching Muttra on April the eighth I first heard echoes about my probable arrest. Before the train had reached Palwal station I was served with a written order to the effect that I was prohibited from entering the boundary of the Punjab as my presence there was likely to result in a disturbance of the peace. I was asked by the police to get down from the train, but refused to do so saying, "I want to go to the Punjab in response to a pressing invitation; not to foment unrest, but to allay it. I am therefore sorry that it is not possible for me to comply with this order."

At last the train reached Palwal. Mahadev Desai was accompanying me. I asked him to proceed to Delhi to convey to Swami Shraddhanand the news about what had happened and to ask the people to remain calm. He was to explain why I had decided to disobey the order served upon me and to suffer the penalty for disobeying it, and also why it would spell victory for our side if we could maintain perfect peace in spite of any punishment that might be inflicted upon me.

At Palwal station I was taken out of the train and put under police custody. A train from Delhi came in a short time. I was made to enter a third-class carriage, the police party accompanying. On reaching Muttra I was taken to the police barracks but no police official could tell me as to what they proposed to do with me or where I was to be taken next. Early at four o'clock the next morning I was roused from sleep and put in a goods train that was going towards Bombay. At noon I was again made to get down at Sawai Madhupur. Mr. Bowring, Inspector of Police, who arrived by the mail train from Lahore now took charge of me. I was put in a first-class compartment with him. From an ordinary prisoner I became a "gentleman" prisoner. The officer commenced with a long panegyric of Sir Michael O'Dwyer. Sir Michael had nothing against me personally, but he apprehended a disturbance of the peace if I entered the Punjab, and so on. In the end, he requested me to return to Bombay of my own accord and agree not to cross the frontier of the Punjab. I replied that I could not possibly comply with the order and that I was not prepared of my own accord to go back. Whereupon the officer seeing no other help told me that he would have to enforce the law against me. "But what do you want to do with me?" I asked him. He replied that he himself did not know but was awaiting further orders. "For the present," he said, "I am taking you to Bombay."

Thus we reached Surat. Here I was made over to the

charge of another police officer. "You are now free," the officer told me when we had reached Bombay. "It would however be better," he added, "if you get down near the Marine Lines where I shall get the train stopped for you. At Colaba there is likely to be a big crowd." I told him that I would be glad to follow his wish. He was pleased and thanked me for it. Accordingly I alighted at the Marine Lines. The carriage of a friend just happened to be passing by. It took me and left me at Revashankar Jhaveri's place. The friend told me that the news of my arrest had incensed the people and roused them to a pitch of mad frenzy. "An outbreak is apprehended every minute near Pydhuni,[7] the Magistrate and the police have already arrived there," he added.

Scarcely had I reached my destination when Umar Sobani and Anasuyaben arrived and asked me to motor to Pydhuni at once. "The people have become impatient and are very much excited," they said, "we cannot pacify them. Your presence alone can do it."

I got into the car. Near Pydhuni I saw that a huge crowd had gathered. On seeing me the people went mad with joy. A procession was immediately formed and the sky was rent with the shouts of "Bande Mataram" and "Allaho Akbar."[8] As the procession issued out of Abdur Rahman Street and was about to proceed towards the Crawford Market, it suddenly found itself confronted by a body of the mounted police who had arrived there to prevent them from proceeding further in the direction of the Fort. The crowd was densely packed. It had almost broken through the police cordon. There was

[7] A crowded quarter of Bombay.
[8] Meaning "Hail Motherland" and "God is Great."

hardly any chance of my voice being heard in that vast concourse. Just then the officer in charge gave the order to disperse the crowd, and at once the mounted police charged upon the crowd brandishing their lances as they went. For a moment I felt that I would be hurt. But my apprehension was groundless; the lances just grazed the car as the lancers swiftly passed by. The ranks of the people were soon broken and they were thrown into utter confusion which was soon converted into a rout. Some got trampled under foot; others were badly mauled and crushed. In that seething mass of humanity, there was hardly any room for the horses to pass, nor was there any exit by which the people could disperse. So the lancers blindly cut their way through the crowd. I hardly imagine they could see what they were doing. The whole thing presented a most dreadful spectacle. The horsemen and the people were mixed together in mad confusion.

Thus the crowd was dispersed and its progress checked. Our motor was allowed to proceed. I had it stopped before the Commissioner's office. I got down to complain to him about the conduct of the police. All about the staircase leading to the Commissioner's office I saw soldiers armed as though for military action. The verandah was all astir. When I was admitted to the office I saw Mr. Bowring sitting with Mr. Griffith. I described to the Commissioner the scenes I had witnessed. He replied briefly: "I did not want the procession to proceed to the Fort as a disturbance was inevitable there. And as I saw that the people would not listen to persuasion I could not help ordering the mounted police to charge through the crowd."

"But," said I, "you know what the consequences must be. The horses were bound to trample on the people. I think it was quite unnecessary to send that contingent of mounted men."

"You cannot judge that," said Mr. Griffith. "We police officers know better than you the effect of your teaching on the people. If we do not start with drastic measures, the situation would soon pass out of our hands. The people are sure to go out of your control. Disobedience of law will quickly appeal to them; it is beyond them to understand the duty of keeping peaceful. I have no doubt about your intentions, but the people will not understand them. They will follow their natural instinct."

"The people are not by nature violent, but peaceful," I replied.

Thus we argued at length. Ultimately Mr. Griffith said, "But suppose you are convinced that your teaching has been lost on the people, what would you do?"

"I should suspend civil disobedience if I was so convinced."

"What do you mean? You told Mr. Bowring that you would proceed to the Punjab the moment you were released."

"Yes, I wanted to do so by the next available train. But it is out of the question to-day."

"If you will be patient, the conviction is sure to grow on you. Do you know what is happening in Ahmedabad? And what has happened in Amritsar? People have everywhere gone nearly mad. Indeed, I am not yet in possession of all the facts. The telegraph wires have been cut in some places. The responsibility for all these disturbances lies on you."

"I assure you I shall readily take it upon myself wherever I discover it. But I should be deeply pained and surprised if I found that there were disturbances in Ahmedabad. I cannot answer for Amritsar. I have never been there; no one knows me there. But even about the Punjab I know this for certain, that had not the Punjab Government prevented my entry into the Punjab I should have been considerably helpful in keeping peace there. By preventing me, they gave the people unnecessary provocation."

So we argued on and on. It was impossible for us to agree. I told him that I intended to address a meeting on Chowpati beach and to ask the people to keep the peace and so took leave of him. The meeting was held on the Chowpati sands. I spoke at length on the duty of non-violence and on the limitations of Satyagraha and said: "Satyagraha is essentially a weapon of the truthful. A Satyagrahi is pledged to non-violence and unless people observe it in thought, word and deed I cannot offer it truthfully."

Anasuyaben too had received news of disturbances in Ahmedabad. Some one had spread a rumour that she also had been arrested. The mill hands had gone mad over her rumoured arrest, struck work and committed acts of violence, and a sergeant had been done to death. So I proceeded to Ahmedabad. On the way I learnt that an attempt had been made to pull up the rails, near Nadiad railway station; that a Government officer had been murdered in Viramgam, and that Ahmedabad was under martial law. The people were terror-stricken. They had indulged in acts of violence and were being made to pay for them with interest.

A police officer was waiting at the station to escort me to Mr. Pratt, the Commissioner. I found him in a state of rage. I spoke to him gently and expressed my regret for the disturbances. I suggested that martial law was unnecessary and declared my readiness to co-operate in all efforts to restore peace. I asked for permission to hold a public meeting on the grounds of the Sabarmati Ashram. The proposal appealed to him and the meeting was held, I think, on Sunday, April the thirteenth. Martial law was withdrawn the same day or the day after. Addressing the meeting, I tried to bring home to the people the sense of their wrong, declared a penitential fast of three days for myself and appealed to the people to go on a similar fast for a day and suggested to those who had been guilty of acts of violence to confess their guilt.

I saw my duty as clear as daylight. It was unbearable for me to find that the labourers amongst whom I had spent a good deal of my time, whom I had served, and whom I had trusted, had taken part in the riots; I felt I was a sharer in their guilt. Just as I had suggested to the people to confess their guilt, so I suggested to the Government to condone the crimes. Neither accepted my suggestion. The late Sir Ramanbhai and other citizens of Ahmedabad came to me with an appeal to suspend Satyagraha. The appeal was needless, for I had already made up my mind to suspend Satyagraha so long as the people had not learnt the lesson of peace. The friends went away happy. There were, however, others who were unhappy over the decision. They felt that if I were to expect peace everywhere and regard it as a condition precedent to launching Satyagraha, then mass Satyagraha would be an impossibility. I was sorry to disagree with them. If those amongst whom I worked, and whom I expected to be prepared for non-violence and self-suffering, could not be non-violent, Satyagraha was certainly impossible. I was firmly of opinion that those who want to lead the people to Satyagraha ought to be able to keep the people within the limited non-violence expected of them. I hold the same opinion even to-day.

Almost immediately after the Ahmedabad meeting I went to Nadiad. It was here that I first used the expression "Himalayan miscalculation" with regard to my failure to see what would happen. Even at Ahmedabad I had begun to have a dim perception of my mistake. But on reaching Nadiad, when I saw the actual state of things there and heard reports about a large number of people from Khaira district having been arrested, it suddenly dawned upon me that I had committed a grave error in calling upon the people in the Khaira district and elsewhere to launch upon civil disobedience prematurely. I was then addressing a public meeting. This confession of mine to have made a "Himalayan miscalculation" has since called down upon me no small amount of ridicule. But I have never regretted it; for I have always held that it is only when one sees one's own mistakes with a convex lens and does just the reverse in the case of others, that one is able to arrive at a just estimate of the two. I further believe that a scrupulous and conscientious observance of this rule is necessary for one who wants to be a Satyagrahi.

Let us now see what that "Himalayan miscalculation" was. Before one can be fit for the practice of civil disobedience one must have rendered a willing and respectful obedience to the State laws. For the most part, we obey such laws for fear of the penalty for their breach; and this holds good particularly in respect of such laws as do not involve a moral principle. A Satyagrahi obeys the laws of society intelligently because he considers it to be his sacred duty to do so. It is only when a person has thus obeyed the laws of society scrupulously that he is in a position to judge as to which particular rules are good and just and which unjust and iniquitous. Only then does the right accrue to him to undertake civil disobedience of certain laws in well defined circumstances. My error lay in my failure to observe this necessary limitation. I had called upon the people to launch upon civil disobedience before they had thus qualified themselves for it; and this mistake of mine seemed to me to be of a Himalayan magnitude. As soon as I entered the Khaira district all the old recollections of the Satyagraha struggle came back to me and I wondered how I could have failed to perceive what was so obvious. I realised that before a people could be fit for offering civil disobedience they should thoroughly understand its deeper implications.

But it may be rightly argued: "How can a people who are in the habit of frequently evading laws, as most people are, suddenly grasp the significance of civil disobedience or keep themselves within its strict bounds? I admit that it is no easy matter for thousands and hundreds of thousands of people to fulfil the ideal conditions mentioned above. That being so, before re-starting civil disobedience on a mass scale, it would be necessary to create a band of well-tried, pure-hearted volunteers who thoroughly understood the strict conditions of Satyagraha. They could explain these to the people and by sleepless vigilance keep them on the right path.

With these thoughts filling my mind I reached Bombay, raised a corps of Satyagrahi volunteers and with their help commenced the work of educating the people with regard to the meaning and inner significance of Satyagraha. This was principally done by issuing leaflets of an educative character bearing on the subject. But whilst this work was going on, I could see that it was a difficult task to interest the people in the peaceful side of Satyagraha. The volunteers too failed to enlist themselves in full numbers. Nor did all those who actually did enlist take anything like a regular systematic training. As the days passed by the number of fresh recruits began gradually to dwindle instead of growing. Thus I realised that the progress of the training in civil disobedience was not going to be as rapid as I had at first expected.

Sir Michael O'Dwyer held me responsible for all that had happened in the Punjab and some irate young Punjabis held me responsible for the martial law. They asserted that if only I had not suspended civil disobedience, there would have been no Jallianwala Bagh massacre. Some even went the length of threatening me with assassination if I went to the Punjab. But I felt that my position was so above question that no intelligent person could misunderstand it.

I was impatient to go to the Punjab. I had never been there before and that made me all the more anxious to see things for myself there at first hand. Dr. Satyapal, Dr. Kitchlew and Pandit Rambhaj Dutt Chowdhari who had invited me to the Punjab were at this time in jail. But I felt sure that the Government would not dare to keep them and the other prisoners in prison for long. A large number of Punjabis used to come and see me whenever I was in Bombay. I ministered to them a word of cheer on these occasions and this would comfort them.

My self-confidence of the time was infectious. But my going to the Punjab had to be postponed time and again. The Viceroy would say "not yet" every time I asked for permission to go there and so the thing dragged on.

In the meantime the Hunter Committee was announced to hold an enquiry in connexion with the Punjab Government's doings under the martial law. Andrews had also reached there, and his letters gave a heart-rending description of the state of things. These letters left me with the impression that the martial law atrocities were in fact even worse than the press reports showed. He pressed me urgently to go and join him. At the same time Malaviyaji sent telegrams asking me to proceed to the Punjab at once. Once more I telegraphed to the Viceroy asking whether I could now go to the Punjab. He wired back in reply that I could go there after October the seventeenth.

The scene that I witnessed on my arrival at Lahore can never be effaced from my memory. The railway station was from end to end one seething mass of humanity. The entire population had turned out of doors in eager expectation, as if to meet a dear relation after a long separation, and was delirious with joy.

CHAPTER XXII

THE AMRITSAR CONGRESS

AS I PROCEEDED WITH MY ENQUIRY into the Punjab atrocities, I came across tales of the Government's tyranny and the arbitrary despotism of its officers such as I was hardly prepared for and they filled me with deep pain. What surprised me was the fact that a province that had furnished the largest number of soldiers to the British Government during the War should have taken all these brutal excesses lying down. The task of drafting the Congress Enquiry Report was entrusted to me; I would recommend a perusal of it to anyone who wants to have an idea of the cruelties that were perpetrated on the Punjab people. All that I wish to say here is that there is not a single conscious exaggeration in that Report. Every statement made in it is substantiated by evidence. Moreover the evidence published was only a fraction of what was in the Committee's possession. Nothing, with regard to which there was the slightest room for doubt was permitted to pass into print. So far as I am aware, not a single statement made in this Report has ever been disproved.

The Congress enquiry had just commenced when I received a general letter of invitation to be present at a joint Conference of Hindus and Musalmans that was to meet at Delhi to deliberate on the Khilafat question. Among the signatories to it were Hakim Ajmal Khan Sahib and Mr. Asaf Ali. Swami Shraddhanand, it was stated, would be attending. The letter went on to say that not only the Khilafat question, but also the question of

Cow protection would be discussed at the Conference.[1] It would, therefore, afford a golden opportunity for a settlement.

I did not like this reference to the Cow question. In my reply, while promising to do my best to attend, I suggested that the two questions should not be mixed up together, or considered in the spirit of a bargain, but should be decided on their own merits and treated separately.

With these thoughts filling my mind, I went to the Conference. It was very well attended though it did not present the spectacle of later gatherings that were attended by tens of thousands. I discussed the question referred to above with Swami Shraddhanandji who was present at the Conference. He appreciated my argument and left it to me to place it before the Conference. I likewise discussed it with the Hakim Sahib. I contended that if the Khilafat question had a just and legitimate basis, as I believe it had, and if the Government had really committed a gross injustice, the Hindus were bound to stand by the Musalmans. It would ill become them to bring in the Cow question in this connexion, or to use the occasion to make their own terms with the Musalmans, just as it would ill become the Musalmans to offer to stop cow slaughter merely as a price for the Hindu support on the Khilafat question. But it would be another matter, and quite graceful if the Musalmans of their own free will stopped cow slaughter out of regard for the religious sentiments of the Hindus. But if the Musalmans considered it as their neighbourly duty to stop cow slaughter they should do so regardless of whether the Hindus

[1] See "Mahatma Gandhi's Ideas," pp. 38 and 56.

helped them in the Khilafat or not. The two questions should be discussed independently of each other and the deliberations should be confined to the question of the Khilafat only. My argument appealed to those present. But in spite of my warning the Musalmans felt called upon at later conferences always to allude to the duty of stopping cow slaughter in grateful recognition of the Hindus' help on the Khilafat question. And at one time it almost looked as if they would really put an end to it.

Maulana Hasrat Mohani was present in this meeting. I had known him even before, but it was only here that I discovered what a fighter he was. We differed from each other almost from the very beginning. Among the resolutions that were passed at this Conference, one called upon both Hindus and Musalmans to take the Swadeshi vow, and as a natural corollary to it, to boycott foreign goods. Khadi[2] had not as yet found its proper place. This was not a resolution that Hasrat Mohani would accept. His object was to wreak vengeance on the British Empire in case justice was denied in the matter of the Khilafat. Accordingly he brought in a counter proposal for the boycott purely of British goods. I opposed it on the score of principle, adducing for it arguments that have now become pretty familiar. I also put before the Conference my viewpoint of Ahimsa. My arguments made a deep impression on the audience. Hasrat Mohani's speech had been received with such loud applause that I was afraid that mine would only be a cry in the wilderness. Indeed, I spoke only because I felt that it would be a dereliction of duty not to lay my views before the Conference. But to my agreeable surprise, my speech was

[2] Home-spun and home-woven cloth.

followed with the closest attention by those present, and evoked a full measure of support among those on the platform, and speaker after speaker rose to deliver speeches in support of my views. The leaders were able to see that not only would the boycott of British goods fail of its purpose, but would, if adopted, make of them a laughing stock. There was hardly a man present in that assembly but had some article of British manufacture on his person. Many of the audience therefore realised that nothing but harm could result from adopting a resolution which even those who voted for it were unable to carry out.

"Mere boycott of foreign cloth cannot satisfy us," said Maulana Hasrat Mohani, "for who knows how long it will be before we shall be able to manufacture Swadeshi cloth in sufficient quantity for our needs? We want something that will produce an immediate effect on the British. Let your boycott of foreign cloth stand, we do not mind it; but give us something quicker and speedier in addition."

Even as I was listening to him I felt that something new, over and above boycott of foreign cloth, would be necessary. An immediate boycott of foreign cloth seemed to me also to be a clear impossibility. At that time I did not know that we could, if we liked, produce enough Khadi for all our clothing requirements; this was only a later discovery. On the other hand I knew, even then, that if we depended on the mills alone for effecting the boycott of foreign cloth we should be betrayed. I was still in the middle of this dilemma when the Maulana concluded his speech.

I was handicapped for want of suitable Hindi or Urdu

words.[3] This was my first occasion for delivering an argumentative speech before an audience especially composed of Musalmans of the North. I had spoken in Urdu at the Muslim League at Calcutta, but it was only for a few minutes. Here on the contrary, I was faced with a critical, if not hostile, audience to whom I had to bring home my viewpoint. But I had cast aside all shyness. I was not there to deliver an address in the faultless polished Urdu of the Delhi Muslims, but to place before the gathering my views in such broken Hindi as I could command. And in this I was successful. This meeting afforded me a direct proof of the fact that Hindi-Urdu alone can become the lingua franca of India. Had I spoken in English I could not have produced the impression that I did on the audience; and the Maulana might not have felt called upon to deliver his challenge. Nor, if he had delivered it, could I have taken it up effectively.

I could not hit upon a suitable Hindi or Urdu word for the new idea that was in my mind. At last I described it by the word "non-co-operation," an expression that I used for the first time at this meeting. As the Maulana was delivering his speech it seemed to me that it was vain for him to talk about effective resistance to a Government, with which he was co-operating in more than one thing, if resort to arms was impossible or undesirable. The only true resistance to the Government was to cease to co-operate with it. Thus I arrived at the word non-co-operation. I had not then a clear idea of all its manifold implications. So far as I remember, this meeting adopted

[3] Delhi is the centre of the Urdu language which is based on Hindi grammatical forms but uses Arabic and Persian words instead of Sanskrit words. Mr. Gandhi believes that a common spoken language combining Hindi and Urdu is possible as the lingua franca of India.

a resolution about non-co-operation, but it was several months before the idea made further headway. It remained buried for months in the records of this Conference.

The Punjab Government could not long keep in confinement hundreds of Punjabis who had been imprisoned under martial law on the strength of the most meagre evidence by tribunals that were courts only in name. There was such an outcry all round against this flagrant piece of injustice that their further incarceration became impossible. Most of the prisoners were released before the Congress opened. Lala Harkishanlal and the other leaders were all released while the session of the Congress was still in progress. The Ali Brothers too arrived there straight from their jail. The people's joy knew no bounds. Pandit Motilal Nehru, who at the sacrifice of his splendid practice at the bar had made the Punjab his headquarters, was the President of the Congress.

The King's announcement on the Reforms had just been issued. It was not wholly satisfactory, even to me, and was unsatisfactory to everyone else. But I felt at that time that the Reforms though defective could still be accepted. I felt, in the King's announcement, the hand of Lord Sinha; and its language lent a ray of hope. But experienced stalwarts like the late Lokamanya Tilak and Deshbandhu[4] Chittaranjan Das shook their heads. Pandit Malaviyaji was neutral.

Pandit Malaviyaji had harboured me in his own room. Being in the same room with him, I was able to observe his daily routine in the closest detail, and what I saw

[4] Lokamanya is a popular title, meaning "loved, or accepted, by the people." Deshbandhu means "friend of the country."

filled me with joyful surprise. His lodging presented the appearance of a free inn for all the poor. You could hardly cross from one end to the other, it was so crowded. At all odd hours chance visitors came who had the licence to take as much of his time as they liked. In a corner of this crib lay my cot in all its dignity.

I was thus enabled to hold daily discussions with Malaviyaji who used lovingly to explain to me, like an elder brother, the various viewpoints of the different people. I saw that my participation in deliberations on the Reforms was inevitable. Having had my share of responsibility in the drawing up of the Congress Report on the Punjab wrongs I felt that much that still remained to be done in that behalf must claim my attention. There had to be dealings with Government in that matter. Then similarly there was the Khilafat question. I further believed at that time that Mr. Montagu would not betray or allow India's cause to be betrayed. The release of the Ali Brothers and other prisoners too seemed to me to be an auspicious sign. In these circumstances I felt that a resolution not rejecting but accepting the Reforms was the correct thing.

Deshbandhu Chittaranjan Das, on the other hand, held firmly to the view that the reforms ought to be rejected as wholly inadequate and unsatisfactory. The late Lokamanya was more or less neutral, but had decided to throw in his weight on the side of any resolution that the Deshbandhu might approve. The idea of having to differ from such reasoned, well-tried and universally revered leaders was unbearable to me. But on the other hand the voice of conscience was clear. I tried to run away from the Congress and suggested to Pandit Malaviyaji and

(*By courtesy of Messrs. J. M. Dent Sons Ltd.*)

"EAST AND WEST"

Motilalji that it would be in the general interest if I absented myself from the Congress for the rest of the session. It would save me from having to make an exhibition of my difference with such esteemed leaders.

But my suggestion found no favour with these two seniors. The news of my proposal was somehow whispered to Lala Harkishanlal. "This will never do," he said. "It will hurt the feelings of the Punjabis." I discussed the matter with Lokamanya, Deshbandhu and Mr. Jinnah, but no way out could be found. Finally I laid bare my distress to Malaviyaji. "I see no prospect of a compromise," I told him, "and if I am to move my resolution a division will have to be called and votes taken."

"You must not absent yourself from the Congress," he insisted.

I capitulated and framed my resolution and with much trembling of heart undertook to move it. Pandit Malaviyaji and Mr. Jinnah were to support it. I could notice that although our difference of opinion was free from any trace of bitterness, and although our speeches contained nothing but cold reasoning, the people could not bear even the hint of a difference. It pained them; they wanted unanimity.

While speeches were being delivered, efforts to settle the difference were being made on the platform and notes were being freely exchanged among the leaders for that purpose. Malaviyaji was leaving no stone unturned to bridge the gulf. Just then Jayaramdas handed over his amendment to me and pleaded in his own sweet manner to save the delegates from the dilemma of a division. His amendment appealed to me. Malaviyaji's eye was already scanning every quarter for a ray of hope. I told him that Jayaramdas's amendment seemed to me to be likely to be acceptable to both parties. The Lokamanya to whom it was next shown said, "If C. R. Das approves I will have no objection." Deshbandhu at last thawed. Malaviyaji was filled with hope. He snatched away the slip of paper containing the amendment, and before Deshbandhu had even pronounced a definite "Yes" shouted out, "Brother Delegates, you will be glad to learn that a compromise has been reached." What followed beggars description. The pandal was rent with the clapping of hands and the gloomy faces of the audience lit up with joy.

CHAPTER XXIII

THE KHADDAR MOVEMENT

THE BEGINNINGS OF THE KHADI MOVEMENT had been more and more occupying my attention. I do not remember to have seen a handloom or spinning wheel till the year 1908 when I described it in my book "Hind Swaraj" as the panacea for India's growing pauperism. In that book I assumed that anything that helped India to get rid of the grinding poverty of her masses would in the same process establish Swaraj. Even in 1915, when I returned to India from South Africa, I had not actually seen a spinning wheel. When the Satyagraha Ashram at Sabarmati, was founded we introduced a few handlooms there. But no sooner had we done this than we were hard up against another difficulty. All of us belonged either to the liberal professions or to business; none of us was an artisan. We needed a weaving expert to teach us how to weave before we could work looms. One was at last obtained from Palanpur, but he did not communicate to us the whole of his art. Maganlal Gandhi, however, was not the one to be easily baffled. Possessed of a natural gift for mechanics he was able fully to master the art before long and gradually several new weavers were trained up in the Ashram.

The object that we set before us was to be able to clothe ourselves entirely in cloth manufactured by ourselves. We therefore discarded the use of mill-woven cloth made from Indian yarn. The adoption of this practice brought us a world of experience. It enabled us to know from direct contact the living conditions among the weavers, the extent of their production, the handicaps in the way of their obtaining their yarn supply, the manner in which they were being made victims of fraud and their ever-growing indebtedness. We were not in a position immediately to manufacture the cloth we needed. So the time slipped by and my impatience increased. I plied every chance visitor, who was likely to have any information about handspinning, with questions about the art. It had been confined to women. If there was some stray spinner still surviving, in some obscure corner, only a member of that sex was likely to find out her whereabouts.

In the year 1917, I was taken by my Gujarati friends to preside at the Broach Educational Conference. It was here that I discovered that remarkable lady, Gangabehn. She was a widow, but her enterprising spirit knew no bounds. Her education, in the accepted sense of the term, was not much. But in courage and common-sense she easily surpassed the general run of our educated women. She had already got rid of the curse of untouchability and fearlessly moved among and served the suppressed classes. She had means of her own and her needs were few. She had a well seasoned constitution and went about everywhere without an escort. She felt quite at home on horseback. I came to know her more intimately at the Godhra Conference. To her I poured out my grief about the Charkha,[1] and she lightened my burden by a promise to prosecute an earnest and incessant search for the spinning wheel.

At last, after no end of wandering in Gujarat, Gangabehn found the spinning wheel in Vijapur in the Baroda State. Quite a number of people there had spinning wheels

[1] Spinning wheel.

in their homes, but had long since consigned them to the lofts as useless lumber. They expressed to Gangabehn their readiness to resume spinning if some one promised to provide them with a regular supply of slivers and to buy the yarn spun by them. Gangabehn communicated the joyful news to me. The providing of slivers was found to be a difficult task. On mentioning the thing to Umar Sobhani, however, he solved the difficulty by immediately undertaking to send a sufficient supply of slivers from his mill. I sent to Gangabehn the slivers received from Umar Sobhani and soon yarn began to pour in at such a rate that it became quite a problem how to cope with it.

I felt ill at ease continuously receiving slivers from him. Moreover, it seemed to me to be fundamentally wrong to use mill-slivers. So I suggested to Gangabehn to find carders who could supply slivers. She confidently undertook the task and engaged a carder who was prepared to card cotton. He demanded thirty-five rupees per month. I considered no price too high at the time. She trained a few youngsters to make slivers out of the carded cotton. Gangabehn's enterprise thus prospered beyond expectation. She found out weavers to weave the yarn that was spun in Vijapur and soon Vijapur Khadi gained a name for itself.

While these developments were taking place in Vijapur, the spinning wheel gained a rapid footing in the Ashram, Maganlal Gandhi, by bringing to bear all his splendid mechanical talent on the wheel, made many improvements in it; wheels and their accessories began to be manufactured at the Ashram. The first piece of Khadi manufactured in the Ashram cost seventeen annas per yard. I did not hesitate to commend this very coarse cloth at that price to friends who willingly paid the amount.

I was laid up in bed in Bombay. But I was fit enough to make searches for the wheel there. At last I chanced upon two spinners, and brought them to the house where I was staying. The wheel began merrily to hum in my room, and I may say without exaggeration that its hum had no small share in restoring me to health. I am prepared to admit that its effect was more psychological than physical. But then it only shows how powerful the physical in man reacts to the psychological. I too set my hand to the wheel, but I did not do much with it at the time.

From its very start the Khadi movement evoked much criticism from the mill-owners. Umar Sobhani, a capable mill-owner himself, not only gave me the benefit of his own knowledge and experience but kept me in touch with the opinion of the other mill-owners as well. The argument advanced by one of these deeply impressed him. He pressed me to meet him and arranged the interview. The mill-owner opened the conversation.

"You know that there has been Swadeshi agitation before now?"

"Yes, I do," I replied.

"You are also aware that in the days of the Partition the mill-owners fully exploited the Swadeshi movement. When it was at its height, we raised the prices of cloth and did even worse things."

"Yes, I have heard something about it and it has grieved me."

"I can understand your grief, but I can see no ground for it. We are not conducting our business out of philanthropy. We do it for profit; we have got to satisfy the shareholders. The price of an article is governed by the demand for it. Who can check the law of demand and supply? The Bengalis should have known that their agitation was bound to send up the price of Swadeshi cloth by stimulating the demand for it."

I interrupted: "The Bengalis like me were trustful in their nature. They believed in the fulness of their faith that the mill-owners would not be so utterly selfish and unpatriotic as to betray their country in the hour of its need and even go the length of fraudulently passing off foreign cloth as Swadeshi."

"I know your believing nature," he rejoined, "that is why I put you to the trouble of coming to me, so that I might warn you against falling into the same error as these simple-hearted Bengalis."

With these words the mill-owner beckoned to his clerk who was standing by to produce samples of the stuff that was being manufactured in his mill. Pointing to it he said: "Look at this stuff. This is the latest variety turned out by our mill. It is meeting with a widespread demand. We manufacture it from the waste. Naturally, therefore, it is cheap. We send it as far North as the valley of the Himalayas. We have agencies all over the country, even in places where your voice or your agents can never reach. You can thus see that we do not stand in need of more agents. Besides, you ought to know that India's production of cloth falls far short of its requirements. The question of Swadeshi, therefore, largely resolves itself into one of production. The moment we can increase our production sufficiently and improve its quality to the necessary extent, the import of foreign cloth will automatically cease. My advice to you therefore is not to carry on your agitation on its present lines, but to turn your attention to the erection of fresh mills. What we need is not propaganda to inflate demand for our goods, but greater production."

"Then, surely, you will bless my effort, if I am already engaged in that very thing," I asked.

"How can that be?" he exclaimed, a bit puzzled. "But maybe, you are thinking of promoting the establishment of new mills, in which case you certainly deserve to be congratulated."

"I am not doing exactly that," I explained, " but I am engaged in the revival of the spinning wheel."

"What is that?" he asked, feeling still more at sea. I told him all about the spinning wheel and the story of my long quest after it. "I am entirely of your opinion," I added, "it is no use my becoming virtually an agent for the mills. That would do more harm than good to the country. Our mills will not be in want of custom for a long time to come. My work should be, and therefore is, to organise the production of handspun cloth and to find means for the disposal of the Khadi thus produced. I am, therefore, concentrating my attention on the production of Khadi. I swear by this form of Swadeshi because through it I can provide work to the semi-starved, semi-employed women of India. My idea is to get these women to spin yarn and to clothe the people of India with Khadi woven out of it. I do not know how far this movement is going to succeed. At present it is only beginning. But I have full faith in it. At any rate, it can do no harm. On the contrary, to the extent that it can add to the cloth production of the country, be it ever so small, it will represent so much solid gain. You will thus perceive that my movement is free from the evils mentioned by you."

"If," he replied, "you have additional production in view in organising your movement, I have nothing to say against it. Whether the spinning wheel can make headway in this age of power machinery is another question. But I for one wish you every success."

To resume the story of the Non-co-operation Movement,—whilst the powerful Khilafat agitation set up by the Ali Brothers was in full progress, I had full discussions with the late Maulana Abdul Bari and others, especially as to the extent to which a Musalman could observe the rule of non-violence. In the end all agreed that Islam did not forbid non-violence as a policy, and further that so long as they were pledged to that policy they were bound faithfully to carry it out. At last the Non-co-operation resolution was moved in the Khilafat Conference and carried after prolonged deliberations. I have a vivid recollection how once, at Allahabad, a Committee sat all night deliberating upon the subject. In the beginning the late Hakim Ajmal Khan was sceptical as to the practicability of non-violent non-co-operation. But after his scepticism was overcome, he threw himself into it heart and soul and his help proved invaluable to the movement.

The All-India Congress Committee resolved to hold a special session of the Congress in September, 1920, at Calcutta, to deliberate on Non-co-operation, which had now been accepted by the Musalmans. Preparations were made for it on a tremendous scale. Lala Lajpat Rai was elected president. Congress and Khilafat specials were run to Calcutta from Bombay. At Calcutta there was a mammoth gathering of delegates and visitors. I was called upon to frame the non-co-operation resolution for the eventful Congress.

In my resolution, Non-co-operation was postulated only with a view to obtaining redress of the Punjab and the Khilafat wrongs. That however did not appeal to Sjt. Vijaya Raghavachari. "If non-co-operation," he argued, "is to be declared, why should it be with reference to particular wrongs? The absence of Swaraj is the biggest wrong that the country is labouring under. Non-co-operation should be directed against this also." I readily accepted his suggestion and incorporated the demand for Swaraj in my resolution, which was passed after an exhaustive and somewhat stormy discussion.

Motilalji was the first to join the Movement. I still remember the sweet discussion that I had with him on the resolution. He suggested some changes in its phraseology which I adopted. He undertook to win the Deshbandhu for the movement. His heart was inclined towards it, but he felt sceptical as to the capacity of the people to carry out the program. It was only at the Nagpur Congress that he and Lalaji [2] accepted it whole heartedly.

I felt the loss of the late Lokamanya [3] very deeply at the special session. It has been my firm faith to this day that had the Lokamanya been then alive, he would have given his benedictions to me on that occasion. But even if it had been otherwise and he had opposed the movement, I should still have esteemed his opposition as a privilege and an education for myself. We had our differences of opinion but they never led to bitterness. He always allowed me to believe that the ties between us were of the closest. Even as I write these lines the circumstances of his death stand forth in a vivid picture before the mind's eye. It was about the hour of mid-night when Yadvadkar

[2] Lala Lajpat Rai.

[3] Lokamanya Tilak.

conveyed over the telephone the news of his death. I was at that time surrounded by my companions. Spontaneously the exclamation escaped my lips, "My strongest bulwark is gone." The Non-co-operation Movement was then in full swing and I was eagerly looking forward to encouragement and inspiration from him.

The resolution passed at the Calcutta special session of the Congress, accepting the non-co-operation program, had to be confirmed at its annual session at Nagpur. Here again there was a great rush of visitors and delegates. The number of delegates in the Congress had not been limited as yet. The figure on this occasion reached about fourteen thousand. Lala Lajpat Rai pressed for a slight amendment to the clause about the boycott of schools, which I accepted. Similarly, some amendments were made at the instance of the Deshbandhu after which the non-co-operation resolution was passed unanimously.

The question of the goal of the Congress formed a subject for keen discussion. In the constitution that I had presented, the goal of the Congress was the attainment of Swaraj within the British Empire if possible, and without if necessary. A party in the Congress wanted to limit the goal to Swaraj within the British Empire only. Its viewpoint was put forth by Pandit Malaviyaji and Mr. Jinnah. But they were not able to get many votes. Again, the Draft Constitution provided that the means for the attainment were to be "peaceful and legitimate." This condition too came in for opposition, it being contended that there should be no restriction upon the means to be adopted. But the Congress accepted the original draft after an instructive and frank discussion.

Resolutions about Hindu-Muslim unity, the removal

of untouchability and Khadi were passed in this Congress; and since then the Hindu members of the Congress have taken upon themselves the responsibility of ridding Hinduism of the curse of untouchability and the Congress has established a living bond of relationship with those "skeletons," the poor of India, through Khadi. The adoption of non-co-operation for the sake of the Khilafat was itself a great practical attempt made by the Congress to bring about Hindu-Muslim unity.

But the time has now come to bring these chapters to a close. My life from this point onward has been so public that there is hardly anything about it that the people do not know. Moreover, since 1921, I have worked in such close association with the Congress leaders that I can hardly describe any episode in my later life without referring to my relations with them. For though Lokamanya, Shraddhanandji, Deshbandhu, Hakim Sahib and Lalaji are no more with us to-day, we have the good luck to have a host of other veteran Congress leaders still living and working in our midst. The history of the Congress is still being made. And my principal experiments with Truth during the past seven years have all been made through the Congress. A reference to my relations with the leaders would therefore be unavoidable, if I set about to describe my experiments further. And this I may not do, at any rate for the present, if only from a sense of propriety. Lastly my conclusions from my current experiments can hardly as yet be regarded as decisive. It therefore seems to me to be my plain duty to close this narrative here. In fact, my pen instinctively refuses to proceed further.

It is not without a wrench that I have to take leave. I set a high value on these experiments. I do not know whether I have been able to do justice to them. I can only say that I have spared no pains to give a faithful narrative. To describe Truth, as it has appeared to me and in the exact manner in which I have arrived at it, has been my ceaseless effort. The exercise has given me ineffable mental peace because it has been my fond hope that it might bring faith in Truth and Ahimsa to waverers.

My uniform experience has convinced me that there is no other God than Truth. And if every page of these chapters does not proclaim that the only means for the realisation of Truth is Ahimsa, I shall deem all my pains in writing these chapters to have been in vain. And even though my efforts in this behalf might prove fruitless, it is the vehicle, not the great principle, that is at fault. After all, however sincere my strivings after Ahimsa might have been, they have still been imperfect and inadequate. The little fleeting glimpses, therefore, that I have been able to obtain of Truth can hardly convey an idea of its indescribable lustre, a million times more intense than that of the sun we daily see with our eyes. In fact what I have caught is only the faintest gleam of that mighty Effulgence. But this much I can say, with assurance, as a result of all my experiments, that a perfect vision of Truth can only follow a complete realisation of Ahimsa.

To see the universal and all-pervading Spirit of Truth face to face one must be able to love the meanest of creation as oneself. And a man who aspires after that cannot afford to keep out of any field of life. That is why my devotion to Truth has drawn me into the field of politics; and I can say without the slightest hesitation and yet in all humility, that those who say that religion has nothing to do with politics do not know what religion means.

Identification with everything that lives is impossible without self-purification; without self-purification the observance of the law of Ahimsa must remain an empty dream; God can never be realised by one who is not pure of heart. Self-purification therefore must mean purification in all walks of life. And purification being highly infectious, purification of oneself necessarily leads to the purification of one's surroundings.

But the path of self-purification is hard and steep. To attain to perfect purity a man has to rise above the opposing currents of love and hatred, attachment and repulsion, and to become absolutely passion-free in thought, speech and action. I know that I have not in me as yet that triple purity in spite of constant ceaseless striving for it. That is why the world's praise fails to move me; indeed it very often stings me. To conquer the subtle passions seems to me to be harder far than the physical conquest of the world by the force of arms. Ever since my return to India I have had experiences of the dormant passions lying hidden within me. The knowledge of them has made me feel humiliated but not defeated. The experiences and experiments have sustained me and given me great joy. But I know that I have still before me a difficult path to traverse. I must reduce myself to zero. So long as a man does not of his own free will put himself last among his fellow creatures, there is no salvation for him. Ahimsa is the farthest limit of humility.

In bidding farewell to the reader I ask him to join with me in prayer to the God of Truth that He may grant me the boon of Ahimsa in thought, word, and deed.

CHAPTER XXIV

CONCLUSION

UP TO THIS POINT, the documents which I have used have been ample enough to cover the whole ground and to give us Mahatma Gandhi's story as he himself has described it in his own words. The outline of the narrative, dealing with more recent events may be found in the second part of *Mahatma Gandhi's Ideas*, which I have called "The Historical Background." It will not be necessary, therefore, to repeat the record of those events in detail here, or to go on still further to describe the last great passive resistance movement which is still unfinished. That must wait for the judgment of future historians in order to be appreciated at its real value and reviewed in its right proportions.

It has appeared to me that I can best bring to a close this work, which has been truly a labour of love, by giving two quotations. In the first place, there is one illuminating passage in Mr. Gandhi's writings, wherein he sums up the chief end and purpose of existence in relation to the soul's deliverance. It was written just after he had passed out of the valley of the shadow of death, in the year 1924. Some of his closest friends had pointed out his inconsistency in agreeing to the surgeon's operation for appendicitis instead of believing in soul force as the remedy for bodily ills. One friend, an old Brahmin ascetic, had urged him to retire to the solitude of some cave in order to regain his spiritual ascendancy over the body. In reply he writes as follows:

"I plead guilty. But that is to admit that I am by no

means a perfect man. Unfortunately for me, I am far from being perfect. I am simply a humble aspirant for perfection. I know my way to it also. But knowing the way is not reaching its end. If I was perfect; if I had acquired full control over all my passions, even in thought, then I should be perfect in body. I am free to confess that daily I am obliged to expend a great amount of mental energy in acquiring control over my thoughts. When I have at last succeeded, if I ever do succeed, think what a store-house of energy would be set free for service! As I hold that my illness was a result of infirmity of thought or mind, so do I concede that my submission to the surgical operation was an additional infirmity of mind. If I was absolutely free from egoism, I would have resigned myself to the inevitable; but I wanted to live in the present body. Complete detachment is not a mechanical process. One has to grow into it by patient toil and prayer. As for gratitude, I have more than once publicly expressed it to Col. Maddock and his staff for all the kindness with which they overwhelmed me.

"Now for the central point of the letter of my friend, in which he compares me with the great prophets of the human race. The confusion in his mind has arisen because of his misconception of the work of the prophets and of an awkward (for me) comparison between them and me. I do not consider myself worthy to be mentioned in the same breath with the race of prophets. I am a humble seeker after truth, impatient to realise myself, to attain spiritual deliverance in this very existence. My national service is part of the training I undergo for freeing my soul from the bondage of the flesh. Thus considered, my service may be regarded as purely selfish. I have no desire for the perishable kingdom of earth. I am striving for the kingdom of Heaven which is spiritual deliverance. To attain this end it is not necessary for me to seek the shelter of a cave. I carry one about me, if I would but know it. A cave-dweller can build castles in the air whereas a dweller in a palace, like Janaka, who was king and *rishi* at the same time, has no castles to build. The cave-dweller who hovers round the world on the wings of thought has no peace. A King Janaka, though living in the midst of 'pomp and circumstance,' may attain the peace that passeth understanding. For me, the road to salvation lies through incessant toil in the service of my country and of humanity. I want to identify myself with everything that lives. In the language of the Gita I want to live at peace with both friend and foe. Though therefore a Mussalman or a Christian or a Hindu may despise me and hate me, I want to love him and serve him even as I would love my wife or son though they hate me. So my patriotism is for me a stage in my journey to the land of eternal freedom and peace. Thus it will be seen that for me there are no politics devoid of religion. They subserve religion. Politics bereft of religion are a death-trap because they kill the soul."

Such, in his own words, is the direct aim that Mahatma Gandhi with a touching sincerity and humility that has won every heart has set before himself to accomplish.

In the second place, as a revealing narrative, I would share with my readers the beautiful description of the Poona hospital with its nurses and doctors and visitors at the time when Mahatma Gandhi's life had been hanging in the balance and had been saved by the tender skill of Colonel Maddock. The picture is faithfully drawn by

Mahadev Desai, and I can personally vouch for its accuracy, because I was present all the while, and shared with him the pathos and the joy of such a unique occasion. The sight of what we saw moved us as a fresh revelation of the beauty of the inner character of the sufferer.

"God in His infinite mercy," writes Mahadev, "has spared to us our Bapu.[1] These have been days which will live in our annals. The Indian nation had the good fortune before to see its revered leader at work, to watch him mould heroes out of clay whilst at work. It had yet to see his gospel go forth from his sick-bed and become translated into act before his eyes. It has done so during the past fortnight. There is in this hospital since Bapu entered it a living atmosphere of love whose effects you begin to feel as soon as you approach the room which happens to possess to-day the light that transcends the bounds of time and space.

"I have had the privilege of being with Bapu these ten days, though not of serving him. That privilege is being entirely monopolised by the hospital nurses. One of them is an Englishwoman of long experience. He cannot help smiling as she approaches him. One day, she comes talking about her pet dogs, and draws Bapu into a conversation about the different varieties of dogs and their usefulness. Another day, she talks about her experience in English and African hospitals, and tells him how she has lived throughout her life the lesson that her doctors taught her of never trying to be popular. A third day she decorates the room with the finest flowers and asks Bapu to admire her work. There was another nurse much younger, but

[1] The endearing name for Mahatma Gandhi used specially in his own Asram; the meaning is "Father."

equally fond of Bapu, who prided herself on having Mr. Gandhi as her first 'private' patient after passing out as a trained nurse. 'Nursing is not always a joy, at times it is a task,' she used to say, 'but it has been a pure joy and a privilege to nurse Mr. Gandhi. The doctor comes and tells me, "You did not use to print your reports like this ever before," and I tell him straightway, "Nor had I such a patient before."' Another day she told me, 'My friends were chaffing me for getting so fond of Mr. Gandhi; I told them they would do the same if they had the privilege of serving him.'

"And the Surgeon's love for him is as undisguised as that of the nurses. The Civil Surgeon has had letters and telegrams pouring in on him to congratulate him for the way in which he was serving Mahatmaji, and it is not without a blush that he says, 'How am I to reply to all of them? Shall I do it through the Press?'

"I do not know if any one attending Bapu has the slightest consciousness that he is serving a state prisoner. For he is still under a guard. A compelling love chokes all other consciousness.

"But why? Even he who has to look upon him as a prisoner seemed scarcely different in his manner from the rest. Col. Murray, the Yerravda Superintendent, came to see Bapu the other day. 'Do you think, Mr. Gandhi, I have neglected you? No. I thought I should not disturb you. And as I see you now after some days I find you very much better. The Colonel also assures me you are quickly improving. Your friends remember you. Mr. Gani especially asked me to tell you that he still gets up at 4 o'clock for prayers. Every one of them is happy, and misses you—I hope they do so permanently.' 'Thank you

Col. Murray,' said Bapu, 'but I assure you nothing will please me better than to be up and doing and under your kind care once again at Yerravda.' You never could tell, if you did not know him, that a jail Superintendent was speaking to one of his prisoners, and you could almost visualise the atmosphere of love created by Bapu in his prison cell at Yerravda.

"But I must say something about Bapu's health, rather than go on talking about his alchemy of love. He looks still emaciated, but he is better than he might have been. His weight which at its best was 112 lbs. in jail cannot be now very much over ninety, though it is difficult to be precise, as he is still in bed, and cannot be moved out of it. There is no doubt, however, that he is getting stronger every day. There is a chain hanging down from the top of his bed of which he gets a hold to enable him to sit up or turn in bed. 'That's for my gymnastics,' he said to a friend the other day. The fingers are still shaky, but not so much as before. His nourishment is nearly half his usual quantity, and consists of about 2 lbs. of milk, a couple of oranges and some grapes. Above all, he gets most restful sleep of the kind which he has never had during the last few years. For even the days in jail were of 'toil unsevered from tranquillity.' From my talks with the surgeons I can say that there is now no cause for anxiety, though the convalescence will certainly be prolonged and even indefinite.

"And need I say anything concerning the torrents of love that have taken their course to Poona from all the parts of India? Devadas, who should be privileged to be with his father all the time, has to content himself by attending to the numerous letters and telegrams coming day and night enquiring after Bapu's health. But the telegrams and letters do not exhaust these acts of affection. One day the residents of far off Tanjore write to say that they did their devotions in a particular temple for Mahatmaji, Hindus from Shiyali, Tirupur, and Dindigul, vie in their love with their Mussalman brethren of Nagore who send special food that has been blessed for him to take. A Parsi sister writes offering her blood if the surgeons thought it necessary to put blood in Mahatmaji; while an English lady writes detailed instructions about Bapu's diet, and Mrs. Gokhale from Bombay writes to say that she will spin an extra couple of hours every day, now that Mahatmaji cannot spin.

"One of the constant visitors at the hospital is an Englishman, an old military pensioner, who makes it a point to come every other day with a bouquet of flowers, and gets into Bapu's room unobstructed by any one. It is simply impossible to stop him. Impatiently he rushes to Bapu, shakes his hand, and delivers his message of cheer in a few seconds and walks away. 'Cheer up!' he cries 'I see that you are very much better than yesterday. I know you must get better. How old are you? Fifty-five. Oh it is nothing. You know I am 82. Get better, please do.' One day he stopped and asked, 'Can I do anything for you Mr. Gandhi?' 'No,' said Bapu. 'Please pray for me.' 'That I will, but tell me if I can do anything for you. Please do tell me. Trust me to be your brother.' To which Bapu replies with a smile, 'Believe me I have amongst my friends a number of Englishmen whom I regard as more than my brothers.' The man is deeply touched, moves out assuring us that he prays thrice every day that Mr. Gandhi may live up to his own age, and also telling us that many Englishmen pray for him, and many officers enquire after him.

"The picture would be incomplete if I did not say a word about the illustrious leaders who are now flocking to Poona to see their leader. They did not come until now, as they knew it would not be well to disturb him. A man like Mr. Jayakar says, 'I will now come, but will only have a sight of him at a distance; for I must not do anything to tire him in his present weakness.' And Pandit Jawaharlal assures Devades that he will come last of all. The big brother, Shawkat Ali, comes, and insists lovingly that Mahatmaji should not talk to him for fear of his becoming too tired. Pandit Motilal Nehru has no heart to get away without bidding him good-bye a second time, and deliberately misses a train. Lajpat Rai comes, eager to have a talk with him, but stands aside, almost in spite of himself, so that he may not draw him into a talk with him. He visits him again before leaving Poona. There is something in him which is struggling to find expression. Probably it checks the tears, or the tears check it. But ultimately it succeeds and bursts out. Bapu with his inimitable smile says, 'Lalaji, the joke is too big for my stomach. I would have a hearty laugh, but for the wound and the stitches.' Lalaji, who would have departed otherwise with a heavy heart, goes away with a much lighter heart, not without assuring others also, that we may not be sad now, but rejoice that God in His infinite mercy has blessed us by preserving the life of the one whom we all love best in the world."

Here then, I would leave "Bapu," where he would wish to be left, in an atmosphere of peace and reconciliation, won through the constant fearless facing of Truth in the Spirit of Love. His devotion to the good surgeon and the gentle nurses and his old English visitor, whose daily visit cheered him, was no less than his love for the dear friends and comrades who had fought the good fight for freedom by his side. The end to be obtained was not any outward victory, however glorious, but rather the supreme victory within the heart. There, in the heart itself, Truth and Inner Purity and Lovingkindness were to have their undivided throne. There, the spiritual test of character was to be carried through to the very end. There, to quote his own words, "When that fineness and rarity of spirit which I long for have become perfectly natural to me; when I have become incapable of any evil; when nothing harsh or haughty occupies, be it momentarily, my thought world, then, and not till then, will my non-violence move all the hearts of all the world."

APPENDICES

BIBLIOGRAPHY

(A)

Mahatma Gandhi. By Romain Rolland. Pub. by George Allen & Unwin, Ltd., London.

(By far the best sketch of his life and thoughts. A work of supreme genius. The book was published in French and has been well translated.)

Mahatma Gandhi's Ideas, including selections from his writings. By C. F. Andrews. Pub. by The Macmillan Company, New York, and George Allen & Unwin Ltd., London.

An Indian Patriot in South Africa. By the Rev. J. J. Doke. Pub. by the *London Indian Chronicle.*

(An invaluable account of Mahatma Gandhi's early days in South Africa; it is now unfortunately out of print.)

My Experiments with Truth: An Autobiography. Pub. by Navajivan Press, Ahmedabad.

(This is the standard work.)

Mahatma Gandhi: By H. S. L. Polak. Pub. by G. A. Natesan, Madras.

(A thoroughly accurate, well-informed, and sympathetic sketch by one of Mahatma Gandhi's closest personal friends.)

Mahatma Gandhi: An Appreciation. By R. M. Gray and Manilal C. Parekh. Pub. by Association Press, Calcutta.

(Compiled with great care from a liberal Christian standpoint.)

Gandhi the Apostle. By H. M. Muzumdar. Pub. by The University of Chicago Press.

(The work of a young and ardent admirer who has deeply appreciated Gandhi's message.)

Mahatma Gandhi: Ethical Religion, with an introduction by John Haynes Holmes. Pub. by S. Ganesan Triplicane, Madras.

(An important little book with an excellent introduction.)

Young India. Current issues. Pub. by Navajivan Press, Ahmedabad.

(Mahatma Gandhi is Editor of *Young India;* therefore this is the main source from whence to discover his own ideas and life-history.)

Golden Number of *Indian Opinion.* Edited by H. S. L. Polak. Pub. at Phoenix, Natal, South Africa.

(A very important document for South African days, admirably edited.)

Speeches and Writings of M. K. Gandhi, with an introduction by C. F. Andrews. Pub. by G. A. Natesan, Madras.

(Contains many early writings not included in *Young India.*)

Economics of Khaddar. By R. B. Gregg. Pub. by S. Ganesan, Triplicane, Madras.

(The one authoritative book on Home-Spinning in India.)

The Ethics of Non-violence. By R. B. Gregg. Pub. by S. Ganesan, Triplicane, Madras.

The Indian Problem. By C. F. Andrews. Pub. by G. A. Natesan, Madras.

The Dawn of a New Age. By W. W. Pearson. Pub. by S. Ganesan, Madras.

The Gospel of Swadeshi. By Prof. Kalekar. S. Ganesan, Madras.

(B)

The main supply of literature concerning Mahatma Gandhi, published in India can be obtained from S. Ganesan, Publisher, Triplicane, Madras.

The following books are now in stock at this publishing house:—

Young India, Vol. I.
Young India, Vol II.
Satyagraha in South Africa. By M. K. Gandhi.
Indian Home Rule. By M. K. Gandhi.
Ethical Religion. By M. K. Gandhi.
Gandhiji in the Villages. By Mahadev Desai.
Gandhiji in Ceylon. By Mahadev Desai.
Seven Months with Mahatma Gandhi. By Krishna Das (2 Vols.).
To the Students. By C. F. Andrews.

The current numbers of *Young India* are published by the Navajivan Press, Ahmedabad, and it may be subscribed for by writing to the Manager. Some special "Gandhi literature" including the Autobiography may be obtained from this Navajivan office.

(C)

The *Modern Review*, 91, Upper Circular Road, Calcutta; the *Indian Review*, Georgetown, Madras; the *Indian Social Reformer*, Bombay, and the *Servant of India*, Poona, are among the most important journals which discuss the problems in India connected with this book. The *Modern Review* also publishes from time to time translations from Rabindranath Tagore's writings. All this literature may be obtained from India. British Postal Orders are current in India, and form a useful means for the payment of small amounts, but checks for larger amounts may also be sent. A rupee in India should be reckoned at one shilling and sixpence.

INDEX

INDEX